BASEBALL
GOES TO
THE MOVIES

BASEBALL GOES TO THE MOVIES

RON BACKER

APPLAUSE
THEATRE & CINEMA BOOKS
An Imprint of Hal Leonard LLC

Published in 2017 by Applause Theatre & Cinema Books
An Imprint of Hal Leonard LLC
7777 West Bluemound Road
Milwaukee, WI 53213

Trade Book Division Editorial Offices
33 Plymouth St., Montclair, NJ 07042

Printed in the United States of America

Book design by John J. Flannery

Library of Congress Cataloging-in-Publication Data

Names: Backer, Ron, 1951- author.
Title: Baseball goes to the movies / by Ron Backer.
Description: Milwaukee, WI : Applause Theatre & Cinema Books, 2017. |
Includes bibliographical references and index.
Identifiers: LCCN 2016054160 | ISBN 9781495075551 (pbk.)
Subjects: LCSH: Baseball films–History and criticism.
Classification: LCC PN1995.9.B28 B33 2017 | DDC 791.43/6579–dc23
LC record available at https://lccn.loc.gov/2016054160

www.applausebooks.com

For my son, Seth,
and for all of the catches
we had in the backyard
and the driveway

CONTENTS

INTRODUCTION

There really was a time when baseball was our national pastime—when people went to the ballpark during the day as often as they went at night; when morning papers were scrutinized for the scores of last evening's games; when people listened intently to the radio to hear who was winning and who was losing; when everyone knew the names Ruth, Gehrig, Robinson, Mays, Musial, and Clemente; and when a taxi driver really wanted to know which base those three Brooklyn Dodgers were on. Things changed in the 1960s and 1970s when football went on national television. Football is faster-paced than baseball and substantially more violent. With only one game per team played each week, every football game is an event. With instant replays and isolated cameras developed back in those early years and seemingly new technological developments every year—such as the more recent electronic line to designate the first-down line for television viewers—football fits television better than baseball ever could. Is there any doubt that football is now our national sport, as it has been for many years?

However, that does not necessarily mean that football is our national pastime. "Pastime" means an entertainment or activity that makes time pass pleasantly; it is something that is laid-back and not intense. That definition clearly fits baseball better than football. With no clock to limit the action, its slow pace between innings and pitches, its bursts of action in between not much happening, its singing of "Take Me Out to the Ball Game" during the seventh-inning stretch, and its very long season after its easygoing weeks of spring training—baseball is much more of a pastime than football. While football may now be our national sport, baseball is still our national pastime.

In the movies, however, baseball has always been our national sport, as well as our national pastime. From the beginning of the cinema in the silent era and continuing to this day, there have always been substantially more significant movies about baseball than football. In fact, there have been more memorable movies about baseball than any other sport. There have been baseball dramas, comedies, musicals, biographical films, family movies, and films about major leaguers, minor leaguers, and Little Leaguers, plus a few mysteries and love stories thrown in. Surprisingly, even when football became more popular than baseball in the 1970s, the number of movies about baseball actually increased over the subsequent decades. Baseball is surely America's cinematic pastime as well as its national pastime.

Baseball Goes to the Movies includes films about baseball from the beginning of the sound era to the current decade. The book is intended for movie fans, of course, and for some films, depending on their content and style, I have emphasized the cinematic features of the film, such as the story, acting, and directing. However, this book is also for fans of the summer game. Thus, as part of the discussions of many of the films, I have emphasized the baseball aspects of the movie, including information concerning the players, the teams, the ballparks, interesting plays, statistics, baseball rules, and the legend and lore of the summer game. As an avid baseball fan myself, I learned much about the game through watching these movies.

Baseball Goes to the Movies covers 74 baseball films that originally played in theaters. As a result, there are films from every category, including dramas, comedies, mysteries, musicals, and biopics. Together these films teach us much about sport and life in America, through the lens of baseball, our national pastime.

MAJOR LEAGUE BASEBALL

✓ *The Natural* (1984)

Along with *The Pride of the Yankees* (1942) and *Field of Dreams* (1989), *The Natural* is one of the best-remembered and best-loved baseball movies of all time. Robert Redford plays Roy Hobbs, a major-league ballplayer who first learns how to play the summer game from his father on the family farm located somewhere in the Midwest. In 1923, a few years after his father dies, Roy receives a tryout opportunity as a pitcher for the Chicago Cubs. On the train to Chicago, Roy meets Harriet Bird, a mysterious and beautiful woman dressed almost all in black. When Roy goes to her hotel room that night for a liaison, Harriet shoots Roy in the stomach with a silver bullet and leaves him for dead.

The story then jumps sixteen years forward to 1939, when Roy signs a contract with the New York Knights, a major-league team in the National League that approximates the New York Giants. As a result of the gunshot wound, Roy can no longer pitch. He has, however, become a fabulous hitter, still using the bat he made for himself back on the farm from a tree struck by lightning. In order to succeed in the majors, Roy has to overcome the antipathy of his manager and the dishonesty of some of the people associated with the Knights. In the background of the story is Iris, Hobbs's childhood love from back home, who has recently re-entered his life.

The Natural is based upon the 1952 novel of the same name by Bernard Malamud. Malamud was an avid baseball fan, and while his novel is a work of fiction, many of the moments in the novel that are carried over into the film, even the fantastic ones, are inspired by true baseball incidents. For example, the shooting of Roy in the hotel room was inspired by the 1949 shooting of Phillies' first base-man Eddie Waitkus by an obsessed female fan who asked Waitkus to come to her hotel room. Waitkus survived the shooting and after four operations was able to return to the game the following season. Similarly, Hobbs's home run, which shatters the scoreboard clock in Wrigley Field, was inspired by a similar feat by Bama Rowell, who, while playing for the Boston Braves in 1946, hit a ball off the Bulova clock on the Ebbets Field scoreboard, shattering the glass. (In the book, the incident happens at Ebbets Field, not Wrigley Field.)

One of the many strengths of *The Natural* is its evocation of the joys of baseball and its importance in American society. (Malamud himself was a son of Jewish immigrants to America and he, along with many other Jews, used baseball as a method of assimilation into American society.) Roy Hobbs expresses the joys of the summer game in several pieces of dialogue; large crowds hang on every pitch as the Knights fight to win the National League pennant; and the film is bookended with scenes of Roy having a catch with his father on the farm back in the early 1900s and Roy having a catch with his son in 1939 in a similar location. Those latter moments—along with scenes of Roy tossing a ball from a train to a young boy and Roy's interactions with the Knights' batboy—display the cycle of baseball in this country, as the game is handed down from one generation to the next. Is there anything more American than a father having a catch with his son in the backyard?

The Natural has one of the best acting ensembles ever put together for a baseball movie. Robert Redford is perfectly cast as Roy Hobbs, believable early in the film as a naïve young man taking his first train ride, to his later reappearance in the movie as a weary but determined ballplayer. Glenn Close received an Academy Award nomination for Best Supporting Actress for the film. She has a small but significant part playing Iris, Roy's lifetime love from back home but now a strong personality in her own right. The film is filled with wonderful character actors, such as Robert Duvall as the officious newspaper reporter Max Mercy; Wilford Brimley as the grumpy manager Pop Fisher; Robert Prosky as the team's dishonest owner the Judge; Darren McGavin as the gambler Gus; and Richard Farnsworth as the team's bench coach Red Blow, with Duvall and Farnsworth being particular standouts.

The direction of the film by Barry Levinson and the cinematography by Caleb Deschanel are superb. As an example, a scene early in the film where Roy is still young and a lightning bolt splits the tree on the farm is shot in the dark, with the only light coming from the storm, in short bursts, giving an eerie feel to the scene. When the tree is sliced by the lightning, sparks fly profusely, presaging the spectacular end of the movie. Throughout the film there are characters shot in silhouette or scenes shot in what little natural light is available. In other films these latter two methods are used to create a noir effect, but in *The Natural* they provide an unworldly backdrop for the movie that is partly a fantasy. A traditional baseball movie would never be shot in these ways, as baseball is played on a bright field, hopefully on a sunny day, but *The Natural*, with its ethereal elements, is not a traditional baseball film.

The baseball scenes themselves are generally shot in the light, but it is a muted light in keeping with the tone of the film. There is pretty good baseball play on the part of the actors. Robert Redford has an excellent pitching motion early in the film and his hitting skills are at least satisfactory. The primary ball field used in the film, Buffalo's War Memorial Stadium, provides the movie with a realistic feel of a ballpark from the 1930s. The scoreboard, in which the inning-by-inning score is placed in the board by hand and the scorekeeper watches the game through the openings in the line score, brings back memories of many of the older ballparks in this country. (Unfortunately, Buffalo's All-High Stadium, which was used by the filmmakers for scenes that are supposed to take place at Chicago's Wrigley Field, looks nothing like Wrigley Field.)

The baseball scenes are well handled, particularly Roy's last at bat in the movie, with a change of pitchers in the middle of the at bat, a long foul ball to raise the viewers' hopes, Roy's favorite bat broken, and close-ups of Roy and the pitcher amid a montage of other players and fans looking on, to delay the big moment, similar to what happens in a real baseball game. While the bolt of lightning that appears would not have happened in a real game, or the game would have been delayed, lightning is a motif of the film, so it properly appears just before the big moment of the film, perhaps predicting what Ray will do in his last at bat.

For all of its other positives, it is still the fantasy elements that make *The Natural* into a classic. Roy Hobbs has three spectacular hits in the film. In his first at bat in the majors, he hits the ball so hard that he literally, as the saying goes, knocks the cover off of the ball. By the time the ball is thrown back into the infield, it is not much more than a pile of unwrapped yarn. As noted above, Roy hits the ball through the scoreboard clock at Wrigley Field, shattering the same, and then there is the spectacular home run at the end of the film, into the light standards at the Knights' home field.

The woman in black, who shoots Roy for no apparent reason, is also an unearthly character. She is first seen by Roy through the smoke of the steam train, implying that she is not quite real. She is beautiful but evil and for some reason uses a silver bullet, the stuff of horror films, to do her dastardly deeds. She contrasts with the very real world Iris, Roy's true love, whose first significant adult appearance in the film occurs when she stands up at a Knights' baseball game so that Roy will be inspired by her. Iris is one of the few females in the stands that day and she is dressed all in white, as if a ghostly figure, particularly as the sun seems to be shining only on her. Roy gets a big hit after spotting Iris in the stands, making the whole incident as eerie as the shooting in the hotel room. Interestingly, on the train, Harriet Bird asks Roy what he hopes to accomplish by breaking every record in the book. Roy replies, "When I walk down the street, people will look at me and say, 'There goes Roy Hobbs, the best there ever was.'" Bird replies, "Is that all?" When Iris asks Roy the same question late in the film and he answers in a similar manner, she says, "And then?" This is an interesting parallel moment in the film, between Harriet and Iris, although its significance is unclear.

The film is substantially faithful to the written work, including reuse of much of the dialogue from the novel. There are, however, two significant changes. In the book, Iris is a minor character. She is not a childhood sweetheart of Roy's. She first meets Roy on the day in Chicago when she stands up during the game. Iris has a grown daughter, not a son, although after a tryst with Roy, she is carrying Roy's son on the day of the championship game.

The most controversial change occurs at the end of the movie. At the end of the novel, Roy Hobbs strikes out. As Malamud wrote, "He struck out with a roar." It is a down moment for a novel, as Hobbs may have accepted a bribe to lose the game. Nevertheless, it is probably the appropriate ending for the novel. In the film, in the same situation, Hobbs hits a three-run homer, winning the pennant for his team. And, it is that change in ending, as controversial as it is, which really makes *The Natural* into the classic film that it has become. Hobbs has had major disappointments throughout his life, but he has still managed to prevail enough that he can play for a league championship on the last day of the season (and, due to the old bullet wound, the last day of his career). In the movie, Hobbs would never take a bribe to lose a game because the sport itself means too much to him. Also, he has Iris again, and he has just learned he has a son. The only way to vindicate Roy's life and his story is with Roy trying to do the right thing, which he does, providing the film with its happy ending.

The ending of the film also provides a special moment of the cinema, one that is hard to forget even years after seeing the movie. Roy hits a walk-off home run, with the ball hitting the light standards high above the park in right field, short-circuiting all of the lights. Sparks shower the field, raining light onto Roy as he rounds the bases and onto the players as they meet to congratulate him, surely the most spectacular home run ever hit in the history of cinema. In many baseball parks today, when a home-team player hits a home run, fireworks are set off in the stadium. In *The Natural*, Roy Hobbs provides his own fireworks for his big hit.

The Natural is about 134 minutes in length, very long for a baseball movie. On viewing, however, the film seems much shorter, because it never loses its interest or seems padded, a result of its myth-like plot, fine acting, surprise moments, and its evocation of the joys of the game. It is a baseball and movie classic, capped by the shattering of the ballpark lights at the end, a truly magic cinematic moment. The film is highly recommended.

Moneyball (2011)

The nonfiction book *Moneyball: The Art of Winning an Unfair Game* by Michael Lewis is a fascinating read for any baseball fan, even more than a decade after its publication in 2003. It must have been particularly fascinating in 2003, when sabermetrics (the science of rigorous baseball statistical analysis) was not well known to baseball fans. The book relates the modern history of sabermetrics, eventually used by Billy Beane, the general manager of the Oakland Athletics, to attempt to field a competitive baseball team in Oakland in an era of free agency and large player salaries. Anyone who loves baseball will love this book, particularly because these statistical analyses have since been adopted by many professional baseball teams. These days, on-base percentage, OPS (the sum of a player's on-base and slugging percentages), fielding shifts, and long at bats are important elements of the game.

On its face, the Lewis book would have little interest for Hollywood, since the book does not have a plot. It is a nonfiction history of a modern aspect of the game, not a drama. Yet, in 2011, after several fits and starts, the book was adapted to the cinema in a film titled simply *Moneyball*. The movie was critically acclaimed upon its release. It was nominated for six Academy Awards, including Best Picture, Best Actor, and Best Supporting Actor.

Philip Seymour Hoffman portrays Art Howe, the manager of the Oakland Athletics, in *Moneyball* **(2011).**

Unfortunately and despite these accolades, the movie is a major disappointment. The core problem with the film is one that anyone could deduce upon reading the book. The film is a straightforward and somewhat accurate account of one season in the life of a baseball team, in this case, the 2002 Oakland Athletics. Any baseball season of any team has its highs and lows, instances of high tension, interesting parts, and moments that are boring. A documentary of any baseball team's season could be fascinating, at least for the hometown fans.

Moneyball, however, is not a documentary. It is a dramatic film, with a little bit of humor thrown in. But a dramatic film needs drama. Where is the tension in *Moneyball*? If by embracing baseball statistical analysis, Billy Beane is the hero of the film, who is the villain? There is none. Without a villain, the film cannot have a true climax. At the end of *Moneyball*, the Athletics make the playoffs, using Billy's new system, but the team loses quickly in the American League Division Series, just as the team did in the playoffs in the prior year. That is hardly the stuff of great movies.

The only conflict in the film occurs early on, when several of Oakland's long-term scouts disagree with Billy's new approach to the game. However, the argument between the two baseball philosophies is only raised; it is not fleshed out. For example, Billy's new approach to the game is called into question when the early season for the Athletics is rocky. Oakland then turns its season around and so Billy's approach is quickly justified. That is about it. If there is not enough drama to carry the story, why make the movie, particularly when the book on the subject is readily available?

That is not to say that *Moneyball* is without interest, particularly in some of its baseball elements, the most compelling of which is the Athletics' winning streak in 2002. The Athletics got off to a very slow start that year but then starting on August 13, 2002, the team unexpectedly started to win game after game without a loss. At seventeen wins in a row, the Oakland Athletics tied the franchise record of the Philadelphia Athletics, set in 1931. At nineteen wins, the Athletics tied the American League record held by the 1906 White Sox and the 1947 Yankees. On September 4, 2002, the Athletics played the Kansas City Royals, hoping to break the American League record for consecutive wins. (The major-league record is twenty-six wins, set by the New York Giants in 1916, although there was a tie game in the middle of the streak.)

By the end of the third inning of that game in September 2002, the record seems to be in hand for Oakland, as it leads Kansas City, 11-0. Then things go south for the Athletics. By the bottom of the ninth inning, the game is tied, 11-11. Then, in spectacular fashion, Scott Hatteberg, one of Billy's signings because of Hatteberg's ability to get on base by walking so much, hits a walk-off home run, bringing the Athletics to the twenty-consecutive-win plateau and the American League record. It is a spectacular baseball moment, aided by the fact that this is a rare moment in the film where the baseball action is new and not just old television footage. (However, the game footage could have done without Billy's memories of his baseball career interrupting the action.)

Also, for baseball fans who like and appreciate sabermetrics, *Moneyball* has its appeal. Billy has become a believer that the most important factor in offense is getting on base, whether by a hit, walk, or error. Long at bats, with the batter fouling off lots of pitches, resulting in the starting pitcher having a high pitch count earlier in the game and hopefully being pulled from the game quicker, are important. That is what Billy emphasizes when he now trades for a player. He is not interested in bunts, stolen bases, or fielding. The film also does an excellent job in detailing Billy's approach to addressing the loss of Jason Giambi, the team's star player, to the New York Yankees. Billy understands that the Athletics are unlikely to ever find another Giambi, and that even if it did, the team would never have the money to pay him. Instead, the team finds three players to replace Giambi's hits, slugging, and on-base percentages at a total cost that is substantially less than Jason Giambi's new compensation with the New York Yankees.

As interesting as the Giambi segment of the film is, the problem is that *Moneyball* simplifies the thought processes and analyses behind sabermetrics, which is a very complicated process. Admittedly, many films have a tendency to do that with difficult concepts, because film is not the best medium for explaining complicated and controversial ideas. Nevertheless, *Moneyball* is successful in introducing the average fan to the basic concepts of what is, in effect, a new strategy for the game, more than a century after baseball was first played professionally.

If *Moneyball* were to be believed, Billy Beane first became acquainted with sabermetrics just before the 2002 season, when he first met Peter Brand, a proponent of the concept, who was then working for the Cleveland Indians. (The character is based upon Paul DePodesta, who came to work for Billy at Oakland from Cleveland, but in 1999.) In fact, Oakland was using some form of sabermetrics prior to 1997, when Sandy Alderson was the general manager of the team and Billy was his assistant. When Billy became the general manager of the team in 1997, Billy continued to use sabermetrics. It was not just something he first adopted in 2002. In addition, some of the player moves shown in the film are either inaccurate or occurred in years prior to 2002.

While it is always disappointing when a film allegedly based on a true story contains new material or inaccurate facts, *Moneyball* deserves a pass when it comes to showing the incorporation of sabermetrics into a baseball philosophy. No movie could be successful by accurately showing the slow adoption of a difficult concept by baseball over many years. Movies need drama, and Billy's story had to be compacted into one year, providing the film with some focus. While that approach does not correct the fundamental flaw of the film, that it has no plot, the filmmakers had to try. For a more accurate portrayal of Billy Beane's early career, the Lewis book is the place to go.

There is an attempt made in the film to find a reason why Billy is so willing to give up baseball's usual way of doing business, by showing flashbacks of Billy being a first-round draft pick of the New York Mets in 1980, forgoing a full scholarship to Stanford University, and then flaming out in his professional playing career. (This is also covered in detail in the book, but primarily as background material for the story that is to follow.)

To tie Billy's backstory to the main plot of *Moneyball*, one of the Athletics' scouts, disgruntled by the new philosophy of the team, says to Billy, "This is about you and your stuff, isn't it? Twenty years ago some scout got it wrong. Now you are going to declare war on the system." The problem here is that, at least in the movie version, Billy was the general manager of the Athletics for several years before the 2002 season and pursued his career just as every other general manager did in the past, employing great players such as Jason Giambi (first baseman and slugger), Johnny Damon (good hitting outfielder), and Jason Isringhausen (right-handed pitcher and closer) and making it to the American League Division Series in 2001. It was the subsequent loss of those star players to free agency after the 2001 season and the limited budget Billy had to work with in Oakland that caused him to change his approach to the game. If that had not happened to Oakland, then Billy, at least according to the movie, would never have changed his approach to the game. Thus, the flashback scenes (and the scout's comments) are irrelevant to the story line of the movie.

Much like many of the biographies of baseball players that have been produced in Hollywood over the years, because there is no inherent drama in the story being told, *Moneyball* comes up short as a film. While the movie holds viewers' interest, a documentary on the same subject would have been just as entertaining and much more informative.

✓ *Eight Men Out* (1988)

Eight Men Out is the story of the 1919 World Series, in which eight members of the Chicago White Sox infamously became involved in a conspiracy to throw the World Series, resulting in the team forever being known as the Chicago Black Sox. The film is based on a nonfiction book of the same name by Eliot Asinof. The Asinof book is an excellent, detailed account of the circumstances that led to the throwing of the World Series, the personalities involved, actual game events, and the aftermath, including the trial of the ballplayers, their acquittal, their lifetime ban from baseball, and their life after baseball. If anyone has an interest in the true story of the Black Sox, Asinof's book is well worth a read.

The film *Eight Men Out* is a generally accurate account of the Black Sox scandal, but, of course, with any cinematic re-creation of historical events, there are a few inaccuracies or misleading elements in the film. For example, a person watching *Eight Men Out* would get the impression that the eight ballplayers never played baseball after the 1919 World Series, because their criminal trial and subsequent banishment seem to take place very quickly in the film. In fact, the players were not indicted until right at the end of the 1920 season. The criminal trial did not commence until June 27, 1921, and the verdict was not delivered until August 2, 1921, at which

These are the eight men out of the 1988 film. Back Row: Eddie Cicotte (David Strathairn), Shoeless Joe Jackson (D. B. Sweeney), Buck Weaver (John Cusack), Chick Gandil (Michael Rooker), Swede Risberg (Don Harvey), Fred McMullin (Perry Lang); Front Row: Hap Felsch (Charlie Sheen) on the left and Lefty Williams (James Read) on the right. In the center is Eliot Asinof, the author of the book, *Eight Men Out*.

time the new commissioner of baseball, Judge Kenesaw Mountain Landis, permanently banned the Black Sox eight from the game. Thus, the eight conspirators played during the 1920 season, except for Chick Gandil, who held out that season for a better salary from Chicago White Sox owner Charles Comiskey. The 1920 season is skipped over in the film for dramatic purposes, because a year delay in reaching the film's climax would have dissipated much of the intensity of the movie.

Given the inaccuracies in the film, the obvious question is: Why produce a film version of the story of the Chicago Black Sox scandal when the book *Eight Men Out* and other historical works are available, which provide more information than any film could and, in fact, provide much more accurate information that most films do? The same question often comes up with biographical films, whether sports-related or not, because biographical films cannot come close to accurately conveying the life of a historical figure. With *Eight Men Out*, however, the better analogy is to the critically acclaimed film *Lincoln* (2012). *Lincoln* is not a biography of Abraham Lincoln. It is primarily the story of a very short period in Lincoln's life, when Lincoln was trying to convince Congress to pass the Thirteenth Amendment to the United States Constitution. The story has an inherent dramatic interest, because of the personalities involved, the monumental issues of the day, and the pressure on Lincoln to pass the amendment before the end of the Civil War.

Similarly, *Eight Men Out* is not a biography of outfielder Shoeless Joe Jackson, pitcher Eddie Cicotte, third baseman Buck Weaver, or owner Charles Comiskey. It is primarily a story of just a few weeks in the history of baseball in October 1919. It is also a story that has inherent dramatic interest, because of the personalities involved, the spreading of the blame for the scandal among many parties and not just the ballplayers, the game action, the trial of the players, and the effect of the scandal on the players and their loved ones. If a true tale has inherent dramatic interest, it is often worth bringing to the cinema. *Lincoln* and *Eight Men Out* are proof of that.

Also, because the purpose of the cinema is primarily to entertain and not to provide an historical reference guide to historical events, filmmakers have the opportunity to artfully adjust the story for dramatic purposes, as noted above, but also to provide some continuity and context to the story. For example, the film of *Eight Men Out* commences with two young boys, fictional characters from Chicago, who, with the help of a quarter one has just earned, are able to buy bleacher seats for a regular season White Sox game. The young fellows are the symbol of the baseball fans of the era in general and White Sox fans in particular, as they are incredibly excited to be able to see their favorite team in person. The two boys turn up again from time to time in the film, as they live in the same neighborhood as Buck Weaver, one of the Chicago players. They talk to Buck about baseball and then the scandal. The two boys provide a human face to the effects of the players' conspiracy, adding to the impact of the film.

In fact, it is one of those two boys who is present late in the film as Shoeless Joe Jackson is leaving the Grand Jury room, re-creating the most famous incident arising from the Black Sox scandal, one known far and wide, even by non-baseball fans. The boy shouts, "Say it ain't so, Joe. Say it ain't so." As handled in *Eight Men Out*, the line is particularly affecting because a young boy, whose love for baseball has already been established in the film, says the lines. The young boy is an avid and loyal White Sox fan, as only young children can be, unsullied by the cynicism of adult life. As a result, this incident, as famous as it is, is one of the most effective moments in the film.

From the perspective of almost a hundred years, most people view the Black Sox scandal as a story of dishonest baseball players only and, of course, to a large degree that is true. Whatever the explanations or reasons for what they did, there is no justification for ballplayers taking money from gamblers to throw any ball game. *Eight Men Out*, however, provides a more nuanced explanation of the events. As to the ballplayers, Buck Weaver was present at meetings in which the conspiracy was discussed, but he never took any money from the gamblers and he played well in the World Series. (Weaver batted .324 in the series and made no errors.) Shoeless Joe Jackson did take illicit money, but he was unsophisticated and naïve, unable to read or write. He also played well in the series. (Jackson batted .375 in the series and made no errors.) When Buck Weaver complains in court that he should have been tried separately from the other ballplayers, there is much to justify that request. Perhaps Shoeless Joe Jackson's actions should also have been considered separately, because Weaver's and Jackson's involvements in the conspiracy were different than the involvement of the other six Black Sox players.

However, the Black Sox scandal was not just a scandal of greedy ballplayers. The film accurately demonstrates that part of the blame for the scandal also goes to the gamblers, who had the temerity to even consider sullying the reputation of the national pastime and its signature event, the World Series. The gamblers even double-crossed the ballplayers, never paying them all that they were promised. It is also a separate scandal that while the ballplayers were prosecuted for their crimes and ultimately banned from baseball, none of the gamblers were ever prosecuted or, it seems, suffered any consequences for their actions. Finally, Charles Comiskey, the owner of the White Sox, deserves much of the blame. He never paid his players fairly, knowing they could not leave him under baseball's reserve clause, and he denied his players bonuses that he had previously promised them. Desperate people do desperate things, and while these players were not exactly desperate (although they were forced to take any salary Comiskey offered them), Comiskey deserves some of the blame for what happened.

The production of *Eight Men Out* is close to flawless. It provides an accurate representation of baseball in 1919, with players wearing small baseball gloves; no numbers on the backs of their uniforms; large advertising on the walls of the ballparks; a man singing the national anthem through a megaphone; and reenactments of the game for people who could not attend in person, by use of a board with dummy figures spread out on a simulated baseball field, with the plays wired in on a ticker. The film is set back seventy years in time from its release in 1988, but the period ball fields, costumes, vehicles, and other locations seem authentic. The baseball itself seems realistic, with some nice plays by the actors in the field and some fairly good cuts at the pitches at the plate. Nevertheless, *Eight Men Out* provides an unusual acting situation, with the actors playing great ballplayers who themselves are trying to play poorly. Thus, even if the actors swing their bats poorly or make weak plays in the field, it is consistent with the story line.

There are no true stars of *Eight Men Out*. The film has an ensemble cast of actors, all of whom do a great job. Of particular interest is Studs Terkel, Chicago historian, writer, and personality, who plays Hugh Fullerton, the writer who helped to unmask the Black Sox conspiracy. Terkel, a non-actor, is spot-on casting for the role.

For all of its positives, *Eight Men Out* exhibits many flaws. Sometimes the film seems more like a historical re-creation than a major motion picture, resulting in it becoming boring at times. It is difficult for any one film to tell a story of eight protagonists and *Eight Men Out* is no different. Except for Cicotte, Weaver, and Jackson, for whom some time is spent fleshing out their characters and providing their personal conflicts and drama, it is hard for viewers to distinguish the players from each other. Who plays what position, who is playing a significant role in the conspiracy, and who is not? There are so many lower level gamblers involved in the wrongdoing, who sometimes seem to be working with each other and sometimes seem to be working against each other, that it is difficult to discern what is going on with all of them. Who is double-crossing whom? People who have not read Asinof's book will probably not know that the character referred to as "Ring" in the film is actually Ring Lardner, a famous sportswriter of his day. A little more exposition of the story line and a more solid foundation for each of the characters would have made *Eight Men Out* a much better film. As it is, the movie can be very confusing.

Film is no substitute for a well-researched work of history. Eliot Asinof's book or several other works on the subject are the best places to go to learn the truth about the Black Sox team and the 1919 World Series. For those who are uninterested in taking that step, *Eight Men Out* is a reasonable substitute, providing a generally accurate recitation of the facts, but in a dramatic manner that only the cinema can accomplish.

Bang the Drum Slowly (1973)

The novel *Bang the Drum Slowly*, written by Mark Harris and first published in 1956, tells the story of a season of a fictional Major League Baseball team, the New York Mammoths, during which the team's slow-witted catcher, Bruce Pearson, is afflicted with a fatal disease and dies. The novel is narrated by one of the characters, Henry "Author" Wiggen, a pitcher on the team.

The same year *Bang the Drum Slowly* was published, it was adapted into a live television drama that starred Paul Newman as Henry Wiggen and Albert Salmi as Bruce Pearson. The most famous version of *Bang the Drum Slowly* is the 1973 film adaptation, made by Paramount Pictures and starring Michael Moriarty as Henry Wiggen and Robert De Niro as Bruce Pearson. The film opens with Wiggen and Pearson leaving the Mayo Clinic in Rochester, Minnesota, where Pearson has been diagnosed with Hodgkin's disease, a fatal illness.

Wiggen tries to keep Pearson's medical situation a secret, particularly from the team's inquisitive manger, Dutch Schnell. However, when news of Pearson's illness leaks out, the team members rally around each other, winning the pennant, with Pearson having the best year of his career, and going on to win the World Series, even though Pearson is too ill to participate in the Fall Classic. As the film ends, Pearson has passed away back in his hometown in Georgia.

The screenplay for the film was written by Mark Harris, so it is not surprising that the film adaptation is faithful to the novel, incorporating some of the memorable lines of dialogue from the novel. In the novel, when Pearson worries that people are being nice to him because they know he is dying, Wiggen responds, "Everyone knows everybody is dying. That is why people are nice. You all die soon enough, so why not be nice to each other?" When Dutch agrees to a contract tying Pearson to Wiggen, he tells Wiggen, "I never done such a thing before and would not do it now except there is a look in your eye that tells me that I must." Then there is the famous last line of the book, spoken by Wiggen after the funeral of Pearson, "From here on in I rag nobody." These and many other lines from the novel make it into the film, giving the movie a richness in its dialogue that is often missing in other baseball movies.

The song "Streets of Laredo" is played over the opening credits (and sung later in the film). "Streets of Laredo" is a traditional cowboy or folk song, in which a dying cowboy tells another cowboy that he has been shot and is about to die. One verse of the song, in which the dying cowboy tells how he wants his funeral to be handled, inspired the title to Mark Harris's book. One version of the stanza goes as follows:

Oh, beat the drum slowly and play the fife lowly / And play the dead march as you carry me along / Take me to the valley, and lay the sod o'erme / I'm a young cowboy and I know I've done wrong.

The words of that stanza have been sung differently over the years and so some singers may have spoken the first phrase as "bang the drum slowly" instead of "beat the drum slowly," but the latter phrasing is the one most commonly used.

Taking a line from "The Streets of Laredo" is unusual for a baseball book and movie, not just because of the different subject matter but also because the cowboy in the song is shot after he takes to drinking and gambling. Although the song does not explain why, the dying cowboy knows that he has done wrong. In the movie, Bruce Pearson has not done wrong to anyone. Through no fault of his own, he becomes afflicted by an incurable disease and is cut down while still a young man. Perhaps it is another line of the song that is more appropriate: "For we all loved our comrade, so brave, young, and handsome."

Bang the Drum Slowly opened to excellent reviews. It contains some noteworthy performances, particularly Vincent Gardenia as

Henry Wiggen (Michael Moriarty) pitches for the New York Mammoths in *Bang the Drum Slowly* (1973).

the team's manager, Dutch Schnell. Gardenia is alternately amusing, irascible, and lovable as the team's manager, finally giving Pearson the chance to play on a regular basis and allowing Pearson to show that he is a not-too-bad ballplayer. Gardenia received an Oscar nomination for his efforts. Robert De Niro's performance as Bruce Pearson, along with his role in *Mean Streets* released later that same year, led to him becoming a star in Hollywood. While De Niro is good in the role, it is a surprisingly small part.

Excellent reviews and all, *Bang the Drum Slowly* is a disappointing film. For a movie that has a serious subject matter, the impending death of a young player, it is surprising to find that *Bang the Drum Slowly* is primarily a comedy. Much of the film is wasted with scenes of Dutch trying to find out why Wiggen wanted a special clause in his contract tying his career to Pearson's, and what happened when Wiggen and Pearson went to Minnesota that winter; Wiggen refusing to change the beneficiary on Pearson's life insurance policy to a prostitute that Pearson likes; and Pearson and the others cheating fans and tourists out of their money in card games they make up as they go along. Pearson's illness is often lost in the details.

Bang the Drum Slowly has a bit of a theme to it. Despite being very talented, the New York Mammoths are having a mediocre season until Pearson's illness brings the team together. At that point, the players stop ragging each other and play up to their potential, underlining the fact that baseball is a team sport, not just a collection of individuals. While that is a worthwhile theme, it seems incredibly insignificant when played against the death of a young ballplayer. Does it really take a dying baseball player to bring a major-league team together?

Despite his disease, Pearson is having his best year ever in the majors. Pearson's father comes to talk to Wiggen about that strange circumstance, not understanding the anomaly and wondering if his son's diagnosis is incorrect. "How can he be so sick and play so well?" It is a poignant moment in a film about death that is surprisingly lacking in many other poignant moments.

There is a good baseball play at the end of the film, when Pearson cannot find a high pop-up around home plate. Wiggen had warned the other players that something like this could happen during the game and so the first baseman comes all the way down the line and to the plate to make the catch, preventing Pearson from having an embarrassing miscue. And finally, at its end, the film achieves the right tone about its core story. The Mammoths win the pennant and then the World Series, but those achievements are downplayed in the movie, subordinate to Pearson's good year behind the plate and then his death. *Bang the Drum Slowly*, though a baseball movie, downplays its most important baseball moment, a wise choice.

For baseball fans, there is an interesting moment in the film. Pearson gets sick in his hotel room and the players call in a local doctor to examine him. The doctor tells the players that he detests baseball. "It is a dying game, I'm told." While the doctor's diagnosis of Pearson in the film may have been correct, his diagnosis of the game is not. More than forty years after *Bang the Drum Slowly* was released, the game of baseball is still thriving.

√ *A League of Their Own* (1992)

A League of Their Own is a fictional account of the Rockford Peaches, a women's baseball team that plays in the All-American Girls Professional Baseball League ("AAGPBL"), a league that would be forgotten today if it were not for the release of *A League of Their Own* in 1992. The AAGPBL was started by Philip Wrigley, the owner of the Chicago Cubs, who, in 1942, was worried that that the ongoing world war could result in cancellation of the entire major-league season the following year. Many major leaguers were in military service and baseball's farm system had already been decimated by the loss of players who joined the military. Wrigley worried that fans would lose interest in the summer game if the quality of play were diminished. He devised the idea of creating a women's league to keep up fan interest, at least until the war was over.

The AAGPBL started in four medium-size cities in the Midwest—Racine, Wisconsin, Kenosha, Wisconsin, South Bend, Indiana, and Rockford, Illinois. (The Rockford Peaches and the Racine Belles are the primary teams portrayed in the film.) About 600 women participated in the league over time. At first the women played a form of softball (the league was originally called the All-American Girls Softball League), but by the 1948 season, they were playing baseball, i.e., pitching overhand with a smaller ball. At one point, Hall of Famers Max Carey (outfielder, primarily for the Pittsburgh Pirates from 1910 through 1926) and Jimmie Foxx (first baseman and slugger, primarily for the Philadelphia Athletics from 1925 through 1935) managed teams. (The Tom Hanks character in *A League of Their Own*, manager Jimmy Dugan, appears to have been inspired by Jimmie Foxx, since Dugan is portrayed as a great home-run hitter when he played in the big leagues, but whose career was shortened by alcoholism, much like Foxx.) Attendance for the AAGPBL was good for a time, but by the early 1950s attendance had dropped considerably, caused perhaps by the competition of television, the lack of a farm system to bring on new players, and changing perceptions of women's employment outside the house. The AAGPBL disbanded after the 1954 season.

The main story line of *A League of Their Own* is bookended by a true event that occurred on November 5, 1998—the opening of an exhibit at the Baseball Hall of Fame, titled "Women in Baseball." On that day, about 150 alumni of the AAGPBL came to Cooperstown to celebrate the opening of the exhibit. There were also about 1,100 visitors, one of whom was Penny Marshall, the director of *A League of Their Own*. That trip was a part of her inspiration to make the film that, more than the Cooperstown exhibit, reignited interest in the history of women's professional baseball in America.

A *League of Their Own* tells the story of a number of young women who are recruited to play in the AAGPBL when baseball owner Walter Harvey, who made his money in candy bars, not chewing gum, decides to form a women's professional baseball league because he is worried that Major League Baseball may be forced to shut down as a result of World War II. (There is some interesting newsreel footage shown of Joe DiMaggio and Bob Feller going off to war.) Ernie Capadino is one of the scouts who goes out to find ballplayers, and he recruits, among others, two sisters, Dottie Hinson, a catcher, and Kit Keller, a pitcher. There is an intense rivalry between the two, as Kit believes she is always under the shadow of her older sister, particularly on the baseball field. That rivalry creates the main subplot of the film, which carries over into the seventh game of the AAGPBL World Series.

While the story of A *League of Their Own* is fictional, many of its elements are based in fact. The AAGPBL insisted that all of the players meet a high moral standard. Destinations for dates had to be pre-approved; the teams had chaperones. The players were required to go to charm school during the early years of the league. The league also insisted on emphasizing the femininity of its players. The women had to show hair outside of the baseball caps and makeup always had to be used. The uniform was a one-piece tunic-like dress with the skirt above the knee (originally a little longer), which resulted in bruises and abrasions when the women slid into bases. Most of these aspects of the game can be seen in A *League of Their Own*.

The film can be viewed as a baseball comedy only. It is very funny throughout, in the dialogue between the women; Coach Dugan's drunken attitude; a society woman going on the radio to protest women playing professional baseball; Dottie and Dugan's battle over whether a batter should bunt or swing away, with their conflicting signs confusing the batter; the charm school scenes; the taunts from the male crowds; the team's promotional activities; and much, much more. There are a lot of good laughs.

In addition to the comedy, there are several poignant moments in the film, such as one woman's father convincing Capadino to allow his less-than-attractive daughter to come to tryouts and later, her falling in love; another player being unable to read her name on the roster and cut lists; the death of a player's husband in the war and the clumsy manner in which it is disclosed to her; and the return from war of the injured Bob, who is Dottie's husband. Even some of the concluding moments of the film at the present-day Hall of Fame ceremony are poignant, as the viewer learns of the deaths of several of the characters. That is not to say that these are the most inventive scenes ever put on film, but they fit nicely with the historical story being told, adding some personal aspects to the history.

In addition to the comedic and dramatic attributes, A *League of Their Own* succeeds because it is a celebration of the game of baseball. The enjoyment of the game comes across throughout the film, including the exuberance of the tryouts; the idea of sparking attendance with some trick plays, such as Dottie doing a leg split when she catches a foul pop-up; the competitiveness of the players as the season moves toward the championship games; and the large crowds that finally attend the games and appreciate the action. The film also provides a good look at 1940s America, with swing music, newsreels, baseball as the national pastime, women moving from the farm to the city, and women taking over many tasks of the men at war, not just baseball.

The seventh game of the World Series for the women is quite dramatic and is cleverly done, clichés and all. Because of the rivalry between Dottie and Kit, including a dispute between pitcher and catcher on the field during a game, Kit is traded from the Rockford Peaches to the Racine Belles. That believable development is used to establish a contrived ending for the film. First, Dottie comes to bat against her sister in the top of the ninth inning, with the Peaches one run behind and two runners on base. Dottie promptly hits a two-run single, putting Rockford ahead. Then, in the bottom of the ninth inning, with Racine behind by one run, with one runner on base and two outs, who comes to the plate? Not unexpectedly, it is Kit, with a chance to tie or win the game. She hits a long ball between the outfielders, scoring the base runner and tying the game. However, that is not enough for Kit who runs through the stop sign at third and crashes into the catcher, her sister, who drops the ball, giving Racine the championship and Kit her first measure of success in her life vis-à-vie Dottie.

Madonna plays "All the Way" Mae in *A League of Their Own* (1992).

Contrived is the word for this, but it is skillfully done. When Kit comes to the plate, Dottie tells the pitcher to throw high pitches, knowing that Dottie cannot hit them or lay off them. This ties back to the opening of the film, where Dottie tells Kit to lay off the high ones in a softball game, leading to one of their recurring arguments. After the hit, when Kit approaches home plate, Dottie already has the ball. Kit has no choice but to crash into her sister and bowl her over, hoping she will drop the ball, which she does. This ending ties into a theme of the film, which is that women can play baseball, not only as well as men but with an equal competitive spirit. That is what makes the ending of the film so satisfying, even if it is contrived.

The acting in the film is excellent throughout, with Jon Lovitz stealing the movie early in the film, playing scout Ernie Capadino in a sarcastic manner, with lines such as, when the sisters jump on the train, "Did you promise the cows you'd write?" or when Marla Hooch is reluctant to board the train at the next stop, telling her, "See, how it works is, the train moves, not the station." As to the baseball play of the actresses, their fielding is good, with some excellent plays shown, such as diving outfield catches, an outfield catch up against the wall, a catch in the outfield after the player falls on her rear, some nice catches of foul pop-ups, line-drive outs, and good fielding of a bunt. The actresses also do a good job sliding into bases, even in their skirts, particularly one headfirst slide by Madonna playing "All the Way" Mae. Unfortunately, many of the women's batting swings are awkward and their runs around the bases seem awfully slow. In other words, the actresses' baseball skills are at least the equal of their male counterparts in other baseball films. Gary Cooper, Anthony Perkins, and Frank Sinatra could have no criticism of the play in A *League of Their Own*.

The film does revert to the baseball storytelling techniques of the 1930s, with a stadium announcer describing the action as it occurs, as if he were a radio announcer, and the championship game ending in a walk-off, inside-the-park home run. At least the home run is shot in an exciting manner, with cuts between the ball in the outfield and the runner on the base instead of the single long shot often employed in 1930s films. Unfortunately, there is a bit of a continuity error in the last home run (which occurs elsewhere in the film) with the ball still so close to the outfield fence when Kit rounds second base that it would be impossible to throw her out at the plate. Yet, that is exactly what would have happened, if the ball had not been dropped by her sister.

A *League of Their Own* has one other important attribute. While many famous lines have come from baseball films, such as "Today I consider myself the luckiest man on the face of the earth" and "If you build it, he will come," the most famous one is spoken in A

League of Their Own. When one of the female baseball players starts to cry after being berated by Dugan, he says to her, "Are you crying? There's no crying. There's no crying in baseball." Long after viewers have forgotten the rest of the film, that line "There's no crying in baseball" remains as memorable as any line in all of the history of the cinema.

Death on the Diamond (1934)

Based upon a 1934 mystery novel of the same name by Cortland Fitzsimmons, *Death on the Diamond* involves the St. Louis Cardinals and their quest for a National League pennant. In spring training, the odds are long against the Cardinals, but the manager and owner, Pop Clark, is confident about his team's chances, primarily because he has signed a young and promising pitcher, Larry Kelly, to the team. However, it becomes clear very quickly that someone wants the Cardinals to lose the pennant, because an unknown person places poison on the players' mitts, tries to bribe Kelly into throwing the games he pitches, and causes Kelly to be injured in a car accident. When those attempts fail, three St. Louis players are murdered. On the final day of the pennant chase, the perpetrator is discovered and St. Louis wins the pennant, but not until after an attempt on Larry Kelly's life.

The baseball scenes in *Death on the Diamond* are filmed in a very dissatisfying manner. Most of the action is clearly stock footage, shot from far enough away that it is unclear which teams are actually playing. (At least the grandstand, field, and second-unit footage were shot at Sportsman's Park in St. Louis, where the Cardinals played their home games in 1934.) Other actions, such as pitchers winding up and pitching the ball, are shot with the camera in front of the pitcher, with no other part of the field being visible, meaning that the action could have been shot in someone's backyard. However, the worse cinematic technique, as unconvincing as can be seen in any other baseball film, is when the batter, catcher, umpire, and sometimes other players perform in front of a rear-projection screen, showing a large crowd watching the pretend games. Everyone knows that the actors are performing in front of a screen and not at a real ballpark. In the eighty years since *Death on the Diamond* was first released, has there been any viewer at any time who has ever been convinced by the not-so-special effects of the film?

In terms of performances, *Death on the Diamond* excels, with Robert Young as Larry Kelly, the lovely Madge Evans as Frances Clark, and David Landau as manager Pop Clark, all giving fine performances. For movie fans, there are some unexpected actors who show up in small roles, such as Mickey Rooney playing the bat boy for the St. Louis Cardinals, Walter Brennan playing a hot dog vendor at one of the games, and Ward Bond appearing as a police guard near the end of the film. Ted Healy, known today for discovering the Three Stooges and appearing with them in vaudeville and some early sound shorts, plays O'Toole, the home-plate umpire for every game shown in the film. Healy has several comedy vignettes with Nat Pendleton, who plays Hogan, the Cardinals' catcher. O'Toole and Hogan are in the film primarily for comic relief, but in a rarity for a B-movie mystery, the two are actually funny, with Hogan making jokes about O'Toole's eyesight and O'Toole making jokes about Hogan's play and his likelihood of being fined. There are even some funny slapstick moments with the two.

The footage of Sportsman's Park gives the film some feeling of verisimilitude. Also, when there is a question of calling off the last game of the season, the Cardinals and the police have a meeting before the "National Commission." The head of the commission is referred to as "Judge" and is played by gray-haired actor Sam Flint. The obvious implication is to Judge Kenesaw Mountain Landis, who became baseball's first commissioner in 1920, with the assignment to clean up baseball after the Black Sox scandal of 1919. In 1934, Landis was still the commissioner of baseball and he still had a full head of gray hair.

By contrast, there are some unconvincing moments in the film. Pop Clark is the manager of the Cardinals and also appears to be the owner of the franchise, which strains credulity, although, admittedly, Connie Mack did manage the Philadelphia Athletics for fifty years while he was an owner of the team. The important final game of the film ends with Larry Kelly hitting a walk-off, inside-the-park home run on a ball that hits off the outfield wall and which should have only been a double. Apparently, 1930s filmmakers believed that inside-the-park home runs were more exciting than out-of-the-park home runs, resulting in a disproportionate use of the former in baseball movies, but the one in *Death on the Diamond* is among the least believable.

In *Death on the Diamond* (1934), the head of the baseball commission is referred to as "Judge" and is played by gray-haired actor Sam Flint. Clearly, the reference is to Judge Kenesaw Mountain Landis, pictured here. *(Library of Congress, LC-DIG-31650)*

The mystery in *Death on the Diamond* is of standard quality for B-movie mysteries in the 1930s and 1940s. While there are lots of suspects, there are no clues provided to the audience members so that they can solve the mystery on their own. Indeed, Jimmie Downey, a newspaper reporter, explains that he knew who the murderer was because when Hogan pointed out the murderer in Hogan's dying breath, the killer went white to the gills, and when Hogan died, the killer was so relieved he almost grinned. As was par for many B mysteries, neither of those moments is shown to the viewer, so the viewer has no possibility of solving the mystery on his own, except for choosing the least likely suspect. However, in *Death on the Diamond*, the actual killer is not exactly the least likely suspect; he is never a suspect at all. Also, the use at the end of the film of shadowy figures and clutching hands was already old-fashioned when used seven years before in the horror classic *The Cat and the Canary* (1927).

Thus, if someone is looking for a quality whodunit that plays fair with the viewer, *Death on the Diamond* is not the film to choose. On the other hand, and as they say in real estate, the most important characteristic of real property is "location, location, and location." In *Death on the Diamond*, what makes the film a good mystery is its setting, setting, and setting. A ballpark with multiple murders, including a runner shot dead on the base paths on his way to home plate, provides a unique setting for a murder mystery, one that makes this film somewhat special. And so, even if the plot and the production cannot withstand much scrutiny, the film is enjoyable enough, both for mystery fans and baseball fans.

The Fan (1996)

The Fan, based on a novel of the same name by Peter Abrahams, is an unpleasant thriller set in the world of Major League Baseball. Robert De Niro plays Gil Renard, a mentally unstable knife salesman who is recently divorced and is about to lose his job. Gil's one solace in life is his beloved San Francisco Giants.

As the film opens, the Giants have just acquired, through free agency, slugger Bobby Rayburn (Wesley Snipes). Rayburn is being paid a large salary, and so his hire has caused some controversy in the Bay Area. Gil, however, is a strong supporter of Rayburn's, even though Rayburn starts the season in a long slump. Gil blames the slump on another Giants' player, Juan Primo, who has refused to relinquish his uniform number 11 to Rayburn, which is the number that Rayburn has worn during his entire career.

After losing his job and having a restraining order issued against him by his former wife with regard to their son, Gil loses it all. After secretly viewing Rayburn arguing with Primo about the uniform number, Gil stabs Primo to death in a hotel sauna. Rayburn is distraught after the death, but his hitting suddenly starts to improve. Later, after Gil saves Rayburn's son from a drowning incident in the ocean and talks to Rayburn, Gil becomes disillusioned by Rayburn's lack of respect for his fans and his failure to thank Gil for turning around Rayburn's hitting slump. As a crazed act of revenge, Gil kidnaps Rayburn's son and refuses to disclose his location unless Rayburn hits a home run for Gil in the next night's game at Candlestick Park.

One of the problems with enjoying *The Fan*, in addition to its simply distasteful story line, made more distasteful because it is employed in a baseball movie, is its ridiculous plot, to the extent there is one. As one example only, the screenwriters needed an avenue for Gil to become personally acquainted with Rayburn so that Gil could kidnap Rayburn's son, Sean. The writers therefore concocted a scene in which Gil is watching Rayburn's beach house one day. It is just at that time that Sean runs into the ocean and starts to drown. Gil, who is unable to accomplish much of anything in his life, manages to make a heroic rescue of Sean, pulling him from the ocean at the last second. Thus, Gil gets to talk to Rayburn personally, setting up the kidnapping of Sean. What a nice coincidence that Gil happened to be there when Sean went into the ocean! To add to the silliness, Rayburn never checks on Sean when Gil leaves the house, even though he has already become concerned about Gil's erratic behavior, and Sean gladly leaves the house with Gil in Rayburn's car, without telling his father or screaming loudly. In a film with little credibility, this scene hardly helps.

Sometimes the baseball elements in a bad baseball film can provide some special interest for a baseball fan, even if a general movie audience may not appreciate those matters. *The Fan* does make some effort in that regard, although it is substantially unsuccessful. Part of the background of the film is the perhaps apocryphal story of Babe Ruth, back in 1926, promising to hit a home run for Johnny Sylvester, a young boy in a hospital, and following through on that promise. Early in the film, Rayburn visits a dying boy in the hospital who asks that Rayburn hit a home run for him the next day. Rayburn accomplishes the feat, remaining in the game after an injury to do so, only to then learn that the young boy slipped into a coma and died before the home run was hit.

This is sometimes referred to in the film as a William Bendix moment, referring to the dramatization of the Babe Ruth/Johnny Sylvester incident in *The Babe Ruth Story* (1948). The fact that Rayburn is upset that he had to visit a dying boy in the hospital and the fact that the boy never heard about the home run before he died makes the film even more distasteful.

Nor is *The Fan* saved by the big game at the end of the movie. In fact, the final game shown in the film is not even a big game. It is just an early regular season contest between the Giants and the Padres, although there is something special on the line. Unless Rayburn hits a home run during the game, Gil has threatened to kill Sean. (Talk about a "do or die" game.) With so much hanging in the balance, this could have been the most suspenseful baseball game in all of cinematic history. It turns out to be a dud.

Rayburn first comes to bat in the second inning, while there is a light rain falling. The scene is shown primarily as pitcher throwing, batter swinging, and umpire gesturing, much the same way that low-budget baseball films from the 1940s and 1950s were shot so that they did not have to be filmed in a large stadium. *The Fan*, however, is not a low-budget film. This style of shooting is a directorial choice, not a budgetary move, and it is a poor one. This approach deprives the scene of any suspense because it provides no context of overall setting for the viewer or the view of the pitcher by the batter as the pitches are thrown. The fact that the pitches are thrown in the semi-dark does not help. Baseball games are not viewed in close-ups and bits of film only; there is a vast expanse of field that provides the true suspense of a game.

Surprisingly, Rayburn's next two at bats in the game are not even shown in the movie, wasting some good opportunities. Rayburn's last potential at bat comes in the eighth inning. First, the pitcher starts to intentionally walk him, then there is a rain delay. When the game resumes, the pitcher decides to pitch to Rayburn. Rayburn swings and misses two pitches. (The time taken between Rayburn's second strike and the next pitch, which seems to be forever, does nothing for the moment.) When Rayburn finally hits the ball, it is shown coming off the bat and next, hitting the top of the wall. As Rayburn runs the bases to attempt to turn the hit into an inside-the-park home run, fulfilling Gil's demand, there are almost no cuts to the outfielders trying to field and throw the ball. Most of what is shown is Rayburn running the bases, so it is never clear if the play is going to be close at the plate. It would seem that a potential inside-the-park home run with a life on the line would have to be suspenseful, but *The Fan* demonstrates that it is not necessarily so.

It is not that *The Fan* would have been much of a film anyway, but director Tony Scott chose style over effectiveness, ruining the ending that might have saved the movie. It is difficult for a baseball film shot mainly in close-ups to be effective. In fact, the baseball scenes in *The Fan* could have been shot indoors on a studio soundstage and they would not have looked much different. Also, there is so much rain coming down at the end of the film that it can be hard to see what is actually going on. Perhaps that is why no viewer is all that surprised to find that Gil has suddenly replaced the real home-plate umpire. It is Gil who calls Rayburn out at home plate. How Gil got into that position is unclear, but by this point in the movie no one cares.

The other baseball aspect of the movie, the dispute over who gets to wear a uniform number when a star player such as Rayburn comes to a team at a time when another player already has that number, is based on fact. The new player often has to pay the first player something or give him something of value to relinquish his rights to the number. (This also happens in other professional sports.) In *The Fan*, Primo originally demands $500,000 for the use of the number, which seems quite a bit high, even for a $40 million player. Of course, murdering Primo for the number seems even more out of line.

The truly strange thing about *The Fan* is that number 11 would have been unavailable to either Primo or Rayburn while they were playing for the Giants. From 1928 to 1943, back when the Giants played in New York, a left-handed pitcher named Carl Hubbell played for the team. Hubbell was a Hall of Famer who famously struck out five of the American League's greatest hitters in a row in the 1934 All-Star Game. Hubbell has the distinction of being the first National League player to have his number retired by his team. Since 1944, no other player has worn number 11 for the Giants. It is true that *The Fan* is not much of a baseball film, but a little baseball research should not have been all that much trouble to try to get at least one important fact right about our national pastime.

2

MAJOR LEAGUE DREAMS

The Rookie (2002)

Of all the films about the dream of playing major-league baseball, *The Rookie* probably best captures the vision and delight of the aspiration. The movie is the true account of pitcher Jim Morris, who made his major-league professional baseball debut in 1999 at the age of thirty-five, making him one of the oldest rookies ever to play the game. The success of *The Rookie* does not come from telling the story of one of the greatest pitchers ever to play the game. In real life, Jim had a short and undistinguished major-league career. Rather, the fascination with the film is that, in addition to its evocation of the joys of the game of baseball, it has a positive theme—dreams are always worth pursuing, no matter how old you are.

The Rookie was adapted from Jim Morris's autobiography, *The Oldest Rookie: Big League Dreams from a Small-Town Guy*, first published in 2001. According to the book, Jim Morris was born on January 19, 1964, in Brownwood, Texas. His father was a military man, causing the family to make multiple moves across the country when Jim was young, until the family finally settled back in Brownwood, Texas, when Jim was in ninth grade. There, Jim played football and basketball for his high school and then baseball in a summer league. When Jim graduated from high school in 1982, he was drafted by the New York Yankees in the eighteenth round of the amateur draft. Because of the illness of his grandfather and financial considerations, Jim turned the Yankees down and enrolled at a nearby college, Ranger Junior College, where he played collegiate ball. Jim was then drafted by the Milwaukee Brewers in the supplemental major-league draft the following year and with a $35,000 signing bonus, Jim agreed to play for the team.

Jim struggled in the minors with the Brewers' teams, never getting above A-ball, part of the problem being the arm injuries from which he suffered. A later stint in the minors with the Chicago White Sox brought little success. Jim then quit baseball and went to college at Angelo State University in Texas, where he became an All-American punter for the college football team. After graduation, Jim got a job as a teacher at Reagan County High School in Big Lake, Texas, a small town about seventy miles west of San Angelo, Texas. The job included being the head baseball coach. Of course, football is king in West Texas and baseball not that important, but Jim attempted to do the best he could with his young ballplayers.

The foregoing summary of Jim Morris's life story comprises more than two-thirds of his autobiography. The story of *The Rookie* (2002) commences with Morris already out of baseball, teaching chemistry at the local high school, trying to raise grass in the outfield of the local baseball field, and trying to improve the baseball play and mindset of his team, the Owls. It is then that a key moment in Jim's life occurs. In a locker room speech outside on the baseball field, Jim exhorts his players to perform to the best of their capacities, saying, "You don't have dreams, you don't have anything." The players throw it back at him, resulting in a deal that if the Owls make the district championship, Jim has to try out for a big-league baseball team.

Of course, that is just what happens, or why make a film about Jim Morris? Without telling his wife, Jim brings his three children, one in diapers, to a tryout with the Tampa Bay Devil Rays. There he throws pitch after pitch registering in the high nineties on the radar gun and after one more tryout with the Devil Rays, this time in a pouring rain, Jim is signed by the team. His first stop in the film is with the Orlando Rays, a class Double-A affiliate of the Devil Rays. Putting aside the taunts of the fans, such as "Hey, Skipper, I didn't know it was Bring Your Dad to Work Night," Jim pitches in his first professional game after a long absence.

These scenes in Jim's first game back in baseball have some special interest. They provide some nice flavor of a Minor League Baseball game, such as Jim having to jump over electric cars racing around the infield as he first approaches the pitcher's mound, fans dancing in the stands to "Wooly Bully," fans wearing balloon hats to the game, and the manager telling Jim to work fast. "We got a long bus trip."

Jim has some success in Orlando and he is moved up to the Triple-A affiliate of the Blue Rays, the Durham Bulls. Coincidentally,

Dennis Quaid plays real-life pitcher Jim Morris in *The Rookie* (2002).

that is the minor-league team that is the subject of *Bull Durham* (1988), another film about major-league dreams. According to *The Rookie*, Jim does not pitch as well as he had hoped with the Bulls, and because of that, and also because of family and financial considerations, Jim decides to quit the game. When Jim phones his wife, Lorrie, about his decision, she tries to talk him out of it, suggesting that he at least pitch for another two weeks, until he has to return to his new high school teaching job in Fort Worth, because Jim cannot deny to Lorrie that he still loves playing the game. Jim decides to continue pitching, and when he returns to the locker room before the next day's game, he walks up to his best friend on the team and with a wide smile, says to him, "You know what we get to do today, Brooks? We get to play baseball."

While these moments in Jim's film story are fictional, as Jim never advised his minor-league manager that he was quitting the game, the dialogue between Jim and Lorrie and Jim and Brooks are important moments in the movie. In these scenes, *The Rookie* reveals the attraction of the game to those who play it and the love for the game for those who can only watch it.

Jim continues to pitch in the minors until one day he is called into the manager's office, not knowing if he is going to be released or called up to the majors as one of the Devil Rays' September call-ups. The manager surprises Jim, telling him that he is being called up to the Devil Rays. It is hard for the audience not to tear up at this moment, at least for an instant, as a lifetime dream has been fulfilled, particularly since it is a dream that involves baseball. Dennis Quaid, who plays Jim Morris in the movie, is particularly effective in this scene as he tries to hold back his emotions, but his face and demeanor show that it is the most astonishing moment of his entire life.

The climax of *The Rookie* occurs in The Ballpark in Arlington, the home of the Texas Rangers. It is a huge edifice, emblematic of its location in Texas. A shot of the inner walkway of the park from above as Jim and another player walk down an entranceway, with its rounded arches, makes the stadium seem like a cathedral (another inadvertent reference to *Bull Durham*). The locker room is spotless and immense as Jim walks down the line, seeing the jerseys of several players in the stalls, including one of future Hall of Famer Wade Boggs. Jim then sees his own jersey in his special stall.

Jim is called into his first game with the Devil Rays in the top of the eighth inning, with two men out, a runner on second, and the score 8–1 in favor of the Rangers. Jim throws three strikes past the batter, ending the inning. Jim has made it to the big leagues.

That is the climax of *The Rookie*, Jim pitching to just one batter. It does not matter what happens in the next inning of the game, a game that is essentially irrelevant. It does not matter what happens in the remainder of the season or the following year. Jim has fulfilled his dream of pitching in the majors, and, as a bonus, his first performance on the mound was a success. *The Rookie* properly ends at this moment, because anything that occurs afterward would only be anticlimactic.

Despite the title of his autobiography, Jim Morris was not the oldest rookie to ever play the game. In the film, Lorrie asks Jim how it feels to be the oldest rookie to play the game in the last thirty years. Lorrie is referring to Minnie Mendoza, who first played for the Minnesota Twins at the age of thirty-six in 1970. Mendoza played in sixteen games that season, his only playing time in the majors. The oldest rookie to ever play a game of major-league baseball was probably Satchel Paige. He debuted as a pitcher with the Cleveland Indians at the age of forty-two in 1948. Of course, Paige had a previous long and successful career in the Negro Leagues.

The Rookie is substantially faithful to the last quarter of Jim's autobiography, although, of course, several portions of the film are fictional. While Jim had trouble growing grass in the baseball outfield for his high school team, the problem was not caused by deer eating the seed at night, and the problem was not remedied by spreading human hair on the field to repel the deer. It is highly unlikely that an electronic sign that measures the speed of cars could measure the speed of a thrown baseball. At the tryouts with the Devil Rays, Jim's father and stepmother came and helped him with the children so that Jim did not have to change his baby's diaper just before he pitched, as shown in the film. In real life, when Jim came in to pitch against the Texas Rangers in The Ballpark in Arlington, he got two quick strikes, a foul ball, and then a swinging strike (after an appeal to the first base umpire). In the film, Jim gets three quick strikes, with the last one being an undisputed swing and miss, a more dramatic scenario.

None of these observations about the difference between the true story and the film's story are meant as criticisms of *The Rookie*. Film is different from real life. Most films need good drama, some humor, and lots of color to be successful. *The Rookie* surely has all of those attributes.

The Rookie does a nice job with the characterization of Jim's wife, Lorrie, as she alternately does not want Jim to throw away their married and financial lives with his impossible dream, but then encouraging him to go on when he almost quits the game. The acting in the film is excellent, not just Dennis Quaid as Jim Morris but all of the performers down to the small parts, such as shopkeepers, scouts, and managers. The baseball action seems authentic, particularly the final game in The Ballpark in Arlington, which was filmed live in the stadium with a large crowd looking on. For Morris's last pitch to the batter, the sound of the stadium slowly filters out and Jim pitches in complete silence except for the musical score. This directorial choice was probably inspired by what Jim wrote about his last pitch in his autobiography: "And I was encased in silence, hearing only white noise" (chapter nine).

Unfortunately, *The Rookie* does not avoid all of the clichés of the cinema. There is the estrangement between Jim and his father, which is never developed well enough in the movie to make it seem more than emotional padding. It is somewhat hard to believe that the entire town of Big Lake, Texas, turned out for Jim's first game in The Ballpark in Arlington, some miles from Big Lake, given that, as a relief pitcher, Jim may not have pitched in the game. Fortunately, the film avoids the biggest cliché of them all—Jim having a long and successful major-league career starting at the age of thirty-five. Of course, the facts would have gotten in the way of that ending, as Jim in real life had arm troubles the year after he made his major-league debut. He therefore had only a brief career in professional baseball. Nevertheless, pitching once in the majors, and successfully at that, is happy ending enough for *The Rookie*, a film about dreams fulfilled, at any age.

✓ *Bull Durham* (1988)

Bull Durham was the first movie set entirely in the minor leagues of baseball. The film involves two baseball players, Ebby "Nuke" LaLoosh, a young pitcher with a strong arm who has difficulty with his control, and Crash Davis, a veteran catcher and good hitter who has been bouncing around the minor leagues for twelve years. The Durham Bulls, a minor-league team in the high-A Carolina League, buys the contract of Davis and brings him to North Carolina, to teach Nuke enough about baseball, pitching, and the mental game so that Nuke's natural abilities can be honed into major-league talent. Tying the story together is a local fan, Annie Savoy, who each year adopts an up-and-coming Bulls player as her lover and, in her own way, hones that player's baseball talent into a potential big-league career. This year, Annie chooses Nuke as her protégé but during the course of the season has regrets about not choosing Crash.

Baseball means different things to different people and one of the strengths of *Bull Durham* is its highlighting of people's differing perspectives on the summer game. For a player such as Crash Davis, who still loves the game but knows he will never make it back to the major leagues, baseball has become more of a job than anything else. When he asks the Bulls manager why he should continue to play baseball after being sent down to A-ball from Triple A-ball, the manager replies, "You can keep going to the ballpark and get paid to do it. Beats the hell out of working at Sears." Davis is still upset, decides to quit baseball, but then quickly changes his mind, obviously concluding that there are worse things in life than playing the summer game. At least Davis still has his memories of his twenty-one days in "the Show," a term the players use to describe the major leagues. They were the twenty-one best days of Crash's life, far better than playing for the Bulls, whose slogan is "The Greatest Show on Dirt."

For some fans, such as Annie Savoy, the narrator of the film, baseball is akin to a religious experience. Annie explicitly makes that reference in the opening moments of the movie, when she says, "I believe in the church of baseball." For Annie, baseball is her own personal religion. Crash Davis does not necessarily treat baseball with the same religious devotion as Annie, but he later accidentally confirms her view, when he refers to a Major League Baseball field as a cathedral.

Of course, for most fans, baseball is not akin to religion. It is just an entertaining experience on a summer eve with, at least in the minor leagues, interest coming from more than the games themselves. In that regard, another strength of *Bull Durham* is its evocation of the slice of Americana that the watching of Minor League Baseball games truly is. The real Max Patkin, sometimes known as the Clown Prince of Baseball, performs before some of the games shown in the film. The thin comedian with the rubbery face wears a baggy uniform with a "?" in place of a number on the back of his uniform and a cap that is tilted toward the side of his head. In the film, he dances on home plate and blows water into the air, delighting the fans. Patkin purportedly performed at over 4,000 baseball games in his career, primarily in the minor leagues. His act is corny and yet for some reason he is a joy to watch in the film, even for sophisticated movie fans.

Other types of special moments that seem to occur only in the minor leagues include a helicopter drop of $1,000 in small bills onto the field and then a drove of Little Leaguers running onto the field to collect as much money as they can. Surely there must have been many serious injuries as the mass of kids runs after the loot that is blowing around! One opposing player hits a home run off a fake bull behind the outfield fence, causing the bull's eyes to light up, its tail to move, and steam to come out of its mouth. The batter also wins a free steak. The Bulls' mascot, a man in a bull outfit and mask, stands on the field behind home plate near the fence during the games, resulting in the creature being hit by a wild pitch on several occasions. One of the players takes his wedding vows on the pitching mound just before a game. Come to think about it, nowadays (and other than the wedding), these are just the types of events that occur at major-league games, which sometimes seem to focus more on entertainment than sports.

There is surprisingly little game action shown in *Bull Durham*. It consists mainly of Crash Davis (Kevin Costner) hitting and Nuke LaLoosh (Tim Robbins) pitching. Robbins, who is young, tall, and seemingly strong, physically fits the role of pitcher Nuke LaLoosh in the film, and his windup and feet movement are realistic. However, as he rears back to throw the ball to the plate, he looks behind his body or up in the air, taking his eye off of home plate, something good pitchers never do. It is not surprising that LaLoosh is often wild in the film, walking lots of batters and even throwing pitches into the stands. It is hard for a pitcher to throw to a spot when he takes his eyes off of the spot during his windup. It is surprising that Annie Savoy, baseball expert and pitching coach extraordinaire, does not notice this defect in LaLoosh's approach to the plate. She never sends LaLoosh a note during the game to help straighten out this significant flaw in his pitching motion. Of course, that could be intentional on Annie's part. No batter would want to dig into the box with a fast pitcher on the mound who looks away from the plate as he delivers a pitch.

There are other interesting baseball-related moments in the film. On two occasions, Nuke shakes off the signs called by Crash, resulting in a mound conference. When the two cannot resolve their disagreements, Crash allows Nuke to throw the pitches he wants. However, Crash tells the two batters what pitches are coming, resulting in long home runs. In order to give his team a spark one day, Crash deliberately gets thrown out of the game after arguing a close call at home plate, with the exchanges between Crash and the umpire being more silly than serious. Given budgetary constraints, the radio transmissions of the Bulls' away games are broadcast with the announcer still in Durham, reenacting the games from wire reports and hitting two wooden mallets together to create the sound of a bat hitting a ball.

At the end of the movie, Nuke has his major-league dreams satisfied and Crash's baseball career may be over. When Nuke tells Crash that he is going to the Show, Crash is not happy, resulting in a small fight with Nuke. Nuke does not understand why his mentor is so upset, until Crash explains, "I got brains but you have talent. See this right arm [grabbing Nuke's arm]? Worth a million bucks a year.

After Nuke LaLoosh (Tim Robbins) gives up a home run to end a shutout, Crash Davis (Kevin Costner) comes out to the mound to talk it over, in *Bull Durham* (1988).

All my limbs put together aren't worth seven cents a pound." After twelve years of baseball, Crash's jealousy of those who have done better in the game he loves is patent.

While the backdrop of *Bull Durham* is always baseball, at its core *Bull Durham* is a love story, not a baseball film. Indeed, the climax of the movie is not the elevation of Nuke from the minor leagues to the big leagues, but rather the recognition by Annie and Crash that they are kindred spirits who, perhaps, should stay together after the end of the season and have a long-term meaningful relationship.

With Nuke up to the big leagues, Crash is no longer of any use to the Bulls (even with the good season he is having). The organization would rather bring in a younger player, with more upside potential, to catch for the Bulls. Crash, who helped make Nuke into a major leaguer, is summarily dropped by the team. In the end, Crash, as knowledgeable as he is about baseball, has never learned one of the truest aspects of the game. Sentiment is not a part of the summer game. Baseball is often not much more than a business and an unfair business at that.

Trouble with the Curve (2012)

Moneyball was the big hit baseball movie of 2011. It tells the story of Oakland's general manager Billy Beane and his successes during the 2002 season. The theme of the film is clear—sabermetrics, the detailed analysis of baseball statistics, is the best way to evaluate baseball players, including decisions on whom to draft out of high school and college. According to the movie, the major-league scouting system and the reliance on the experience and intuition of seasoned baseball scouts are seriously out-of-date. *Moneyball* makes a convincing argument for its thesis.

Trouble with the Curve was the big hit baseball movie of 2012. It tells the story of an aging scout, Gus Lobel, who works for the Atlanta Braves. The baseball theme of the film is clear—old-fashioned scouting still has a significant role in baseball decisions and no major-league team should rely solely on computers to make hiring decisions. *Trouble with the Curve* makes a convincing argument for its thesis. Thus, the two films, when viewed in tandem, raise but do not resolve what has recently become an age-old dispute in baseball, i.e., personal scouting versus computers.

Gus Lobel is nearing the end of his contract with the Atlanta Braves, and some in the front office believe he is long past his prime. Pete, the head of scouting, supports Gus but worries that Gus is having health problems. Pete asks Mickey, Gus's daughter, to spend a few days with her father to see if he is okay. Mickey agrees to do so, despite being on the partnership track at the large law firm in which she works, with almost no time for days off, and also being somewhat estranged from her father. Then, when Mickey discovers that Gus's eyesight is failing, she goes on the scouting trip with her father as he evaluates a top prospect, Bo Gentry, with the two traveling from field to field in the Carolinas.

Trouble with the Curve opened to mixed reviews. The primary criticism was the film's clichéd plot. Most viewers of the movie will know, after about fifteen minutes, that Mickey and Gus will come to terms with their lifelong differences; that Mickey will fall in love with Johnny Flanagan, the good-looking young scout for the Boston Red Sox; Gus will be proven right when he evaluates Bo Gentry based on Gus's scouting skills, not Bo's computer stats; and that by the end of the film, Mickey will give up her unsatisfying life in the legal profession and somehow move into the world of sports. (The last story arc is particularly satisfying to baseball fans who are also attorneys.)

Other negatives of the film are its Disney-like villains. Bo Gentry is portrayed, not just as a very good baseball player, but as a conceited, loudmouth creep, always telling people about the money and the women he will have once he reaches the majors and even charging for his autographs while he is still in high school. The man gunning for Gus in the Braves' front office, Phillip Sanderson, is portrayed as insensitive, greedy, and dishonest, even sending a second scout to watch Bo Gentry, unbeknownst to Gus.

All of these criticisms are fair, and if viewers cannot get past them, they will not like the movie. Viewers who can will surely enjoy the location shooting on baseball fields of the South; an excellent performance by Clint Eastwood as Gus, with the Hollywood star embodying his age-appropriate character; the beautiful and engaging Amy Adams as Mickey; and the love of baseball that comes through in the film. *Trouble with the Curve* is also very amusing in spots, particularly in Gus's mutterings under his breath or his sarcastic remarks to others; the banter among the other old baseball scouts; and Johnny's charming way in which he pursues Mickey. Indeed, the love story itself is quite entertaining. It complements the baseball story rather than detracts from it.

Trouble with the Curve does a good job of showing the life of a baseball scout, staying in a cheap motel because there is nothing better in sight; spending evenings at local bars; going to games to view just one player but having to watch them all; and sitting with scouts from other major-league teams on a daily basis, because how many unknown prospects are out there these days? Most of the scouts are older. They easily joke with each other because they have probably been sitting together for years, trying to evaluate young talent. The high school baseball scenes are also a nice slice of Americana, with play on small fields with limited seating and fans sometimes sitting on the grass, but with the crowd always enthusiastic. These high school baseball games are important to the families of the players and to the locals. Baseball does thrive as the national pastime in these settings.

The love of the game comes through in these surroundings, but also in Gus's unwillingness to leave the game after many years as a scout; Johnny Flanagan's desire to stay with the game after his pitching career flamed out, now as a scout and later hopefully as a member of the Red Sox broadcasting team; and the trivia contests between Mickey and Johnny over obscure baseball facts. Mickey is a true feminist, close to becoming the youngest partner at her law firm, but still enthralled with the game she learned as she traveled with her father as a young girl. For baseball fans, the film also addresses one very old and one very new idea in the game. The old concept is that the inability to hit a curve ball has ended the potential careers of many young players. The new concept is that, particularly in recent years, the first-round pick of a team in a Major League Baseball draft has significant importance, even though it is still not quite as important as the first-round picks in football and basketball.

All of that said, the ending of the film is a little hard to take. Matters seem to take a bad turn for Gus and Mickey when the Braves choose Bo Gentry as the team's first pick, over Gus's advice. Suddenly, Mickey discovers a pitching prospect in Rigo Sanchez, apparently the son of the owner of the motel at which she is staying. Rigo has a good fastball and a wicked curve, yet he never played baseball in high school. This is all a little hard to believe, particularly when

Bo Gentry cannot hit Rigo when Rigo pitches against him at a tryout in Turner Field, thereby confirming that Gus was right about Bo all the time. To top it off, coincidentally, a prior draft pick of Gus's who was struggling in the minors is now playing very well, just because Gus recognized that the kid was homesick and brought his parents down to see him play. As the screen fades to black, the hero and heroine are happy and the villains are punished, but only after a *deus ex machina* climax. The ending of *Trouble with the Curve* is unconvincing.

Early on in the film, Gus says to Pete, the head of Braves' scouting, "Anybody who uses computers doesn't know a damn thing about this game." He goes on to explain, "A computer, that can't tell if a kid's got instincts or not; or if he can hit a cutoff man or hit behind the runner; or look into a kid's face that has just gone 0 for 4 and know if he's going to be able to come back the next night like nothing's happened. No, a computer can't tell you all that crap. I'll tell you." Gus believes that good scouts are the heart of the game. This is the antithesis of Billy Beane's philosophy in *Moneyball*. In fact, that dispute between old and new baseball philosophies is at the core of *Moneyball*.

In *Trouble with the Curve*, while Gus's opinion about the value of scouts to baseball is an important aspect of the film, it is not a core element, because all of the major-league teams who are interested in Bo Gentry have sent scouts to see him. The core baseball dispute in *Trouble with the Curve* is not the value of scouting but whether Gus is over the hill and should be replaced by a younger scout. Thus, *Trouble with the Curve* tees up the dispute over the baseball philosophies expressed in *Moneyball* but never tries to resolve it. Nevertheless, if Gus Lobos had worked for the Oakland Athletics in 2002, he probably would have been fired by Billy Beane. Also, Beane would have probably drafted Bo Gentry, to his ultimate chagrin.

Problems and all, *Trouble with the Curve* is a first-class production, with an excellent cast and a strong plot amid the clichés. It is well worth seeing for its entertainment value but also as a cinematic response to the baseball philosophy of *Moneyball*.

Pastime (1990)

The protagonist of *Pastime* is career minor-league pitcher Roy Dean Bream, who made only one appearance in the big leagues, giving up a grand-slam home run to Stan Musial. It is 1957 and Roy Dean is now forty-one years old. He is a relief pitcher for the Tri-City Steamers, a Class-D minor-league team playing somewhere in California. As the film opens, Roy Dean is struggling with his pitching. The owner of the club would like the old man fired; the manager is standing behind him.

Roy Dean has a role model that keeps him going, a pitcher named Jack Quinn. In real life, Jack Quinn was a major-league pitcher for twenty-three seasons, winning 247 games playing for several different teams, including the New York Yankees, Philadelphia Athletics, and Boston Red Sox. Quinn made his major-league debut on April 15, 1909, at the age of twenty-five, pitching for the New York Yankees (then known as the Highlanders). In 1928, at the age of forty-five, Quinn had his best major-league season ever. He won eighteen games while losing only seven, for the fifth-best winning percentage in the American League that year. On October 12, 1929, the forty-six-year-old Quinn became the oldest pitcher to start a World Series game, and the following year, on October 4, 1930, he became the oldest pitcher to finish a World Series game. Quinn's last game in the majors was for the Cincinnati Reds in 1933 at the age of forty-nine. After his major-league career was finished, Quinn pitched a few more times in the minor leagues, with his last game in 1935 at the age of fifty-one or fifty-two.

Early on in the film, Roy Dean mentions Jack Quinn as the oldest pitcher ever to play the game and still third-highest in career pitching appearances. Roy is just six games behind Quinn's career pitching statistic and even though Roy Dean's appearances have all been in the minor leagues except for one, Roy Dean wants to first pass Quinn in appearances and then perhaps continue pitching for several more years. (If Roy Dean is accurate about Quinn being in third place in career pitching appearances in 1957, those pitching appearances must include Quinn's minor-league appearances as Quinn was not in third place in major-league appearances at that time.)

Passing Quinn's career statistic, unfortunately, is not to be. When Roy Dean throws a wild pitch with the bases loaded and allows the winning run to score in a seventeen-inning game, the team owner finally gets his way. Roy Dean is fired. Roy Dean, for whom baseball is his entire life, is unable to accept the end of his long career. He sneaks into the minor-league stadium at night, turns on the lights, and throws his heart out pitching into the backstop, to the cheers of the imagined fans. Roy Dean then succumbs, dying on the pitcher's mound that he loved. After the fact, it is learned that he suffered from high blood pressure.

There is a lot to like in *Pastime*. Set in 1957, it evokes the atmosphere of the low minor leagues as perhaps no other film has. There is the obtrusive public address announcers; long bus rides, including one on a bus that breaks down and the players having to take turns pushing the bus; the owner of the team having to sell hot dogs in the stands when the high school vendor calls in sick; and the players smoking when they are practicing in the field.

There are also some good baseball scenes, such as when Roy Dean comes in as a relief pitcher with the bases loaded and gets an out before throwing the wild pitch, or when Tyrone, the newest pitcher on the team, is ordered to throw at the first batter he faces since the other team deliberately hit a batter of the Steamers in the previous half-inning. Tyrone is reluctant to throw such a pitch, wondering why the managers do not just throw at each other, but he finally manages to throw a pitch at the batter, resulting in his ejection from his first game. Roy Dean also mentors Tyrone, helping him to avoid giving away his curve ball by the way he raises his leg when he is about to throw that pitch.

One incentive for baseball fans to see *Pastime* is the appearance of several baseball greats in cameo roles. Ernie Banks, Duke Snider, Harmon Killebrew, Bob Feller, Don Newcombe, and Bill Mazeroski are in the film as fans, a flag raiser, and attendees at Roy Dean's funeral. Unfortunately, if the viewer blinks, these former players, most of whom are Hall of Famers, will be completely missed, and even if the viewer does not blink, these ballplayers were so old and so long past their playing careers in 1990 that few will recognize them.

Baseball fans enjoy movies that extoll the virtues of the game, elevate the game to far greater importance than other sports, have a feel for the past of the game, and have real ballplayers in the film. *Pastime* displays all of these characteristics, but there are simply not enough of these baseball moments. The rest of the film seems to be just a hodgepodge of unfocused ideas and events, such as a hint of racism in the treatment of Tyrone and an uninteresting romantic element, making the film a hard view for even the most devout fans of the summer game.

Talent for the Game (1991)

California Angels baseball scout Virgil Sweet will do just about anything to find baseball talent. As *Talent for the Game* begins, Virgil rides a mine elevator down into a deep pit and gives a tryout to a young mineworker who has a wicked fastball and potential professional baseball talent. The tryout occurs in a low passageway with inches of water on the floor. Virgil is clearly dedicated to the sport, but, unfortunately, the California Angels no longer appreciate Virgil's contributions to the team. The Angels' new owner, Gil Lawrence, who has no experience in baseball, has decided that the team's scouting system is too expensive. He wants to fire all of the team's scouts and rely instead on Major League Baseball's central scouting system. Unless Virgil can find a hot prospect quickly, he will be out of a job.

Fortune then smiles on Virgil, and more out of luck than anything else, he discovers a pitching phenom in a rural area in Idaho. The pitcher's name is Sammy Bodeen, and although Sammy has never played in organized baseball, he has the talent for the game. Bodeen impresses the Angels in his tryout, and then, more as a publicity move than anything else, Gil Lawrence decides to have Bodeen make his major-league debut immediately (or immediately after Lawrence's publicity machine goes into effect). Virgil is opposed to that decision, believing Bodeen needs more seasoning in the minors, but there is nothing Virgil can do. Sammy starts the next Saturday-night game for the Angels, pitching against the Kansas City Royals.

There are several mentions in *Talent for the Game* of two former major-league pitchers, Eddie Bane and David Clyde, and worries about whether Sammy Bodeen's fate could be similar to the two of them. Eddie Bane was a first-round draft selection of the Minnesota Twins in 1973. Without spending any time in the minors, he made his professional pitching debut on July 4, 1973. Pitching against the Kansas City Royals, Bane had a good start that day, allowing only three hits. However, his lack of minor-league experience caught up with him quickly and his record for his entire season was a very poor

0–5. Although Bane came back to pitch for the Twins for a short time a few years later, most of the rest of his brief career was spent in the minors.

Similarly, David Clyde was drafted out of high school by the Texas Rangers as the first overall pick in the 1973 draft. Clyde may actually be the inspiration for the fictional Sammy Bodeen of the movie, just as the then-owner of the Rangers, Bob Short, may be the inspiration for Gil Lawrence. Just out of high school, Clyde had his first major-league start on June 27, 1973, when he pitched against the Minnesota Twins. Clyde had a rocky first inning, walking the first two batters, but thereafter pitched well and won the game. The Rangers had originally intended to have Clyde pitch two games in the majors and then be sent to the minors for more teaching. However, because Clyde was such a big draw for a franchise that then had serious financial problems, Bob Short, who had no baseball experience, kept him on the major-league roster, essentially as a marketing ploy. Clyde did not perform that well over the rest of the year. His record was 4–8 and he had an ERA of 5.01. Clyde only played five years in the majors (not all consecutively), with a lifetime record of 18–33.

Most baseball professionals believe that Bane and Clyde were brought along too quickly, and that they should have spent some time in the minors before pitching in the majors. In other words, their long-term careers were sacrificed for short-term results. That same issue comes up in *Talent for the Game*, as a result of Gil Lawrence's decision, for marketing purposes only, of pitching phenom Sammy Bodeen in the majors before Bodeen acquires the requisite minor-league experience. Gil Lawrence is the epitome of the baseball owner who is a businessman only, in the game just for a profit. He is willing to risk Bodeen's career for a full house at the end of the season just because the home team is having a poor financial year.

Talent for the Game directs its criticism against Lawrence, not so much for his greed but for his lack of experience in baseball. Lawrence's previous business experience has been in advertising. However, most baseball owners have little experience in baseball, so the criticism is directed at all of them. Of course, if an owner did have substantial baseball experience, he would probably not have enough money to buy a team.

Talent for the Game has its baseball heart in the right place. It conveys the joys of the game, from Virgil scouting talent in the boondocks of the country to a filled Anaheim Stadium anxious to see the major-league debut of Sammy Bodeen. Bodeen's debut with the Angels is shown in detail, taking up substantial screen time, even though the action consumes only an inning and a half. Fans are there on the mound with Bodeen, as he suffers through a first inning of pitching in which he gives up four runs. The audience agonizes along with Bodeen as he keeps pitching in an excruciating situation, perhaps hoping he will be taken out of the game.

Virgil Sweet always wanted to catch in the major leagues, but after being hit in the head with a pitch, his career was cut short. Virgil finally fulfills his dream of playing in the majors when he impersonates the regular Angels catcher during the second inning of the game so that he can catch Bodeen, hoping that Bodeen will start to pitch well once he has a familiar catcher. Virgil is unrecognizable with all of the catcher's gear on, although it is hard to believe that no one notices Virgil's mustache. This is an endearing moment in the film, as Virgil fulfills a lifelong dream. The audience is happy for him, even though Virgil can never tell anyone what he did or he will be thrown out of baseball.

While an endearing moment for the film, it is also a dumb one. Could anyone have truly gotten away with that stunt in a real game? Virgil is lucky that there were no pop-ups behind home plate. Due to his training as a catcher, Virgil surely would have taken off his mask to catch the ball, revealing his cheating conduct.

In fact, the entire ending of *Talent for the Game* is dumb. Virgil Sweet tries to convince Gil Lawrence not to pitch Bodeen so soon, before he has some experience and training in the minors. Lawrence refuses to budge, and because Virgil does not want to lose his new position as assistant general manager of the team, he acquiesces in the folly. As expected, Bodeen has a miserable first inning, giving up four runs on hit after hit. Virgil's position is correct! Then, in the second inning, Bodeen turns it around, with a three-up, three-down inning. Virgil's position is incorrect! In fact, as Gil Lawrence then says, "When I'm right, I'm right."

Is Virgil correct or incorrect? The careers of Eddie Bane and David Clyde suggest that Virgil was correct and that there are bad times ahead for Sammy Bodeen. Nevertheless, the contrived ending of the film completely ignores this likelihood. *Talent for the Game* sacrifices a logical ending for an illogical one, solely in its quest for a happy ending. *Talent for the Game* is enjoyable enough, but its dumb ending weakens the movie so much that it is a hard film to recommend.

Million Dollar Arm (2014)

Walt Disney Pictures has a long track record of producing sports films based on true stories, including *Cool Runnings* (1993) (about the Jamaican bobsled team that competed in the 1988 Winter Olympics), *Miracle* (2004) (the story of the American hockey team that won the Gold Medal in the 1980 Olympics), *Remember the Titans* (2000) (the story of an African-American football coach in a Virginia high school in the early 1970s), and *McFarland, USA* (2015) (about a 1987 cross-country team from a Mexican American high school that won the state championship). For baseball, there are *The Rookie* (2002) (about a pitcher who first pitched in the major leagues at the age of thirty-five) and *Million Dollar Arm* (2014) (about the first ballplayers from India to ever sign professional baseball contracts in the United States).

The plots of these films have much in common. They involve sports teams or individuals with only a long shot chance at success, their hard work toward achieving their impossible dreams, disappointments along the way, and then, when least expected, a happy conclusion, with the teams or individuals finally achieving at least some success in their sport of choice, satisfying the audience's desires for a positive ending.

The frameworks of these films are clichés of sorts, with very few surprises along the way. However, these Disney films are also known for their excellent production values, likable performers, and light-hearted scripts, usually making these films highly enjoyable. *Million Dollar Arm* is no exception.

Down-on-his-luck sports agent J. B. Bernstein concocts an idea to bring baseball to India and two Indian players to America by way of a talent contest he has dubbed "Million Dollar Arm." Backed by a wealthy investor, Mr. Chang, Bernstein travels throughout India, a country in which few play baseball, auditioning young men to see who can throw a baseball with speed and accuracy, leading to a final televised contest in India in which two young men will be chosen from the finalists to come to America, be trained as pitchers, and then given a tryout before several major-league scouts.

After some early difficulties in India, two young athletes, Rinku Singh and Dinesh Patel, win the contest and come to America with Bernstein, where they are trained by Tom House, the coach at USC. However, Chang has decreed that the two players must be ready for a tryout within one year of Bernstein leaving for India. No one with any knowledge of baseball believes that goal is a realistic possibility. Nevertheless, most people in the audience will undoubtedly expect that, despite the long odds, Bernstein's hopeless dream will be fulfilled by the end of the movie and Singh and Patel will get that tryout, or why make the movie?

Million Dollar Arm is a very likable film, clichés and all. Jon Hamm is engaging as J. B. Bernstein, hard to dislike even when he is acting selfishly, such as not attending the boys' practices, or saying unknowingly cruel things, such as referring to the boys as his investment. Pitobash Tripathy is hilarious as the Indian interpreter and baseball fanatic hired by Bernstein to translate for the boys. Alan Arkin is amusing as Ray Poitevint, the baseball scout who comes to India with Bernstein, sleeps through most of the tryouts, but can still tell the speed of a pitch just by the sound of the ball.

The film is genuinely amusing in spots. With regard to the baseball, most of the players at the early tryouts in India cannot throw above thirty miles an hour. Singh acquires the nickname "The Flamingo" because he holds his front foot up for quite a while before throwing to the plate. When Singh and Patel first pitch in practice in America, they either bounce the balls or throw them over the catcher's head. When he sees a fielding glove for the first time, Patel asks if it is really necessary to use one.

After the boys have their successful tryout, the film discloses the futures of most of the characters. However, with regard to Singh and Patel, the film only reveals that "Rinku Singh and Dinesh Kumar Patel were both signed by the Pittsburgh Pirates 10 months after the day that they first picked up a baseball. They were the first Indian athletes to be signed by a major American sports league." This is a type of before-the-final-credits reveal that is common to films inspired by true stories and even some that are not (i.e., *Amer-*

ican Graffiti [1973]). In this case, however, Disney does not tell the whole story.

Singh and Patel were signed by the Pirates in 2008; *Million Dollar Arm* was released in 2014. Most viewers would probably want to know more of what happened to the two young players after they were signed by the Pirates. In fact, Singh did pitch for the Pirates in the low minor leagues, as well as for teams in Australia and the Dominican Republic. In 2013, in an American baseball tradition, he underwent Tommy John surgery on his left elbow. As of this writing, it appears that Singh's professional baseball career has ended. Patel pitched for two seasons in the low minor leagues for the Pirates but was out of baseball for good after the end of the 2010 season.

Even though the facts about the baseball careers of Singh and Patel are not as positive as the hope, it still would have been nice for Disney to tell the whole story. Reality is not always depressing, even in a Disney film. Nevertheless, the omission of the full after-stories of Singh and Patel is ameliorated somewhat by pictures and film of the real Singh and Patel, shown behind the closing credits, as they take their journey through the world of professional baseball with celebrity status.

For some reason, *Million Dollar Arm* does not explain all of the facts of its premise. For example, if Bernstein is looking for a million-dollar arm, why does the winner of the contest, Singh, only win a $100,000? The filmmakers forgot to mention that in the real-life try-outs, the winning player could only be awarded $1,000,000 if he threw three consecutive strikes over ninety miles per hour in a bonus session.

When a film is designated as "based on a true story," that is a significant clue that the film will not be totally accurate in its facts. *Million Dollar Arm* is no exception, from big matters, such as it not being Bernstein's sole idea for the *Million Dollar Arm* television reality show in India and that Bernstein's agency was not in financial trouble at the time, to small matters, such as Brenda, Bernstein's love interest in the film, being a business executive in real life instead of a doctor. Much like other films of its type, there are several other embellishments to the story line of *Million Dollar Arm* for purposes both of comedy and drama.

However, the basic concept—that two young men from India who had never heard of baseball before Bernstein traveled to their country had a tryout with major-league teams within one year and received professional baseball contracts with the Pittsburgh Pirates—is truly amazing, The story of Singh and Patel is surely worthy of a motion picture and *Million Dollar Arm* does not disappoint.

Big Leaguer (1953)

Big Leaguer is a slight tale about a tryout camp of the New York Giants and several young men taking their shot at playing in the major leagues. The film is best known today, if it is known at all, as the first film directed by Robert Aldrich and as the movie that provides an opportunity for movie buffs to see Edward G. Robinson in a baseball uniform, although admittedly viewers had the chance to see Robinson in a prison baseball uniform in *Larceny, Inc.* (1942).

Robinson plays Hans Lobert, a former third baseman for the New York Giants, who has been relegated for many years into running the Giants' spring-training camp in Florida for potential ballplayers who have not yet signed with any other team. Hans's niece, Christy, who works in the Giants' front office, has come to Florida to assist her uncle. She warns Hans that the front office is unhappy with the results Hans has been obtaining and that the Giants may replace Hans with someone else if he cannot find a good crop of players this year.

While there are over a hundred players in camp that year, the film focuses on Adam Polachuk, the son of an immigrant coal miner from Pennsylvania, who wants his son in college rather than playing baseball. Therefore, Adam did not tell his father that he was trying out for the New York Giants. At the conclusion of the film, when the Giants prospects are playing the Dodgers rookies in a game that may determine whether or not Hans continues to run the camp, Adam's father unexpectedly appears. He wants Adam to quit baseball and go off to college, but after seeing the big game, he has a change of heart.

Edward G. Robinson is good, as always, in the film, but he is miscast as a former major-league ballplayer who now runs a training camp for prospective ballplayers. The part of Hans Lobert is often described as "avuncular," and Robinson simply does not have an avuncular screen persona. Also, Robinson never looks quite right in that New York baseball uniform. Perhaps it is because he buckles the pants too high on his belly, or perhaps it is because he

Adam Polachuk (Jeff Richards) comes to bat in the last inning of the exhibition game between the Giants and Dodgers rookies in *Big Leaguer* (1952). Richards was once a Minor League Baseball player.

just appears to be too small to have been a ballplayer. Whatever the reason, Robinson seems out of place during much of the film.

Brian McLennan, a fictional sports columnist for one of the New York papers who has decided to write a story about the Giants tryout camp, narrates *Big Leaguer*, sometimes making the film seem more like a documentary than a work of fiction. That impression is aided by the fact that the story does not have a strong narrative. In addition to the scenes concerning Adam's personal conflict about playing baseball and Hans's job situation, there is a young player named

Tippy Mitchell who cannot live up to the accomplishments of his father, major-league first baseman Wally Mitchell, and a hotshot young pitcher whom Hans cuts from the team, perhaps to Hans's regret. These story arcs are simply not strong enough to carry a film, which is why the film sometimes seems more like a documentary than a Hollywood movie.

The story arc of an aging coach or scout pitted against the front office (or, in other films, the parents at a school) fighting for the survival of his career is a well-used plot point for sports films, from *Hoosiers* (1986) to *Trouble with the Curve* (2012). As every moviegoer knows, Hans will produce an excellent player at the tryout camp and prove to the front office brass that his camp is a worthwhile endeavor for the Giants. But surprisingly, that never happens. *Big Leaguer* is so unfocused in its story lines that the issue as to whether or not Hans will continue to run the camp is never resolved by the end of the film. In fact, the issue seems to have been completely forgotten as the film comes to its conclusion. Instead, *Big Leaguer* ends with a cliché. Adam comes to the plate against the Brooklyn rookies with two men on and two men out and his team trailing by two runs. Adam hits a walk-off home run, winning the game for the underdogs.

Big Leaguer also has its good moments. The baseball is believable, aided by the fact that the film was made on location at the Giants' training camp in Melbourne, Florida, and that Jeff Richards, who plays Adam Polachuk, was once a minor-league player. Chuy, the Cuban player who needs a dictionary to understand English, is often amusing. The ending, with Mr. Polachuk in the stands, learning about baseball from Wally Mitchell and having a change of heart about baseball, is endearing and amusing.

Mr. Polachuk, who is of Polish descent, is particularly impressed by the story of Joe DiMaggio, the son of Italian immigrants, who has become successful at baseball both in terms of status and compensation. Chuy, the Cuban native, holds his own against the American ballplayers. Hans, the former big leaguer, is of Dutch descent. Thus, *Big Leaguer* may actually have a little bit of a theme to it. Baseball is the great equalizer. A person's nationality and background are not important; it is only his ability to play the game that counts. Of course, if that were the theme of *Big Leaguer*, it would have been nice to see a few African American players in training camp. The major leagues had been integrated for many years prior to 1953.

There are several real-life sports figures in the film, the most famous of whom is Carl Hubbell. Hubbell spent his entire career with the Giants, being voted the National League's Most Valuable Player on two occasions. The Hall of Fame pitcher is probably most famous for his legendary performance in the 1934 All-Star Game, when he struck out Babe Ruth, Lou Gehrig, Jimmie Foxx, Al Simmons, and Joe Cronin, future Hall of Famers all, in succession. At the time of *Big Leaguer*, Hubbell was the director of player development for the Giants, similar to his role in the film, so it was not much of a stretch for him to appear in the feature. The Hans Lobert of the film is loosely based on a Major League Baseball player named John Bernard "Hans" Lobert, who played third base for several teams, including the New York Giants, and then went on to become a manager and a scout.

Summer Catch (2001)

Baseball is played on many different levels, with players usually starting with Little League Baseball and, if they are good enough, working their way up to PONY, Colt, American Legion, or AAU ball, then high school and college ball, to finally the professional leagues, both minor and major. Less well known are the college summer leagues, where talented college baseball players go to hone their skills and play against the best competition available and, not incidentally, to be tracked by major-league scouts.

These days there are more than fifty summer college baseball leagues operating in the United States. To be eligible, a player usually must have completed at least one year of college and have at least one year of college eligibility left. The players generally report to their summer league once their college baseball season is over. Volunteer local families often house the players, who receive no pay so that they can retain their amateur status. Many players, however, get day jobs in the towns in which they temporarily live, such as working as a camp counselor, painter, cook, or member of a grounds crew so that they can make at least a little money during the summer.

The Alaska Baseball League, the New York Collegiate Baseball

League, the Texas Collegiate League, the California Collegiate League, and the Cape Cod Baseball League (CCBL) are among the top leagues in the country, although most experts consider the CCBL to be the best. The CCBL plays its games on the peninsula of Cape Cod in Massachusetts, about fifty miles southeast of Boston.

At present, the CCBL has ten teams, playing games from mid-June to mid-August. It is estimated that close to 1,000 big-league ballplayers are alumni of the CCBL, with recently, on average, more than 200 alumni of the league on major-league rosters each year. Today, the league is a major tourist attraction for Cape Cod, providing visitors a chance to get a close look at potential major leaguers.

All of that is background for the 2001 film *Summer Catch*, about a local baseball prospect, Ryan Dunne, who gets a chance to play for the Chatham Athletics in the CCBL one summer, hoping, just as everyone else in the league is hoping, to become a Major League Baseball player one day. Ryan is an atypical player for the CCBL in recent years, since he is a native of Cape Cod. During his summer of baseball on the Cape, Ryan falls in love with Tenley Parrish, who is vacationing with her family. Most of the film concerns the relationship between the two young lovers. As a result, *Summer Catch* is more of a romance than a baseball film, although the CCBL is always in the background of the story.

As a romance, there is little that is original to the story. Tenley is rich, beautiful, and sophisticated; Ryan is the poor son of the local gardener. Tenley's father is opposed to the romance. He has someone from his own class in mind for Tenley. He also wants Tenley to become an investment banker; she wants to become an architect. Ryan has his own family problems, with a father and brother who do not always support him. Despite all of these apparently irreconcilable differences, no one will be surprised with the ending of the film.

Although *Summer Catch* is filled with clichés, it has its interest. There are two attractive performers in the lead roles, Freddie Prinze Jr. as Ryan and Jessica Biel as Tenley. The members of the supporting cast of mainly unknowns (except for Brian Dennehy as the coach) are all quite good. The play in the field seems realistic. The direction of the movie is adequate. Also, the film does provide a fair approximation of baseball in the summer on Cape Cod, despite the fact that most of the picture was shot in North Carolina. *Summer*

Freddie Prinze Jr. plays Chatham Athletics pitcher Ryan Dunne in *Summer Catch* (2001).

Catch shows the high quality of the game that is played by the collegians, the closeness of the fans to the field, the pressure on these young men to succeed, and the recognition, to a degree, that these are still young men, not professional athletes.

Unfortunately, although the setting seems real, the climax of the film is not. Near the end of the film, Ryan is pitching a no-hitter through one out in the ninth inning, while at the same time Tenley is leaving Cape Cod to go to San Francisco to become an investment banker, instead of following her dream of becoming an architect. When Ryan sees Tenley leave the ball field, he decides to voluntarily quit the game he is pitching, so that he can pursue Tenley. His explanation to his catcher is that no one will remember a no-hitter thrown in a summer league, but the right girl is forever. For some reason, his coach and a Philadelphia Phillies scout have no problem with Ryan leaving the game with just two batters left, even though his relief pitcher has to pitch with no warm-ups. Most baseball fans, however, will be flabbergasted, believing that pitching a no-hitter carries great significance and that the summer game is more important than a love that will probably never last. If there is any difference of opinion on this, it will probably be between female viewers, who see *Summer Catch* as a romance, and male viewers, who see *Summer Catch* as a baseball film.

Among the several famous people who appear in the film are Hank Aaron, the legendary hitter who played for the Braves both in Milwaukee and Atlanta and broke Babe Ruth's career home-run record in 1974, who has a surprise cameo as a scout watching the game at the climax of the film, and Ken Griffey Jr., a prodigious home-run hitter both for the Seattle Mariners and the Cincinnati Reds, who, in the epilogue to the movie, playing for Cincinnati, hits a home run off Ryan in Ryan's first major-league appearance, pitching for the Philadelphia Phillies. Curt Gowdy, one of the most successful broadcasters of all time, who called many World Series, NFL games, and Final Four basketball games for television (including, coincidentally, Hank Aaron's record-breaking home run), plays himself as the radio voice of the Chatham A's.

Summer Catch generally did not receive good reviews upon its release. Its clichéd story line, its sex scenes that are played for laughs but which are more embarrassing than funny, and its unbelievable conclusion, justify those poor reviews. However, the film still has some interest for baseball fans, as a result of its setting on Cape Cod and its evocation of an important aspect of baseball, the collegiate summer leagues.

3

YOUTH BASEBALL

The Great American Pastime (1956)

Long before the Bad News Bears began to play baseball and even longer before the Bad News Bears went to Japan, there were the Panthers, the first Little League team of the baseball cinema. While the Bad News Bears performed in two sequels and one remake, the Panthers are long forgotten, and for good reason. *The Great American Pastime* is a difficult film to watch.

Of course, young people have been playing baseball in America since forever, but it was not until 1939 that Little League Baseball was founded as a separate legal entity in Williamsport, Pennsylvania. By the 1950s, Little League Baseball had become very popular, with leagues in all forty-eight states and some foreign countries. MGM therefore must have concluded in 1956 that it would be a good idea to make a film about Little League Baseball with its apparent built-in audience.

However, *The Great American Pastime* was both a critical and box office failure. In fact, with the exception of *Moochie of the Little League*, a television movie shown on *Walt Disney Presents* in 1959, and some episodes of television shows in the 1950s and 1960s featuring Little League Baseball, *The Great American Pastime* was so unsuccessful that it seems to have ended this subgenre of baseball entertainment for about twenty years.

The core problem with *The Great American Pastime* is that the film is more about the adults than the young ballplayers. The film is introduced by the Panthers' new coach, Bruce Hallerton, who, speaking directly to the camera, complains about how bad Little League coaching has been for him and his standing in the community. The film then goes on to show some of the reasons for Bruce's dissatisfaction, concentrating on matters such as a banker inviting Bruce and his wife, Betty, over for dinner in order to pressure Bruce into allowing the banker's son to pitch for the Panthers (outside of the house, the son promptly makes an errant pitch, smashing

Tom Ewell plays Little League coach Bruce Hallerton, and Anne Francis plays his wife, Betty, in *The Great American Pastime* (1956).

Bruce's car window); parents criticizing Bruce for his managerial style or asking him why the team does not play better; a player's mother, Doris Patterson, flirting with Bruce in order to convince Bruce to play her son; and Betty becoming upset about the attention Bruce is giving to Doris.

While all of this is going on, the Little League kids are lost in the shuffle. Because the film makes little effort to introduce the youngsters to the audience on an individual basis, it is impossible to tell them apart, with or without a scorecard. The film has no time to concentrate on the kids because it spends so much time on Bruce's real and imagined problems. The silly ending of the film, in which Bruce inexplicably becomes the hero of the neighborhood after winning a single ball game, is once again all about Bruce and not the kids.

Little League Baseball may have been different in the 1950s than it has been in the past sixty years, but it seems very strange that Bruce's son plays for a different team than the one coached by his father; that the kids seem to be playing on a field that is the size of a high school field, if not larger; or that coaching involves mainly calisthenics and not much else. On the other hand, it is surely within the scope of believability to have one coach load his team with the best players; to have another coach supportive of a young player just because his mother is attractive; or to have the parents more stressed out as to who has won or lost than the players themselves.

Not surprisingly, the best parts of *The Great American Pastime* are the scenes of actual games. In the Panthers' first game, there are easy ground balls missed by the Panthers fielders; easy fly balls dropped by the outfielders; a fly ball dropping in front of four fielders who have surrounded it; and Bruce telling his third baseman to play off the line at third, with the next ball then being a grounder just over third. The Panthers' pitcher seems to be lobbing the ball toward home plate rather than employing a proper pitching motion. (The parents are right; Bruce is not much of a coach.) When the Panthers come to bat, it is usually quick outs for the team, with the Panthers only having three base runners during their entire first game. Unfortunately, one of them is picked off first base, another is doubled off first base, and the third is thrown out by a mile trying to steal second base. In the final game of the season, a runner's pants slip down as he is caught between third base and home plate, but he still scores the winning run, essentially stealing three bases in the process.

Even with the many films that were made subsequent to *The Great American Pastime* about youth baseball and the players' antics on the field, it is hard not to smile at these scenes from *The Great American Pastime*. Not only are moments like these often the highlights of youth baseball films, they are also some of the minor delights of watching Little League Baseball in person, as very young players try to do their very best at a very difficult game. If *The Great American Pastime* had concentrated on the ball games and the players rather than on the adults and their petty pursuits, the film could have been worthwhile. Unfortunately, that is not the case and *The Great American Pastime* is not worth the while of any baseball or movie fan.

The Bad News Bears (1976)

The Bad News Bears involves a team named the Bears that is forced upon the very competitive North Valley Little League due to litigation brought by a disgruntled parent whose child was not allowed to play in the league. The league is none too happy about the Bears playing that year, and the league's attitude is reflected in many ways. While all of the other teams have beautifully printed nameplates on the scoreboard, the Bears' name is handwritten; the team is given the worst equipment; and perhaps most important, the team has the worst coach and the worst (although most ethnically diverse) players.

The coach is Morris Buttermaker (Walter Matthau), sometimes referred to sarcastically in the film as Boilermaker and other pejorative names. Buttermaker is a former Minor League Baseball pitcher but now an alcoholic, who cleans swimming pools in Southern California as his primary vocation. Buttermaker's only claim to fame is that he struck out Ted Williams once or twice in spring training many years ago. Buttermaker has to be paid to coach the Bears, probably a violation of little league rules, but then who else would agree to coach this team of misfits on short notice?

At the beginning of *The Bad News Bears*, Buttermaker is only in it for the money, providing very little coaching for his players and being content to allow the kids see him smoking and drinking on the bench. After the team's disastrous first game, Buttermaker finally develops an interest in the Bears, actually doing some teaching and also recruiting some better players for the team. However, as the Bears start to play better and have a shot at making it to the championship game, Buttermaker loses perspective on sportsmanship. For example, he instructs his best outfielder to try to catch any ball he can get to, resulting in the outfielder practically taking the ball out of the gloves of his teammates, obviously upsetting and humiliating the other players on the Bears.

Walter Matthau plays the manager of the Bears, Morris Buttermaker, in *The Bad News Bears* (1976).

Then, in the championship game against the Yankees, Butter-maker keeps the team's best pitcher, Amanda, in the game, even though she has a sore arm. He directs another player to be deliberately hit by a pitch on two occasions, just to get on base for the next hitter. For one of the first times in the film, Buttermaker yells at his players when they make mistakes. Buttermaker has become so involved in his rivalry with the Yankees manager, Roy Turner, that they both treat the championship game as a contest between the two of them, with the players only innocent bystanders. Suddenly, after seeing the reaction of his team to his conduct and finally recognizing what the other coach is doing just to win a youth baseball game, Buttermaker sees the errors of his ways. He reverts to his former approach to the game, plays in a sportsmanlike manner, and inserts all of his kids into the championship game, even at the risk of losing the championship, thus providing a theme for *The Bad News Bears*, and an important one at that.

Even though the Bears lose in the end, it is not a personal loss for Buttermaker. It is the vagaries of youth sports. *The Bad News Bears* reiterates the concept that Little League is for the kids, and the parents and coaches are there only to facilitate matters. While *The Bad News Bears* is primarily a comedy and therefore this theme can be lost in the humor, it is still an important concept, not just for Little League coaches but also for coaches of all youth sports.

Of course, the highlights of any youth sports film that involves a team of misfits are the misplays in the field. *The Bad News Bears* has many of them. There are the balls through the infield that bounce off the leg of the center fielder; the third baseman stepping on third instead of tagging the runner sliding into third; five players, including the shortstop, chasing a ball hit into the outfield so that when the ball is thrown into the infield there is no shortstop to catch it; an outfielder catching a ball and then dropping it; the catcher running out to field a bunt and throwing the ball back toward the home-plate umpire; and an outfielder trying to throw the ball into the infield and on each try, throwing the ball only about one foot. It is hard not to laugh at these misplays in the field.

The Bad News Bears is known for its raunchy dialogue and politically incorrect language, most spewing out of the mouths of kids who are twelve years old or younger, providing some additional humor for the movie, although in the forty years since the film has been released, the humor quotient of the kids' language has decreased while the inappropriateness of the language has increased. In fact, it is the jokes told only by the visuals that are some of the best in the film. The Bears are sponsored by Chico's Bail Bonds and the company's motto, "Let Freedom Ring," is printed on the backs of the Bears' jerseys. The championship trophy won by the Yankees at the end of the film is huge and outlandish. The second place trophy won by the Bears is diminutive and bland. Buttermaker is holding a can of beer in the team photo.

For all of the humorous moments in *The Bad News Bears*, the best baseball moment in the film is not a funny one. It is an endearing one. Late in the championship game, Buttermaker puts Lupus, one of the worst players on the team, into right field. A high fly ball is hit in his direction. Lupus puts up his glove, takes a few steps back, and the ball lands in his glove, just before it would have gone over the fence. It is his first catch of the season. The players on the field and the fans in the seats are thrilled. Lupus is as excited and surprised as anyone watching the game. It is the high point of the film, just as similar incidents are the high points of many real Little League games. It also ties back into the theme of the movie, that Little League Baseball is for the kids, whether they are great or mediocre players.

The Bad News Bears was both a critical and box office success. It initiated a new subgenre of movies about youth sports. While it has aged just a bit since its first release, it is still well worth a view today.

The Bad News Bears in Breaking Training (1977)

The Little League team known as the Bears is back in its second feature film, *The Bad News Bears in Breaking Training*, and there are so many things wrong with the movie that it is hard to describe them all. Actually, it is not quite clear if the Bears are still a Little League team, since "Little League" is never mentioned in the movie, the opposing players are awfully big for Little Leaguers, there are several references to junior baseball, and the runners lead off bases and steal before the pitches cross the plate.

One of the problems with *Breaking Training* is that while films about little kids and their mishaps in sports are often quite enjoyable, the charm starts to wear off as the kids get older. However, the most significant problem with the film is that the story line is just too unbelievable. The filmmakers would have an audience believe that the Bears, a mediocre baseball team at best, which did not win the championship game in its own league (as shown in the original film), is now the California champion and has been invited to the Houston Astrodome for a game against a local team to see which team will earn the right to travel to Japan for an international baseball contest. The whole event has apparently been put together by the players themselves, as the local league is not involved. The team has no coach, and the parents know nothing about it.

To add to the unbelievable nature of the story, the parents are willing to let their children be stuffed into a van and then driven from California to Texas, without knowing who is chaperoning their kids. The van is driven by one of the players, Kelly Leak, even though he is apparently only thirteen years old. The Bears are without a manager because early on, the kids, on their own, fired the manager who was assigned to their team.

If a viewer is somehow willing to accept that unbelievable premise, that same viewer will likely be disappointed in the fact that Walter Matthau and Tatum O'Neal, who had significant roles in the first film, do not appear in the sequel. While several of the young actors who played the Bears players in the first film carry over to the sequel, the loss of the two stars is significant. Also, one of the highlights of the first film was the poor play of the Bears on the field, moments in a baseball film that can almost always get a good laugh out of a moviegoer. In *Breaking Training*, the requisite scene of the players making silly errors in the field occurs in a practice session before the big game. However, the scene falls flat because the play of the Bears had already improved by the end of the prior film, so it is not clear (or believable) that the team's skills deteriorated so quickly. In any event, since the Bears are on their way to an important game in the Houston Astrodome, an honor that could only be given to a good baseball team, their incompetent play in those scenes does not make sense.

There are also some new matters in *Breaking Training* that are very disappointing. When the team gets to Houston and still does not have a manager, Kelly Leak finds his father, who deserted him eight years ago, and convinces him to coach the team. That, unfortunately, leads to some excruciatingly obvious scenes of disputes and then reconciliation between father and son, with Kelly suddenly leaving the team and then coming back in time for the big game, as if anyone was surprised by that chain of events. (What great luck that the father knows a lot about baseball and is a good coach!)

All of that said, *Breaking Training* redeems itself, in a small way, by the baseball game between the Bears and the Houston Toros, the Texas state champions, at the end of the film. The contest, which is supposed to last four innings, is played between games of a Houston Astros doubleheader in the Houston Astrodome. In choosing the Astrodome for the location of the big game, the filmmakers made a wise choice. Just in the shots of the outside of the building from afar, it is clear that the Astrodome will be an impressive venue for the game, validating its nickname as the Eighth Wonder of the World.

Breaking Training also makes good use of the inside of the Astrodome, with its high, spherical glass roof that Tanner first marvels at by looking straight up at the top of the dome, turning in a circle and then falling down from dizziness; the visuals on the scoreboard, including the explosions; Ahmad Abdul Rahim seeing his name on the huge scoreboard for the first time; the pitcher unable to reach home plate until the umpire moves the rubber closer to home plate; and just the overall experience of a team of youngsters having the opportunity to play in such a spectacular facility. The director of the film, Michael Pressman, continually emphasizes the vast size of the facility and contrasts that with the diminutive size of the players on the field. The kids also get to meet a few of the then-current Houston Astros, including Manager Bill Virdon, center fielder César Cedeño, and first baseman and outfielder Bob Watson.

Unfortunately, the baseball play in the Astrodome is not all that convincing, with strange swings by the batters (such as swinging down at balls thrown over their heads), strange defensive plays (a ball Tanner catches on one bounce is an out), unusual umpiring (a clear strike is called a ball by the umpire), very slow base running (such as the batter crossing first base and running into foul territory instead of running straight through), and batting orders that are inconsistent. However, the game is still enjoyable, primarily because of its surprise internal climax when, because of time constraints, the game is called after two innings with the Toros in the lead, 5–0.

That leads to the best moments in the film, when Tanner refuses to leave the field and, all alone on the huge field, continues to shout, "We're not finished. The game isn't over yet." Two security guards come out and try to remove Tanner from the field, but he continually eludes them, running between them and around them (a type of incident always good for a laugh). The game finally resumes and the Bears win. If that happy ending is a little difficult to swallow, well, the enthusiasm of the players does carry the moment, and, in any event, the whole film does not make a lot of sense either.

The Bad News Bears in Breaking Training does provide baseball fans with a chance to see the Houston Astrodome being used for baseball, at a time when the facility was still in its prime, along with a mildly interesting youth baseball game. Other than that, there is little to like in the film, an unworthy successor to *The Bad News Bears* (1976).

The Bad News Bears Go to Japan (1978)

The quality of the Bad News Bears franchise dropped quickly after the original 1976 film, with *The Bad News Bears in Breaking Training* (1977) very disappointing but still far better than *The Bad News Bears Go to Japan*, which is hardly watchable at all. Of course, that drop in quality does not even come close to the precipitous drop in the career of Tony Curtis, with major starring roles in the 1950s (*The Defiant Ones* [1958] and *Some Like it Hot* [1959]), continuing through the 1960s (*The Boston Strangler* [1968]) and then hitting bottom with *The Bad News Bears Go to Japan*. What is Tony Curtis doing in this awful film?

For those who watched *The Bad News Bears in Breaking Training*, they know that by winning an exhibition game against the Texas champions, the Bears earned the right to travel to Japan and play the Japanese champions. Thus the opening of *The Bad News Bears Go to Japan* should have been obvious, with the entire Bears team from the last game, including their coach, being sent to Japan courtesy of Anheuser-Busch, the sponsor of the Texas exhibition game. However, nothing is easy or logical in Bears country, so, once again, the Bears have no coach, they have no money to travel to Japan, and apparently none of the kids has any parents. The Bears, on their own, hook up with a small-time hustler, Marvin Lazar (Tony Curtis), and it is Lazar who takes the Bears to Japan. Among the missing players are Tanner, the irrepressible shortstop from the prior films, and Carmen, the team's new pitcher from the prior movie. *Go to Japan* does not have very much in common with the prior two films in the series.

Of course, there is the requisite scene of the Bears having fielding woes, missing balls, and making errant throws. A loyal viewer of the *Bad News Bears* films might wonder what happened to the team that just beat the Texas champions in the Astrodome. How did they lose their championship playing skills so fast? Once again, these scenes are not funny, as they have already been done before in the prior two films. Also, since the Bears are representing the United States in an international contest, the scenes are embarrassing.

Go to Japan does have a staple of the series, the usual foul language and sarcastic comments of the young players. In *The Bad News Bears* (1976), the youngsters' language made them delightful, probably because it was so unexpected from kids that seemed so young.

Tony Curtis plays the newest coach of the Bears, Marvin Lazar, in both of these photos of *The Bad News Bears Go to Japan* (1978). In the top photo, the overweight catcher, Mike Engleberg, is played by Jeffrey Louis Starr, and in the bottom photo, the manager of the Japanese team is played by Tomisaburo Wakayama. The other individuals are unidentified.

By the third film in the series, the language makes the kids seem obnoxious, partially because it is repetitive but partially because the players no longer seem to be young boys anymore. The Bears now have so many adult attributes, such as the ability to negotiate contracts and fall in love with a geisha, that *Go to Japan* seems like a youth baseball film in name only.

Actually, *Go to Japan* is a baseball film in name only. Much of the film is taken up by irrelevancies, such as Kelly Leak pursuing the young geisha girl (how old is Kelly Leak supposed to be in this movie?); famous Japanese wrestler Antonio Inoki competing in a karate exhibition against an American athlete, Mean Bones Beaudine; Inoki competing in a wrestling match with a masked wrestler who turns out to be Marvin Lazar, with the play-by-play called by former figure skater Dick Button (who describes the action in the ring in skating terms, giving the film a Woody Allen aura); and Lazar's promotional activities for the big game, including an unbearable appearance of the Japanese team on a Japanese television variety/talent show. Surprisingly, even with all of the interaction between the Americans and the Japanese, there is nothing of significance shown in the film concerning the differences between Japanese and American cultures. Even *Mr. Baseball* (1992) was able to do that.

Of course, many otherwise mediocre baseball films have been saved by their climactic baseball games. Unfortunately, *Go to Japan* is not one of them. The game itself is uninteresting and it is suddenly called after just a couple of innings, because of a fight between the players. Even the creators of *The Bad News Bears in Breaking Training*, a very bad film, had sense enough to try to end the film with an interesting ball game.

The one positive attribute of the film is Tony Curtis playing Marvin Lazar. Curtis must have felt the part was demeaning to him after a long and successful screen career, but that does not prevent him from giving a convincing and funny performance in the role. Curtis surely looks the part, always dressed well, usually wearing an open shirt and a gold chain around his neck. He is the epitome of the Hollywood hustler, not all that different from his role as a New York press agent in his early screen success, *Sweet Smell of Success* (1957).

The Bad News Bears Go to Japan is not a film about baseball, is not a film about youngsters, and is not a film about Japan. It is not even a film about the Bad News Bears of the prior films. It is difficult to discern why it was ever made, and it is hard to understand why anyone would ever watch it.

Bad News Bears (2005)

After the Bad News Bears broke training and went to Japan, Paramount Pictures apparently decided that the next best thing to do was to do it all over again, thus the remake of the original 1976 film, *Bad News Bears* (2005). Less than thirty years had passed between the makings of the two films. The original film was in color. The use of foul language went unrestrained in that movie. The new film has almost an identical plot to the old film. What was the purpose of producing a remake?

The changes made for the 2005 film are primarily an attempt to go for a more outrageous, or at least a more gross, approach wherever possible. In the old film, Coach Buttermaker cleaned pools for a living, which was surely enough of a demeaning job to make its point. In the new film, Buttermaker is a rat exterminator, allowing for the showing of some disgusting matters, such as Buttermaker carrying dead rats in the Little League team's drink cooler or the kids having a fight with rat spray. In the old film, the players' uniforms were sponsored by Chico's Bail Bonds, whose slogan was "Let Freedom Ring." In the 2005 film, the uniforms have the advertisement "Bo-Peeps, a Gentlemen's Club" on the back. (Frankly, the older slogan is much more clever, but in a moment of homage to the older film, Buttermaker stops at Chico's in the 2005 film to see if it will sponsor the team. Apparently, the company turns down Buttermaker.) In the older film, the kids use foul language. In the new film, the kids also swear profusely, but so does Coach Buttermaker.

Billy Bob Thornton, who plays Coach Buttermaker, was a solid star when *Bad News Bears* (2005) was made. However, Thornton is not a comedian and humor is not his forte, despite his then-recent appearance in *Bad Santa* (2003), with a broadly similar plot and similar role for Thornton. Walter Matthau's dour expression, beat-upon personality, and comedic skills carried the 1976 film. Thornton does not come close to the performance of Walter Matthau in the identical role. Similarly, Tatum O'Neal, who played Amanda, Buttermaker's daughter and the team's pitcher in the earlier film, was already a star when the 1976 film was made, having won an Academy Award for Best Supporting Actress at the age of ten for *Paper Moon* (1973). O'Neal was believable and funny as the overpowering pitcher who was a little bit of a juvenile delinquent. In the newer film, the role of Amanda is played by Sammi Kane Kraft, who never appeared in a film before or after the *Bad News Bears* (2005). Kraft had a sports background, so she is convincing when on the field but not anywhere else.

Normally it is unfair to continuously compare a film to an older movie or stage version of the same. After all, many people, especially youngsters, will come to *Bad News Bears* (2005) without having seen the earlier film and without having preconceived notions of what the film should look like. For those viewers, there may be a lot to like in the film.

For example, the movie can be very funny. It has the usual youth baseball practice hijinks, such as a fielder fleeing from a ball hit to him; a pop-up that hits the fielder's glove, knocking the fielder down; a bunt in front of home plate that no one moves to pick up and throw; and an errant throw from the catcher that goes over the first-base fence and breaks the window of Buttermaker's car. The kids do some research and find that Buttermaker's only major-league experience was pitching for the Seattle Mariners for two-thirds of an inning in 1984, as a September call-up. Buttermaker achieved a life-time ERA of 36. In the first game of the season, there are the usual bad fielding plays, as Buttermaker watches from the bench, smoking a cigar and drinking a beer.

The baseball scenes themselves are always engaging, bad plays or not, and the direction of the film in those scenes is good. Substantial portions of the final game are shown, which is always a plus for a baseball movie. The child actors are fun to watch, a veritable League of Nations, as Buttermaker points out.

Even with these few positives, however, *Bad News Bears* is still a lackluster film. By 2005, the plot of the movie was a true cliché, because so many others sports films, youth or otherwise, had already stolen the basic framework of the original movie—a hopeless group of players managed by a disgruntled coach turns it all around and play for the championship at the end of the film. How many more times can that same story be told? In addition, it is never made clear in this movie how the Bad News Bears ever became a good team. Sure, But-termaker convinces Amanda to pitch for the team and Kelly Leak, a good hitting and fielding player, agrees to play for the team. Those two players are important additions to the Bears, but once they join the team, the other players start to play the game much better, hit-ting and fielding with some skill. Why does that happen? Surely it is not Buttermaker's influence. The film seldom shows him providing any substantive advice about the game to his players.

The original *Bad News Bears* has a bit of a theme to it, that adult coaches should stop taking the game so seriously and treat youth sports as if they are for the young, not for the adults. In the championship game in that film, Buttermaker realizes he is overreacting to the other coach and allows all of his players to play in the final game at the risk of losing the championship. In the remake, almost the exact same events happen, and yet, somehow, the same theme of the movie does not come through. Buttermaker is much more disgusting in the second film than in the first, and his last-minute conversion is completely unconvincing, obscuring any theme that the film might otherwise have.

Similarly, a high moment of the championship game in the earlier film was when the worst player on the team, Lupus, catches a fly ball in the outfield. In the newer film, the same event happens, except that the ball bounces off of Lupus's glove and is caught by Hooper, a wheelchair-bound player. While the scene in the latter film is clever, it does not carry the significance of Lupus catching the ball in the first film, because it rings untrue. Having a player in the field in a wheelchair makes so little sense that his catch of the ball seems like a Hollywood concoction, which it is, not just one of those special moments that makes Little League so great.

So while it may be unfair to continually compare a remake with its original version, *Bad News Bears* almost demands the comparison, since it was made so soon after the original film and has an almost identical plot. In almost every way, the 2005 film comes up short in the comparison, and in an era of cable television, DVDs, and Blu-rays, it is well worth locating a copy of the earlier film and watching that in lieu of this pale imitation.

√ *The Sandlot* (1993)

Probably nothing is more exciting for movie fans than starting to watch a film on television or at a theater with low expectations only to discover that the film is truly excellent. *The Sandlot* is just such a movie. It seems to be just another silly film about youth baseball, but this one turns out to be much, much better.

The Sandlot has the slightest of story lines. It is just a tale of some young boys who have little to do in the summer but play baseball. Scotty Smalls, the new kid in the neighborhood, tries to make friends with eight young boys who play the game every day at the local sand-lot. Unfortunately, Scotty cannot throw or catch and the boys make fun of him, until the best player on the team, Benjamin Franklin Rodriguez, takes Scotty under his wing and teaches Scotty to play the game. Scotty then becomes a participant in the daily baseball game and in the other activities of his teammates, such as beating a rival gang of snooty Little Leaguers (who have uniforms and team caps) and watching when one of the young players, Squints, pretends to be drowning at the local swimming pool so that he can steal a kiss from Wendy, the pretty lifeguard.

Much like the television program *The Wonder Years*, *The Sandlot* is narrated in the future by a grown-up Scotty Smalls, and through-out the narration Scotty foreshadows some upcoming trouble for his friends by telling the audience that he got his friends into a pickle that summer. Now, the word "pickle" has a special meaning in base-ball. It refers to a situation where a runner is caught between two bases and has to get to one of those bases before being tagged out. In baseball jargon, the synonym for "pickle" is "rundown." The use of the term in baseball probably comes from the old expression "in a pickle," which means to be in a difficult situation.

At the beginning of the film, when the narrator first mentions the word "pickle," there is a moment from a baseball game shown where Rodriguez is caught in a pickle between first and second base. Rodriguez gets out of the rundown safely, presaging the moment when he will get the team out of a much more serious pickle later that summer, because in *The Sandlot*, when Scotty says he got his team into a pickle, he is definitely not referring to a rundown. The team's pickle begins when Rodriguez hits the team's only baseball so hard that the cover comes off in mid-air, ending their daily game. Scotty then retrieves a ball from his stepfather's trophy room that was signed by Babe Ruth so that the game can continue. As luck would have it, Scotty smashes his first home run ever that day, hitting the valu-able ball over the outfield fence and into Mr. Mertle's backyard. Not much is known about Mr. Mertle, but he has a reputation of being very mean and very scary. His backyard is guarded by the "Beast," a huge monster that once ate a kid (or so the story goes). Somehow the boys must retrieve the ball from the Beast without getting themselves killed, or Scotty will be in lots of trouble when his stepfather gets home and finds that his Babe Ruth ball is missing.

For television fans of a certain age, part of the plot of *The Sandlot* may bring back memories of an episode of the *Leave It to Beaver* television series, titled "Ward's Baseball," which first aired on ABC television in April 1960. Beaver's father, Ward Cleaver, has a baseball that was signed by such luminaries as Babe Ruth, Lou Gehrig, Lefty Grove, Kiki Cuyler, Augie Galan, Bill Dickey, and Grover Cleveland Alexander. Beaver's friend Larry talks Beaver into playing catch with the ball, but when Larry overthrows Beaver, the ball rolls into the street and is crushed by a truck. In order to avoid the wrath of Ward, Beaver substitutes a different ball, on which Larry has re-signed the names of all of the ballplayers. Fred Rutherford discovers the fraud when he sees that the ball now bears the names of Baby Ruth, Kiki Gehrig, and Augie Dickey.

That episode of *Leave It to Beaver* seems dated by today's standards. *The Sandlot*, on the other hand, is still a wonderful film. It is very funny in spots, such as when Squints goes to such lengths to get a kiss from the pretty lifeguard; the banter between the kids; Scotty not knowing who the Great Bambino was and thinking that the name Babe Ruth on the baseball meant that it was signed by a girl; the Beast chasing Rodriguez through the town during the Founder's Day celebration, including knocking down a man on stilts, thereby causing the town's multitiered celebratory cake to fall on the chefs' heads; and the strange devices the kids employ to retrieve the treasured ball from behind the fence. But, for all of that, the true joy of *The Sandlot* is in its celebration of the game.

The nine boys play baseball every day, starting at around nine in the morning and continuing for much of the day. They play among themselves (except for one informal game with another team). There are no adults organizing the games, no adult coaches, and no umpires. This accurately reflects the time frame of the film, 1962, when young boys simply played pick-up baseball or softball all summer, without the help of any parents. Nowadays, all youth sports are completely organized, sometimes seeming to be more for the adults than the children. In the process, the youth version of the national pastime may have lost some of its spontaneity and some of its "every man" image.

The boys do not keep the score of their games. When the game ends on one day, they just pick up the game where they left off the next day. There are no winners or losers. They are truly playing for love of the game. Little can interrupt the daily game, except on July 4th. That is the day the kids play their one night game of the year, with the field illuminated by the fireworks in the sky. Even though the boys love playing baseball, they are still youngsters at heart, and it is difficult for them to take their eyes off of the beautiful sky, with the fireworks flashing. This is a brief moment in the film but a magic moment, with the awe on the boys' faces shown as they watch the fireworks, while Ray Charles sings his stylized version of "America the Beautiful" in the background.

The joy of the game comes back at the end of the movie when the boys finally meet Mr. Mertle. It turns out that Mertle is not a figure of foreboding. (He asks the boys why they didn't just knock on his door. He would have gotten the ball back for them.) Mertle is actually a former professional baseball player who is now blind, the result of being hit in the head by a pitch when he was batting. Mertle knew Babe Ruth and Lou Gehrig personally; he even refers to Babe Ruth as "George." Recognizing that the Babe Ruth ball has taken quite a beating since the Beast got it into his mouth, Mertle replaces it with a ball signed by Ruth and the other members of the 1927 Yankees, famously known as "Murderers' Row." Mertle considers it a fair trade, so long as the boys come by just once a week to talk baseball with him. (The Beast is actually Mertle's dog, Hercules, who, while quite large, is hardly a beast. Perhaps the story about Hercules eating a kid was greatly exaggerated.)

Mertle's love of the game, his mention of Murderers' Row, his description of how he crowded the plate while batting so that the strike zone almost disappeared, a photograph he has of himself between Lou Gehrig and Babe Ruth, his smile when he recalls the old days, and his simple desire to talk baseball with the boys adds to the film's celebration of the national pastime. There is, however, one false note in this scene. In the picture with Ruth and Gehrig, Mertle appears to be wearing a Major League Baseball uniform, and Mertle says that if he had not been injured, he would have hit more home runs than Ruth. Mertle is played by James Earl Jones, an Afri-

Babe Ruth makes an unexpected appearance in *The Sandlot* (1993). Here, Ruth is pictured at the 1924 World Series (10/4/24) between two of baseball's all-time greatest hitters, from left to right, George Sisler and Ty Cobb. *(Library of Congress, LC-USZ62-103759)*

can American actor, and, of course, there were no African American baseball players in the major leagues in the 1920s and 1930s.

The Sandlot starts to get ridiculous when the boys attempt to retrieve the Babe Ruth ball from the clutches of the Beast, employing several Rube Goldberg devices that have little chance of success. The film starts to turn into both a science fiction and horror movie at this time, and the audience's credulity starts to waver. But, in some ways, this is also very believable, as memories of childhood often become magnified and exaggerated when looking back after many years. The filmmakers are then able to cleverly tie this incident back to baseball. The night after the ball is lost, Rodriguez has a dream of Babe Ruth coming to his room and advising him that the best way to retrieve the valuable baseball from the Beast is simply to hop over the fence and get it. While actor Art LaFleur looks nothing like Ruth, it is a good scene, with the Babe imparting the wisdom of the ages to Rodriguez, helping Rodriguez become a local legend. The moment ends with a nice touch as Babe handles a baseball card of

Henry Aaron and asks Rodriguez, "I don't know why, but can I have this, kid?" While Mertle would never have been able to beat Babe Ruth's record for lifetime home runs, Henry Aaron could and did.

The Sandlot ends with a few more surprises as Scotty tells what happened to the kids when they grew up, cleverly presented as the image of each of the boys disappears from the sandlot. Rodriguez became a professional ballplayer, and, surprisingly, Scotty became a baseball play-by-play announcer, presumably one who now knows who Babe Ruth was. The biggest revelation, however, is that Squints married the pretty lifeguard and they have nine children.

Almost every baseball film, except baseball biographical films, ends with a big game, whether a championship game, a playoff game, or a grudge match. *The Sandlot* is a rare exception, with the main part of the movie ending with the boys retrieving the Ruth ball and meeting Mr. Mertle. *The Sandlot* is about the love of the game, not the competition of the game, and perhaps, in the end, that is why it is so special.

Hardball (2001)

Hardball is based on a work of nonfiction by Daniel Coyle, titled *Hardball: A Season in the Projects*, published in 1993. The setting of the book is the Cabrini-Green housing projects in the inner city of Chicago where, in 1991, two men started a Little League, backed by the sponsorship of several large Chicago corporations. This Little League, known as the Near North Little League/African-American Youth League, became Chicago's only Little League based in a housing project. At the time of the events in the book, Cabrini-Green, filled with high-rise apartments, was the second-largest housing project in the United States. Gunfire and death were a way of life in the projects, with one person shot each week, one person killed each month, and double those numbers in the summer. It was a difficult place to coach a Little League team.

The movie *Hardball* uses the setting of Coyle's book, a dangerous slum in Chicago, and the concept that Chicago corporations have provided equipment and coaches for the youngsters. However, the plot of the film is totally original and very few incidents in the movie are even inspired by the book. The protagonist of the film is Conor O'Neill, a down-on-his-luck gambler, who bets large sums of money on Chicago sports teams. Conor's only other source of income appears to be scalping sports tickets and borrowing money from acquaintances. As the film opens, Conor is in serious trouble. He has large debts with two Chicago bookies who are not afraid to use physical violence to get their money back. Desperate, Carter goes to a friend who works with a securities firm and begs for another loan. Instead, the friend pushes Conor into coaching the Kekambas, a Little League team in the slums, for a payment of $500 per week.

Although there are some funny moments in the film, *Hardball*, because of its setting in the slums, is not a comedy. Nevertheless, the film follows the same pattern of youth baseball films that are comedies, with a reluctant coach, a group of poor ballplayers, sudden character changes for no reason, and a shot at the championship at the end of the film. There must be another way to tell this story!

The setting and culture of the film do provide *Hardball* with some unique aspects. None of the youngsters playing the kids are professional actors. Their dialogue and cadence when they speak seems natural; they really seem like boys from the slums. The well-worn field that the team plays on is introduced by an aerial shot between tall slum apartment houses, clearly indicating that this is no California suburban Little League. While the ball field is an oasis within the projects, the real world quickly intrudes into the film when one player, Jefferson Albert Tibbs, has to walk home in the dark after a late practice. The audience is scared right along with him as he tries to make it home safely with a pizza, without being beat up or worse. In school, one player, Kofi, criticizes a book he has read because in the book a girl hopes her father will come back, which is ridiculous, as Kofi says, "'Cause where I'm from, don't nobody's father come back." On one occasion, Conor drives one of the boys home after dark, and when Conor sees everyone sitting on the floor in the lower apartments and asks why, Conor is told that the residents are afraid of bullets.

The problem with *Hardball* is that despite some positives, the film usually focuses on Conor O'Neill, not the kids. That creates two problems for the movie. For baseball fans, there is very little baseball shown. Most of it are mere snippets, until the playoff game near the end of the film. More importantly, without an emphasis on the kids, the danger and difficulties inherent in their lives are generally overlooked, undercutting the film's unique setting.

In fact, most of the violence and potential death in the movie involve Conor O'Neill. He is constantly on the run from the bookies to whom he owes money, being beaten up, threatened with a baseball bat, and surely afraid for his life. Conor's life is saved in the film, not by working with young boys but by a buzzer beater in a basketball game that allows Conor to win a long-shot bet. Because Conor also lives a life of violence and fear, the desperate lives of his Little Leaguers is de-emphasized, once again misusing the unique setting of the movie.

Another difficulty with the film is highlighted by a line of dialogue. Elizabeth Wilkes, a teacher at the boys' school, tells Conor that she trusts him, saying, "Because those kids trust you. And they don't trust anybody." The problem is that despite what Miss Wilkes says, there is nothing in the film to back up that point. The only bit of coaching Conor appears to do during practice is break up fights on the field and tell his players not to criticize each other. During their early games, Conor coaches the bases while standing near the dugout. (He never gets an assistant coach.) At one point he quits the team without good reason. The kids' trust is apparently based on Conor taking them out for pizza and then taking them to a Major League Baseball game. That is not the stuff that forms the basis of long-term trust.

Hardball does turn serious at the end when G-Baby, one of the players, is killed, an innocent bystander in a shootout near the apartment where he lives. While this incident seems obvious and heavy-handed, it does lead to the best moment in the film. Conor speaks at the funeral of G-Baby, and in his speech he completes the story of the playoff game, which had been left hanging with the score tied, two out in the bottom of the last inning and the winning run on third. G-Baby, who was too young to play regularly for the team, was called to bat as a pinch-hitter, his first appearance in a game that year. As Conor describes it to the audience at the funeral, G-Baby, who was very small, had two strikes on him. On the next pitch, all of the fielders moved in on him, believing he could not hit the ball very far. G-Baby managed to punch a ball over the first baseman, normally an easy out if the fielder were in the correct position, but because he was playing in, it was a game-winning hit. As Conor describes it at the funeral, G-Baby jumped for joy, his big smile now filling his face, a striking moment in the movie. The joys of playing baseball, slum field or not, come through in that special moment.

Hardball attempts to explore a theme—giving one's time to the community can work wonders in one's personal life. Conor gives his time for the kids, resulting in a metamorphosis of his character and life goals, or so the film posits. Of course, many adults give their free time to Little League and other organized youth sports. It is a fun and rewarding experience. However, few would consider it a life-changing event.

Likewise, it is not a life-changing experience for Conor. In *Hardball*, Conor is paid $500 a week for coaching; it is not an altruistic endeavor on his part. If he had not won that long-shot bet, he would be running for his life to get out of Chicago, not coaching some Little League team. The film implies that working with the Little Leaguers changed Conor's outlook on life, but nothing in the film truly supports that conclusion.

The film ends with a weak theme. Woody Allen is often quoted as saying, "Ninety percent of life is just showing up." When the Kekambas appear for the championship game and Kofi, G-Baby's older brother, is not there, it looks like the team will have to forfeit for lack of players. Conor gathers the boys together and says, "What I've learned from you is that, really, one of the most important things in life is showing up." While that sentence may seem profound, it really makes no sense in a manager's speech to the Kekambas because the players did, in fact, do much more. The team made it to a playoff game. Conor is really talking about himself. The one thing he really did for the boys was to show up, even if for the wrong reasons, and so he did help his kids. But, in real life, people have to do more than show up to be effective.

In the end, the themes of *Hardball* are either not borne out by its story line or they are trivial. The plot itself is duplicative of many prior youth sports films. *Hardball*, a film with a unique setting, is hardly a unique film.

Mickey (2004)

Mickey involves Tripp Spence, a widowed lawyer who coaches his son Derrick in Little League Baseball in a town somewhere in the eastern United States. As the film opens, twelve-year-old Derrick, a dominating pitcher and hitter, is completing his final season in Little League. Once the game ends, Tripp, who knows that he is about to be arrested for bankruptcy fraud and tax evasion, goes on the lam with Derrick. Through a less-than-legal connection of Tripp's, the two acquire the identities of a father and a son who were killed several years ago in a boating accident in Florida. Tripp is now Glen Ryan and Derrick is now Mickey Ryan. Since Derrick/Mickey now has a fake birth certificate, he has officially become twelve years old again, allowing him to play another season of Little League Baseball in another town.

Tripp/Glen arranges for Derrick/Mickey to be drafted by the Moose, the best team in the local Little League in Las Vegas, Nevada. Mickey is such an overwhelming performer at bat and on the field that the Moose wins the local championship, the Las Vegas All-Star team wins the Little League regional championships in the West Region, and then the Las Vegas All-Star team makes it all the way to the championship finals in Williamsport, Pennsylvania. The nationwide publicity, however, causes Tripp and his son to be tracked down by the IRS, resulting in Tripp going to jail after the end of the championship game.

Mickey is a rare youth baseball film about a team that is very good from the start of the film. Most youth baseball films are about crummy teams that, for no realistic reason, somehow turn into good teams by the end of the movie. The Moose, on the other hand, is the favorite team in the Las Vegas league from the beginning of the season. Thus, *Mickey* avoids a baseball cinematic cliché. In fact, screenwriter John Grisham obviously sought to avoid many of the clichés of baseball cinema in his script. In another example, the big hit in the championship game does not come off of Mickey's bat. It is surprisingly hit by the diminutive catcher on the team.

Mickey has several strong attributes. There are quite a few good acting performances in the film, particularly Mike Starr as Tony, the coach of the Moose, and Mark Joy as Seeger, the relentless IRS agent who is chasing Tripp. Each of their characters has some of the best lines in the film. When Tripp asks Tony if he is going to take Mickey on his team after a tryout in which Mickey, at the suggestion of Tripp, pretended to be a poor player so that the other teams would not draft him, Tony says, "Oh, I want the kid. I don't know about the father."

(Which Little League coach has not had the same feeling from time to time about one of his players?) Near the end of the film, in Williamsport, Pennsylvania, when Tripp asks Seeger how he caught him, Seeger replies, "Well, let's put it this way. If Mickey were playing soccer this summer, I wouldn't be here."

The baseball in the film is also well done, with significant action shown for several of the games. In fact, the last two games were shot at the actual Little League field in Williamsport that is used for the real Little League World Series, with enthusiastic crowds on hand, providing some authenticity to the game. The final games are called by Brent Musburger and Harold Reynolds, who called the real Little League championships for ABC television back in the early 2000s. The young boys appearing as the ballplayers, even Shawn Salinas, who stars in the film as Mickey, were all youth ballplayers when they were cast in the film, adding to the realism of the play on the field.

All that being said, *Mickey* has a significant problem, the same one from which *It Happens Every Spring* (1949) suffers. Both films are about cheaters. Both Mickey and his father know that since Mickey is over twelve years of age, he is too old to play Little League Baseball, but Mickey still plays, knowing that if caught, the Moose and the All-Star team will have to forfeit all of their games, to the chagrin of teammates and local fans. Additionally, when Patty, an administrator at Mickey's school and a regular date of Tripp's, learns of the deception, she does not seem particularly upset, a surprising reaction from one involved in youth education. When Mickey's teammates have to forfeit the championship game, they are also not overly upset. They actually comfort Mickey.

In fact, no one in the film, whether teammates, coaches, or fans, seems bothered by the humiliation of forfeiting the Little League championship or by the fraud committed on them. They also do not seem to be bothered by the fact that Tripp/Glen is not just an overly enthusiastic Little League father. He is a legitimate crook, having gone on the lam when he was about to be caught by the IRS, and who is now about to be sent to jail for at least one year.

Thus there is an immoral core at the center of *Mickey*. Is the audience supposed to root for Mickey, the cheater, as he blows pitches past legitimate twelve-year-olds on his way to the championship season? Is the audience supposed to root for Tripp to escape when the IRS is about to catch him, just so that he can be with his son?

This moral dilemma of the audience is hardly helped by the contrived ending of the film. In the championship game, the West All-Stars, Mickey's team, plays the Caribbean team from Cuba. The kids on the Caribbean team seem to be awfully big for twelve-year-olds, and although that violation cannot be proved, it also appears that the players are not all from the Havana area, a violation that is easier to establish. Is the audience supposed to forgive Mickey and root for him because the other team, from Castro's Cuba, at the time an enemy of the United States, also cheats? Do two wrongs make a right? Hopefully, that is not the message of a film that is supposed to be for the whole family.

Major League Baseball disassociated itself from *It Happened Every Spring*, since the film was about cheating. The Williamsport Little League did not disassociate itself from *Mickey* and, in fact, assisted with the making of the film. The apparent difference is that the official Little League comes out looking quite good in *Mickey*. After learning of the illegal players on both the Caribbean and West All-Stars teams, the organization immediately decrees that the Western All-Stars and the Caribbeans forfeit their last wins. The league then schedules a new championship game the next day, between the two former runner-ups.

As noted in the film, the official Little League does have a strong record in enforcing its rules against cheating. *Mickey* makes reference to the 1992 Little League World Series in which Zamboanga City, a Filipino team that represented the Far East at Williamsport, was disqualified after it won the championship game when it was discovered that the team used several players from outside the Zamboanga City district. Similarly, the 2014 champions from Jackie Robinson West in Chicago were disqualified for using out-of-district players. The incident that is closest to the scenario in *Mickey*, and one that many baseball fans may remember, involves Danny Almonte, the star for the Bronx area team that won the 2001 Little League World Series. Danny's team was later disqualified when it was discovered that Danny was fourteen years old at the time he played in the tournament.

The strong record of the Little League in policing its tournaments, as shown in the film and based on fact, is another positive of *Mickey*. Along with the film's strong performances, good baseball scenes, location shooting, and celebration of the youth pastime of Little League Baseball, there is much to appreciate in the movie. Nevertheless, the film is difficult to recommend, because of its ambivalence about the integrity of the game and the lack of integrity of its characters.

Block Busters (1944)

On October 28, 1935, Sidney Kingsley's famous play *Dead End* opened on Broadway. The production introduced six young actors to the world: Leo Gorcey, Huntz Hall, Gabe Dell, Billy Halop, Bernard Punsly, and Bobby Jordan. The six played juvenile delinquents operating on the streets of a tenement section of New York City, right next to an upscale apartment building. The show was a huge success, running for 687 performances. It was then adapted into a movie in 1937 starring Joel McCrae, Sylvia Sidney, and Humphrey Bogart. The six youngsters reprised their roles as the street urchins for the film, thereafter always being known as the Dead End Kids. The gang was such a success in the movie that Warner Bros. signed them to a contract with the studio.

Even before Warner Bros. released the Dead End Kids from their contracts in 1939, the group split up for different film series, with some going to Universal for the Little Tough Guys movies (twelve films and three serials) and others going to Monogram for the East Side Kids series (twenty-two films). Additional actors joined the gangs for those two series of films. In 1946, parts of the various groups coalesced at Monogram for the Bowery Boys movies, a series that continued until 1958.

Block Busters is part of the East Side Kids series, a group of very low-budget films featuring semi-delinquent teens roaming the East Side of New York City. *Block Busters* features three of the original Dead End Kids, Leo Gorcey, Huntz Hall, and Gabriel "Gabe" Dell. The three are still playing teenagers in the film, even though each of those actors was in his mid- to late-twenties at the time of filming.

The main plot of the movie involves a newcomer to the neighborhood, a French-born teenager named Jean, and his interactions with the gang. The kids are initially wary of Jean, because of his upper-class affections and good manners. In particular, the leader of the

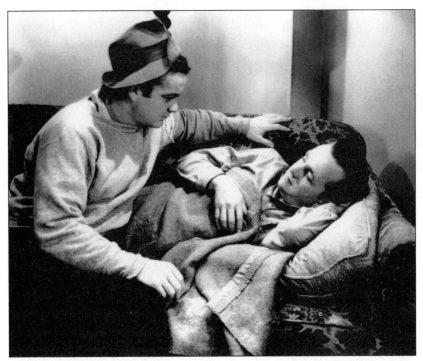

Team captain Muggs McGinnis (Leo Gorcey) comforts one of his ailing teammates (Bill Chaney) in *Block Busters* (1944).

gang, Muggs (Leo Gorcey), does not want Jean to play for the gang's baseball team. Eventually matters work out and the East Siders win an important game, aided by the last-minute heroics of Jean.

Even though most lists of baseball movies exclude *Block Busters*, it is clearly a baseball film. *Block Busters* focuses on baseball, East Side style. In the opening scene, the East Siders are playing their rival, Five Points, in a high-scoring game. As the film opens, the score is already 29 to 15 and it is only the fifth inning. After a couple of pitches, the game degenerates into a ridiculous fight about a pitch out of the strike zone that the umpire correctly called a ball.

The most significant baseball part of the film is the big game at the climax. As a result of his jealousy of Jean, Muggs originally refuses to allow Jean to play in the game, but when Mr. Lippman, a local fan who supplied the team with its uniforms, complains, the team reluctantly allows Jean to play. Not surprisingly, Jean hits a walk-off grand-slam home run, winning the game for the East Side Kids. The win entitles the gang to a summer-long trip to camp in the Catskills, courtesy of Mr. Lippman, which is very fortunate since an ailing member of the team, Tobey Dunn, has been told by the doctors that he can only be cured by a long stay in the country.

One of the reasons that *Block Busters* is seldom considered to be a baseball film is that there are many frolics and detours from the baseball plot, including street fights, a costume party, musical numbers, some dancing, and the usual East Side Kids shenanigans. Another reason may be that baseball is not the usual sport of the East Siders. They generally go in for petty stealing of fruit, harassing people walking on the street, and murdering the English language.

Perhaps the main reason for the exclusion of *Block Busters* from a list of baseball movies is that there is little attempt to provide a realistic depiction of baseball on-screen. When the gang brings Jean to one of its practices and teaches him baseball, a game that he has never played before, Jean quickly learns how to play, thrilling the many spectators at the team's well-attended practice with his new-found skills. However, Jean's fielding style and technique is hardly convincing to the viewer or, apparently, to Muggs, who afterward comments, "He stood there like he was nailed to the ground and still caught the ball!" When some of the batters at the big game swing and miss, they take a 360-degree swing and fall to the ground. When Jean runs the bases on his grand-slam home run, he actually slows down at each base and practically makes a right angle turn.

Some of these baseball issues may have to do with Fred Pressel, the actor playing Jean. In addition to his unconvincing fielding, he never really moves the bat back while he is taking a swing. He must have been a very poor batter in real life, because his big hit in the final game is not shown on-screen. Only the sound is heard. In addition, the baseball scenes in *Block Busters* are poorly shot, with limited camera angles.

For baseball fans, the film has some mild interest. It is actually nice to see the East Side Kids off the streets of New York and on a ball field. The ball field appears to be a typical city ball field of the era, with no amenities (not even a good backstop) and the field in only fair condition. There are a few neat baseball jokes, such as when Glimpy (Huntz Hall) takes three strikes while he is warming up in the batter's box and bragging about what a great hitter he is, and the umpire having to put on glasses to read the rule book. For movie fans, *Block Busters* has some special interest. The great silent film comedian Harry Langdon has one of his last screen roles, playing the landlord's agent, Mr. Higgins. Bernard Gorcey, Leo's father, makes an appearance in the film as Mr. Lippman. Gorcey was just a few years away from screen immortality, when he landed the coveted role of sweet shop owner Louie Dumbrowski in the Bowery Boys series.

The Final Season (2007)

As fans of *Field of Dreams* (1989) know, baseball in Iowa can be very special. As viewers of *The Final Season* will learn, one place in Iowa where baseball was once very special was the town of Norway, located about seventeen miles southwest of Cedar Rapids. For many years, Norway had less than 600 residents and its high school had only about 100 students, yet despite its lack of size, Norway was a powerhouse in Iowa high school baseball, winning twenty state championships in twenty-five years. Unfortunately, Norway's high school was consolidated into a larger school district in 1991, and that was the last year for the Norway high school baseball team.

The Final Season is a partly fictional, partly true account of that last season of high school baseball in Norway, before the team and the local school merged into the much larger Madison School District. The merger and the end of baseball in Norway were caused by the state's interest in creating larger school districts with more diverse subjects at a lower cost, and the local school board's inexplicable determination to eliminate Norway High School. The film addresses those issues early on in the film, but its focus quickly turns to the school's last baseball season and the hope of winning a record twentieth state championship. Due to local politics, the team's long-standing and revered coach, Jim Van Scoyoc, is dismissed from his job and the coaching duties are turned over to Kent Stock, the team's former assistant for part of a year. At the climax of the film, the Norway Tigers do the impossible, defeat a school from a much larger district and win their twentieth state championship.

The Final Season is different than just about every other film about youth sports, including those about football, basketball, and soccer. The Norway Tigers are not a collection of misfits, juvenile delinquents, or poor ballplayers who must somehow be melded into a championship team. In fact, the Tigers won the state championship the year before their final season, so they have a lot going for them in their last campaign. Also, this is not a film in which a coach reluctantly decides to coach a youth team for publicity purposes or to right some wrong he has committed in his life. Rather, Kent Scott, a college baseball player and one who is very knowledgeable about baseball, happily agrees to coach Norway in its final season.

While it is great to avoid the clichés of the genre, that avoidance presents a significant problem for the film. Where is the conflict? Where is the drama? The most significant conflict in the film arises between the school board and citizens of Norway, but as good a conflict as it is, the issue disappears partway through the movie. Other subplots—one about a romance between Kent Stock and Polly Hudson, the representative of the state at the school board meetings, and another about a juvenile delinquent who takes up baseball—are little more than cinematic clichés. (They also did not happen in real life.) Without a significant point of conflict in a film, it can become uninteresting quite fast, and so it is not surprising that *The Final Season* received a poor critical reception.

For baseball fans, however, *The Final Season* is a joy to watch. *The Final Season* is a baseball film that really is about baseball. In addition to some extended practice sessions, there is substantial game action shown in the movie. Indeed, the final game for the state championship between the Norway Tigers and the South Clay Spartans consumes about 25 percent of the film's total running time of approximately two hours. Contrary to most youth baseball games in movies, it is a game without stunts or screwy plays. Instead, it is about good, hard-fought baseball action between two quality teams. Even though there is little doubt as to who will win the championship game (or why make a movie about the Norway team), the action itself is always engaging, with the Spartans' pitcher throwing over ninety miles an hour, a Norway batter who crowds the plate so that he can be hit by a pitch, some slick fielding plays, a successful suicide squeeze bunt, and close plays at the bases. What more could a baseball fan desire?

Much of *The Final Season* is shot outdoors, and the authenticity of the film is aided by the location shooting in Iowa. From time to time, a train comes by the outfield of Norway's home field, just as a railroad line actually runs on the outskirts of Norway in real life. The railroad is a true slice of rural America, as is the young girl who sings the national anthem before the championship game. When she finally manages to get through the entire song, it is truly a great sports moment. Another nice feature of the movie is the use of some television footage from the actual 1991 season, showing some real residents of Norway talking about baseball and the real Kent Stock being interviewed after the championship game.

Sean Astin as Kent Scott and Rachael Leigh Cook as Polly Hudson are lightweights in their roles, not significant enough personalities to carry their moments in the movie. Also, Sean Astin seems a little pudgy for a young high school baseball coach. By contrast, Powers Boothe is excellent as Jim Van Scoyoc, the former coach of the Norway Tigers. Boothe brings a gravitas to the role that is particularly important in this film, because he is the symbol of what baseball means to this small community, and by analogy, what baseball means throughout much of the country.

Although the Norway Tigers win the final game, it is still a sad day for the residents of Norway, as the baseball victory will do nothing to bring back the local high school and the high school baseball team. Thus, because the film has a somewhat gloomy conclusion, *The Final Season* avoids the most common cliché of sports movies, a happy ending. To paraphrase Terrence Mann in *Field of Dreams*, the one constant through all the years in Norway has been baseball. With the end of the championship game, the only constant in Norway will be its memories of its fine high school baseball teams.

4

BASEBALL BIOGRAPHIES

The Pride of the Yankees (1942)

Before *The Pride of the Yankees*, baseball films were generally low budget and without major directors or performers, except for a few comedians who had name recognition but who could hardly be considered important stars. *The Pride of the Yankees* was different. The film was produced by Samuel Goldwyn, already a legendary name in films at the time, and directed by Sam Wood, who previously directed significant films such as *Goodbye, Mr. Chips* (1939) and *Kings Row* (1942). *The Pride of the Yankees* starred Gary Cooper, one of Hollywood's most popular leading men, who had just won an Academy Award for Best Actor for *Sergeant York* (1941). *The Pride of the Yankees* was nominated for eleven Academy Awards, including Best Picture. It was one of the top-ten box office films of the year and was truly a major film production.

The Pride of the Yankees relates the life of Henry Louis Gehrig with some surface accuracy, beginning with his growing up in the Washington Heights area of Manhattan with parents of limited means. The film covers his matriculation to Columbia University, where he plays football and baseball. The film shows Gehrig being signed by the New York Yankees while still in college, thus never obtaining a degree. Gehrig is then shipped to the Yankees' affiliate in Hartford, Connecticut, to begin his baseball career in the minor leagues. Gehrig is eventually called up to the major leagues, and when first baseman Wally Pipp becomes sick one day, Gehrig is put into the lineup in his stead. Thereafter, the Iron Horse never leaves the Yankees' starting lineup, playing in 2,130 straight games over fourteen different seasons, a record that many thought would stand forever. (Of course, Cal Ripken Jr., playing for the Baltimore Orioles, finally broke Gehrig's record. Ripken's streak ended on September 20, 1998, after he played in 2,632 consecutive games.)

The Pride of the Yankees (1942). This is a photograph taken at the 1937 All-Star Game (7/7/37), which shows, from left to right, Lou Gehrig, Joe Cronin, Bill Dickey, Joe DiMaggio, Charlie Gehringer, Jimmie Foxx, and Hank Greenberg. *(Library of Congress, LC-DIG-hec-22989)*

Gehrig marries Eleanor Twitchell of Chicago in a ceremony conducted in New Rochelle, New York, by its mayor, while workmen are still working on the Gehrigs' new abode. After the ceremony, Gehrig receives a motorcycle escort to Yankee Stadium so that he can play in that night's ball game. Eleanor and Lou never manage to take a honeymoon, even in the off-season. *The Pride of the Yankees* ends with Gehrig's illness, taking himself out of the lineup on May 2, 1939, ending his long streak of consecutive games, and his famous speech to a sold-out Yankee Stadium on July 4, 1939.

Surprisingly, many significant moments from Gehrig's life that would seem to be made for the cinema are overlooked. For example, there was that occasion in June 1920, when Gehrig, still in high school, played for a team that traveled to Chicago for a game at Wrigley Field. In the ninth inning, Gehrig hit a home run so far out of the park that it landed on the porch of a small house that faced the stadium. The home run was said to be prodigious, especially for a young man of high school age. It gained some notoriety at the time for Gehrig and put Gehrig in the baseball spotlight for the first time in his life. *The Pride of the Yankees* skips this important incident in Gehrig's life, as it almost had to, because it would have strained the movie's credulity even more if Gary Cooper, who was over forty years of age when the movie was filmed, played Gehrig in high school. As it is, it is difficult enough to watch Cooper playing a very young Gehrig during the time he is in college.

In addition to events in Gehrig's baseball life, *The Pride of the Yankees* skips over aspects of his personal life. Although the film addresses the problems between Eleanor and Gehrig's mother, if the film were to be believed, those problems were mainly about the furniture and wallpaper in the newlyweds' home, and these problems were amicably resolved in a short period of time. In real life, Mom Gehrig constantly meddled in Lou and Eleanor's affairs, and although Lou's mother and Eleanor maintained a polite relationship, they were never close, usually sitting apart on the days they were both at the ballpark. While Gehrig was a friend of Babe Ruth's early in Gehrig's career, their relationship soured over time, and by the end of their baseball life together, they were barely speaking with each other. Indeed, when the Babe spoke to Gehrig after Gehrig's famous speech at Yankee Stadium in 1939, it was purportedly the first time they had talked to each other since 1934. (There is a famous still of Ruth hugging Gehrig on the day of the speech, itself a legendary moment in baseball history.) The film gives a totally different impression of the relationship between the two Yankees sluggers.

The Pride of the Yankees glosses over the severity of Lou's illness and its cruel effects on his ability to function. After Lou stopped playing in Yankees games, he went to the Mayo Clinic in Rochester, Minnesota, where he finally received the true diagnosis for his illness. For some reason, the name of the disease, amyotrophic lateral sclerosis, or ALS, is not mentioned in the film. ALS causes a person's muscles to progressively weaken, atrophy, and then become paralyzed. Even though the disease is painless, death is guaranteed. (Of course, the disease is now better known as Lou Gehrig's disease.)

The already serious effect of the disease on Gehrig is illustrated by the fact that after Lou took himself out of the Yankees lineup that summer of 1939, he stayed with the team for the remainder of the year, retaining the captain's honor of bringing the daily lineup out to the umpire. However, Gehrig was already so ill that he sometimes struggled with that task, and as a result, he had to be accompanied by another player or a coach to ensure that he would not fall down. By ending the film with Gehrig's farewell speech at Yankee Stadium, *The Pride of the Yankees* avoids showing Gehrig's subsequent heart-breaking physical deterioration and death.

The filmmakers may simply have believed that all of these incidents, not just the ones relating to Gehrig's illness, were not in keeping with the tone of the film and its celebration of the life of Lou Gehrig, who had passed away at the age of thirty-seven, only about a year before the film's opening in New York City. In any event, the decision to end the film with Gehrig's farewell speech was the right choice, as it was the emotional high of Gehrig's life and is just about the most memorable ending any baseball movie could ever have.

Other incidents and dialogue are simply made up in *The Pride of the Yankees*, sometimes making the film seem more like a work of fiction than a biography. For example, Pop Gehrig and Lou's idea of pretending to Mom Gehrig that Lou is attending Harvard while he is really playing baseball in Hartford is fiction, and also somewhat mean to the mother, as all of the Gehrigs' neighbors in the film apparently know exactly what Lou is actually doing. The incident where Lou hits two home runs in a game—to fulfill a promise to a hospitalized boy who cannot walk, and the cured boy showing up on Lou Gehrig Day—is complete fiction, and schmaltzy fiction at that. When Gehrig went into the lineup and replaced Wally Pipp on that historic day in the summer of 1925, he did not slip on a line of bats outside the dugout, his wife-to-be was not in the ballpark at the time, and, accordingly, she never dubbed him "Tanglefoot," at that time or, for that matter, at any time. (According to Gehrig's biographer, Richard G. Hubler, Lou's fellow Yankees called him "Tanglefoot" early in his career, referring to Gehrig's weak fielding abilities at first base.)

Some scenes take real-life incidents and turn them into partial fiction. In real life, Lou was discovered playing baseball at Columbia by a Yankees scout, Paul Krichell, and not by a newspaper reporter, as shown in the film. Lou replaced Wally Pipp in the lineup at the start of a game, not during a game. (Gehrig's consecutive game streak actually started the day before, when he pinch-hit for a different Yankees ballplayer.) When Lou finally took himself out of the Yankees lineup, it was not a spur-of-the-moment, during-the-game decision but one made in advance before the beginning of the game, not as shown in the movie. While all of these incidents have some truth to them, the film modified the facts in an attempt to make the movie more dramatic. In fact, there are so many completely or partially fictional incidents in *The Pride of the Yankees* that it is difficult to find the truth among the fiction.

Then there is the dialogue that could only have been concocted by Hollywood writers. When the doctor from the clinic comes out to inform Lou about the results of his tests, Lou tells him he wants the true diagnosis, saying, "Go ahead, Doc. I'm a man who likes to know his batting average." When Lou wants to know the severity of his illness and whether it could result in his death, he asks, "Is it three strikes, Doc?" The doctor somberly replies, "It's three strikes." What should have been a moving moment in the film is, instead, a cringe-worthy moment, as if a baseball player can only understand non-baseball subjects by expressing the concepts in baseball jargon.

Perhaps because Gary Cooper could not play baseball well or perhaps because of bad decisions on the part of the filmmakers, there are actually very few baseball scenes in the movie. Most occur during two montages, the first being a standard series of quick baseball clips and the second being a montage of newspaper headlines, not baseball scenes. In the few times actual baseball scenes are shown with Lou Gehrig playing, the viewer is never invested in the scenes because the opposing team, the score, and the season standings are never identified. These are baseball scenes without substance or tension. Instead of additional scenes of baseball, viewers are treated at one point in the film to the dancing of Veloz and Yolanda and the singing of Bettye Avery, performing with Ray Noble and His Orchestra, people that were probably known back in 1942 but surely have no interest today. What are they doing in a baseball movie? Even the farewell speech by Lou Gehrig suffers somewhat early on by an inexplicable decision of the filmmakers. The beginning of the event is partially narrated by a radio announcer, instead of showing the event in its entirety.

Babe Ruth, in his tenth and last screen appearance, plays himself in the film. It is a significant character part, not just a cameo appearance. Other Yankees who appear in *The Pride of the Yankees* are Bill Dickey, the Yankees catcher for many years starting in 1928,

Bob Meusel, an outfielder for the Yankees in the 1920s, and Mark Koenig, who played shortstop for the Yankees in the 1920s. Dickey actually gets a chance to punch another Yankees player when that player slurs the ailing Gehrig. The radio announcer shown during the film is Bill Stern, a well-known broadcaster of the era. Although there is some stock footage of Yankee Stadium in the film, the baseball scenes were shot at Wrigley Field in Los Angeles, a common and convenient shooting location for Hollywood baseball movies.

Most film biographies, whether about baseball players or not, have the same problem. It is not enough for a movie to just depict events in a person's life in chronological order. Such an approach lacks dramatic content. Also, if someone wants to learn about a historical figure, baseball player or not, the best way to go about it is to read a book about that person, not watch a movie. A movie is never able to convey as much factual information as a book and, in any event, a film is likely to be far less accurate. Therefore, a film needs to develop a strong plot to justify the film's production or an interest-

Babe Ruth's screen career ended with *The Pride of the Yankees* (1942). The Babe is on the left. On the right is Gary Cooper in his role as Lou Gehrig.

ing theme to tie the elements of the story together. *The Pride of the Yankees* has neither.

Nevertheless, this particular film biography works to a degree, even without a strong plot or theme, because it has a form of dramatic irony, i.e., even while the Lou Gehrig of *The Pride of the Yankees* is living an idyllic life, the audience knows that his life will be short-lived and end in tragedy. In 1942, at the time of the film's release, Lou Gehrig was probably one of the most famous names in America and his manner of death was well known to the moviegoing audience. Even today, over seventy years since his death, most people who watch *The Pride of the Yankees* know in advance how Lou Gehrig will die in the film.

As noted above, the film does not go into the specifics of Gehrig's disease or its effects on him. The first revealing moment in the film occurs when Lou experiences some pain in his shoulder while clowning around in his house. Then there is a deterioration of his baseball skills, with Lou no longer the hitter he used to be. The audience is far ahead of the characters in knowing what is really happening. The most telling moment, one that did happen in a similar manner in real life, is when Gehrig, trying to untie his shoe, falls off a chair in the clubhouse. His teammates try to pretend that nothing has happened. After Gehrig manages to get back onto the chair by himself, the perplexed look on Gehrig's face is revealing.

The Pride of the Yankees re-creates the most famous non-sports moment in all of sports, thereby crafting an iconic moment in the history of film. On July 4, 1939, almost 62,000 fans were present in Yankee Stadium for Lou Gehrig Day. The ceremony took place in between games of a doubleheader with the Washington Senators. As the current Yankees stood with the former Yankees teammates of Gehrig's near home plate, there were speeches about Lou and gifts given to him. Lou was then reluctantly brought to the microphone to talk to the fans. This quiet, reserved, and shy baseball player then gave one of the most famous speeches of all time. The first lines and the last one are memorable:

> Fans, for the past two weeks you have been reading about a bad break. Yet today I consider myself the luckiest man on the face

of the Earth. . . . So I close in saying that I might have been given a bad break, but I've got an awful lot to live for.

The phrase "I consider myself the luckiest man on the face of the Earth," while perhaps not the cleverest line ever spoken, is surely one of the most effective. It is one of the most-remembered speech lines of all time.

One of the reasons that sentence is so memorable is that it was heard around the world, on the radio and in newsreels, for sure, but also in *The Pride of the Yankees*. The scene is staged slightly differently in the film than it was in real life, adding to its iconic stature. The face of Babe Ruth is prominent in the shot as Gehrig begins to speak. The echoing of his speech on the field's loudspeakers provides some realism for the scene. A tearful Eleanor Gehrig listens to the speech by herself in the runway of the stadium; in real life she was sitting in the ballpark with her in-laws. For dramatic effect, the most famous line of Gehrig's speech is moved to the end of Gary Cooper's speech, which closes with these words, "People all say that I've had a bad break. But today . . . today, I consider myself the luckiest man on the face of the Earth." After the speech in the movie, Gehrig, head down and cap in his left hand, walks the long distance to the dugout by himself to the cheers of the crowd. There are no cuts in this shot, and the camera remains stationary so that the image of Gehrig grows constantly smaller as he walks off the field. Then, in the last shot of the film, Gehrig disappears into the darkness of the clubhouse runway. The direction and staging of this scene are superb, adding to the emotional effect of a very emotional moment.

Most people remember Lou Gehrig's speech in the form and setting in which Gary Cooper delivers it. Cooper is excellent; the staging is superb. Moving the most famous line of the speech to the end heightens the emotion. While the actual newsreel footage of Gehrig's speech still delivers an emotional wallop today, the film actually improves on the moment.

When Lou Gehrig passed away on June 2, 1941, almost two years after he delivered his famous speech, it was sixteen years to the day that he replaced Wally Pipp as the first baseman for the New York Yankees. Lou Gehrig's number 4 had been previously retired by the

Yankees. It was the first time that any athlete's number in any sport was retired.

Although *The Pride of the Yankees* is still included on just about every list of great baseball movies, its stature has dropped over time. The film is now seriously out-of-date, not aided by the fact that many better baseball films have been made since 1942. Indeed, *The Pride of the Yankees* might even be forgotten today if it were not for its emotional and memorable ending with Lou Gehrig's final speech at Yankee Stadium, as performed by Gary Cooper and as directed by Sam Wood.

The Babe Ruth Story (1948)

Most sports biographies provide a somewhat accurate though superficial outline of a player's life, along with the usual embellishments for dramatic or comedic purposes. *The Babe Ruth Story* is different. The film is almost completely fictional, and the made-up scenes provide neither drama nor comedy. Those are some of the reasons why critics have called *The Babe Ruth Story* the worst sports film biography of all time.

Viewers will learn that Babe was born in Maryland, lived at an orphanage named St. Mary's for a while under the tutelage of Brother Matthias, entered baseball for the Baltimore Orioles of the International League as a pitcher, was traded to the Boston Red Sox where he excelled as a pitcher, and then was sold to the Yankees, where he became a popular slugger, setting records for most home runs in a season and a career. That is about the same amount of information that a young boy could learn from the back of one of Babe Ruth's baseball cards from the 1930s.

Despite the credits to the film that state that the movie was based on Babe's autobiography of the same name, it is essentially a work of fiction. That would not necessarily disqualify the film from serious consideration, provided the fictional scenes highlighted some of Babe Ruth's attributes or conveyed some important moments in his life in a metaphorical way. Unfortunately, that is not the case, as three scenes in the film demonstrate.

The first of those scenes is probably the most well-known moment in the film, which, regrettably, is not a compliment. Babe is at spring training with the Red Sox, learning how to play the outfield. A young invalid boy is watching the game while lying flat on his back in his father's car behind the outfield fence because he is physically unable to stand. A doctor has said that the boy will never walk again. The Babe hits a home run and later as he is walking along the outfield fence, he shouts hello to the boy. Apparently cured by a few words from Ruth, the boy stands up by himself and waves to the Babe.

Another moment involves Babe autographing baseballs for kids prior to a game. He meets a young boy, Tony, and his dog, Pee Wee. During batting practice, Pee Wee falls out of the stands and is nailed by a ball hit by Babe. The dog's injuries seem fatal, alarming both Tony and the Babe. He rushes the dog to the hospital with Tony in tow. At the hospital, the teary-eyed youngster says to Babe, "Please don't let Pee Wee die, Babe. You said you wouldn't." Babe finally manages to convince regular doctors, not veterinarians, to operate on the dog. The operation is successful; Pee Wee will live. However, Babe has missed the entire ball game, leading to a fine and suspension by Yankees manager Miller Huggins.

After the 1927 season, according to the film, Miller Huggins, the manager of the Yankees, falls ill. Babe and his new wife, Claire, just after getting married, return to Miller's hospital room to cheer him up. However, as Babe is starting to talk to him, a doctor pulls a sheet over Huggins's head. That sad moment does not prevent Babe from giving a speech to Huggins's dead body, apologizing for all of the grief he gave Huggins off the field, but reminding Huggins that he always did his best for him on the field, and finally saying, "Whatever team you're playing on now, Hug, I know they'll be winners."

There is simply nothing that can be written about these scenes that can do them justice. They have to be seen, not to be believed, but to believe that they could ever have been inserted into a motion picture made for adults. These scenes epitomize how truly bad *The Babe Ruth Story* is, as it substitutes sap for facts and awkwardly tries to play on the heartstrings of the audience.

The only fictional scenes in the film that do highlight a real attribute of the Babe and are therefore appropriate to the film are his scenes with young boys and orphans, signing autographs, buying up their unsold newspapers, taking them to dinners at upscale restaurants, and visiting them in hospitals. While these specific scenes may be fanciful, Ruth in real life did have a soft spot for young children, whom he considered his greatest fans. Ruth always went out of his way for his young fans, and these scenes appropriately show that to the audience.

In addition to the completely fictional aspects of the film, *The Babe Ruth Story* is inaccurate on many of its facts. For example, in that scene in Miller Huggins's hospital room, the film would have viewers believe that Huggins died just after the 1927 World Series and that Babe was first married that year. In fact, when Babe Ruth moved to Boston to play for the Red Sox, he met and courted a pretty young waitress, Helen Woodford, who was working at a coffee shop. Ruth married her on October 17, 1914, about three months after they met. The two adopted a daughter in 1921, separated several times thereafter but never divorced. Helen died in a house fire in 1929.

On the right is Miller Huggins, the Yankees manager whose death is portrayed in *The Babe Ruth Story* (1948). On the left is Red Sox manager Frank Chance. The photo was taken on Opening Day, April 18, 1923. *(Library of Congress, LC-DIG-ggbain-35754)*

Helen's story is completely ignored in *The Babe Ruth Story*. Substantial attention is paid to Babe's courting of, and marriage to, Claire Hodgson, but there is also substantial fiction in that portion of the film. While Claire was in show business in her younger days, as shown in the film, she did not meet Babe when she gave him advice on his pitching technique. Also, the two were not married until early in 1929, and Huggins died near the end of the 1929 season. Babe Ruth was playing in a baseball game when he received news of

Huggins's death. Much like the Babe, this was a second marriage for Claire. She also had a daughter from a previous marriage.

The Babe Ruth Story even mixes up its apocryphal stories. It combines a 1926 incident in which Ruth allegedly visited a dying boy in a hospital and promised to hit a home run for him in that day's game, miraculously curing the boy, with an incident in the 1932 World Series in which Babe Ruth allegedly called his shot, gesturing that he would hit a home run on the next pitch, which he did. *The Babe Ruth Story* combines those incidents (if they actually occurred) into one, making the stories even more unbelievable than they already are.

The film correctly shows that at the end of his career, Babe Ruth played for the Boston Braves of the National League and hit his last three home runs on a single day, May 25, 1935, at Forbes Field in Pittsburgh. However, after accomplishing that feat, Ruth did not quit baseball on that day, as shown in the movie, although several people, including his wife, Claire, suggested that he should. Ruth continued to play for a few more days, playing in the first game of a Memorial Day doubleheader in Philadelphia on May 30, 1935, and then retired a few days later.

Another statement in the movie that looks like a mistake is not. After Ruth hits those three home runs in Pittsburgh and is walking off the field, Phil Conrad, a longtime friend and perhaps press agent of Ruth's (a fictional character created for the film), speaks to him. Conrad tells Ruth that he now has 729 career home runs. Now, just about every fan of the game knows that Babe Ruth ended his career with 714 home runs. However, Ruth did hit 15 World Series home runs, so Conrad must have included those home runs in his count to reach the total of 729 career home runs.

Oddly, for a film that unnecessarily builds Babe Ruth up to being a greater ballplayer and person than he ever was in real life, the filmmakers missed an opportunity in those three home runs in Pittsburgh. The last one, in the seventh inning, was one of the longest balls Ruth hit in his entire career, which was amazing given his age and health. The ball cleared the roof of the double-decked right-field stands of Forbes Field and purportedly landed across the street from the ballpark. It was the first time anyone had ever hit a ball over the Forbes Field roof. How nice would it have been to end the story of Babe Ruth's career with a colossal moment in his life, hitting a monumental home run on the last significant day of his career, instead of continuing the movie for quite some time with a series of made-up moments after his career ended?

If those were not already enough reasons to pan the film, *The Babe Ruth Story* is, quite simply, poorly done. It starts with a prologue at the Hall of Fame in Cooperstown, wasting valuable time explaining to viewers that Ruth was a Hall of Famer, as if anyone watching the film did not know that. The last part of the film, comprising about 20 minutes of the film's total running time of 105 minutes, is about Ruth's post-baseball career, the least interesting part of his life, or so it seems after watching this film. The narrator of the movie sometimes seems to be making a speech rather than providing segues for the viewer to better understand the film. On several occasions, his unnecessary narration becomes hysterical. Also, the direction of the film is uninspired, except for one nice shot of Yankee Stadium, with the elevated train running outside center field, bringing back memories of a similar moment in *The Cameraman* (1928), starring Buster Keaton.

William Bendix is almost universally criticized for his performance as the Sultan of Swat in *The Babe Ruth Story*. Bendix, however, is pretty good while he is portraying the large personality that Babe Ruth was, confident, brash, and a big spender. However, in his death scene, he reminds viewers more of Lou Costello than Babe Ruth. In fairness to Bendix, many of the scenes in the film are silly, with ridiculous dialogue, and it is unlikely that any actor could have played the part well. At the age of forty-two, Bendix was required to play a teenager in some of the early scenes at St. Mary's, performing with other actors who were actually teenagers. That was not an easy assignment for any actor.

Babe Ruth was an incredible baseball player. The film posits that he almost single-handedly saved baseball after the Black Sox scandal, a historically defensible position. Surely, Ruth made the long ball a highlight of the game, continuing to the present day. Yet, for all of Ruth's attributes, which should have been enough to carry the film on their own, the filmmakers felt the need to concoct a new ending to Babe's life, calling Ruth a hero for taking an experimental drug to extend his own life (because the drug could potentially then help others). Although late in his life Ruth did take an experimental drug to treat his cancer, it was not at the very end of his days and it was not done to help mankind.

Thus the ending of *The Babe Ruth Story* is a total Hollywood fiction, demonstrating that the filmmakers were bereft of the necessary filmmaking skills and baseball knowledge to tell the story of the greatest of them all. The critics are right. *The Babe Ruth Story* is an awful film.

The Babe (1992)

Babe Ruth, the most famous American athlete of all time, has had difficulties with his film biographies. The first alleged one, *Headin' Home* (1920), a silent film, is almost 100 percent fiction, suggesting that Ruth grew up in a small town in the South and courted the banker's daughter before he became a slugger for the New York Yankees. *The Babe Ruth Story* (1948) gets it right about where Ruth grew up (Baltimore, Maryland) and then touches on his pitching days in Boston before moving on to his years with the New York Yankees as the premier slugger of his generation. Almost all of the rest of *The Babe Ruth Story* is fiction. In addition to the inaccuracies in their story lines, both films are among the worst baseball movies ever made.

The most recent cinematic biography of the Sultan of Swat is *The Babe* (1992), with John Goodman in the title role. In life, the third time is often a charm. In baseball, the third one is usually strike three. Unfortunately for *The Babe*, the film falls into the latter category.

The broad outline of Ruth's life is accurately told in the film, from being sent at an early age to St. Mary's orphanage (portrayed in the film as something straight out of Charles Dickens), learning to play baseball there, first playing professionally with the Baltimore Orioles, a minor-league team, before moving on to Boston and then New York City. Considerable time is spent on the Babe wooing and then marrying Helen Woodford in Boston, their subsequent marital problems, and their adoption of a daughter. Babe's long-term affair with Claire Hodgson and their subsequent marriage are also covered in detail. The film ends with Babe being released by the New York Yankees, signing with Boston, and hitting his last three home runs in Pittsburgh.

The Babe (1992). This is a photo of Babe Ruth's first wife, Helen Woodford Ruth, taken in 1921. *(Library of Congress, LC-DIG-ggbain-33200)*

Nevertheless, much of the film is pure fiction or, at best, factually inaccurate. Babe did not meet Claire in Boston; he first met her once he moved to New York City. Helen's death in a house fire occurs much later in the film that it did in real life. Instead, the film states that Helen and Ruth divorced, which never occurred. Ruth had his troubles with manager Miller Huggins, but Ruth never threatened him by holding him over the back side of a moving train (although the story itself has become another of the legends about Ruth). If *The Babe* were to be believed, Ruth was a home-run hitter from the first game he played in Boston through his last innings there. Of course, Babe was really known as a pitcher in Boston, setting the record for consecutive scoreless innings pitched in a World Series in 1918 (29 2/3 innings), a record that stood until 1961, when Whitey Ford pitched 33 2/3 scoreless innings. Although the film does show Babe pitching on at least one occasion in Boston, striking out Ty Cobb twice in a game, the movie generally overlooks Ruth's pitching success and focuses on his slugging abilities in Boston, which did not become his trademark until he was sold to the Yankees after the 1919 season.

In fact, if *The Babe* were to be believed, every hit that Ruth ever had was a home run. No singles, doubles, or triples are ever shown (except for the one time he bats right-handed, a piece of fiction). One of Ruth's pop-ups was hit so high in the infield, according to the film, that before it hit the ground, Ruth had an inside-the-infield home run. One wonders if that fictional incident was rejected by the screenwriters of *The Babe Ruth Story* as being too far-fetched.

Two of the most legendary moments in Babe Ruth's life are shown in *The Babe*. One is the time Ruth visits young Johnny Sylvester, who is dying in a hospital. Ruth promises to hit two home runs the next day for Johnny, in exchange for Johnny's promise to get better. Of course, the next day, the Babe succeeds and, after rounding the bases on the second occasion, tells Johnny over the radio that the home runs were for him. The other is the moment in the 1932 World Series when Babe Ruth called his shot, a home run to center field.

The true story behind the Johnny Sylvester incident is more mundane, according to Ruth biographer Robert W. Creamer. In 1926, eleven-year-old Johnny Sylvester was hurt in a fall from a horse and hospitalized. (The movie has the incident taking place in 1921.) To cheer him up, a friend of Johnny's father brought him a baseball autographed by the Yankees team and a promise from the Babe that he would hit a home run for Johnny in the World Series. Ruth hit four home runs in the series that year, and after it was over Ruth paid a visit to Johnny in the hospital, something Ruth did for lots of children. That is all there is to the story. (The real Johnny Sylvester recovered from his injury, went to college, served in the navy during World War II and became president of a manufacturing company, dying in 1990 at the age of 74.)

As for the called shot in the World Series, there is controversy to this day as to whether the Babe actually called his home run that afternoon in 1932. Eyewitnesses dispute the account that Babe called his shot, and supposedly Ruth later admitted that he did not. Fortunately, there is film and a photograph available of that moment, and it shows that after Ruth took two pitches for strikes, he raised his arm with two fingers pointed outward, telling the Chicago bench and the pitcher that he only had two strikes on him. He was not calling his shot.

However, apocryphal or not, most people believe that both stories about Ruth are true. There will never be a biographical film about Babe Ruth that does not include those two incidents, because, as a newspaper reporter says in *The Man Who Shot Liberty Valance* (1962), "When the legend becomes fact, print the legend."

Much like *The Pride of the Yankees* (1942), *The Babe* struggles to find a theme that is important enough to tie the long story together and is also interesting for viewers. The first attempt concerns Ruth's weight. The kids at St. Mary's kid him about his size, as do his teammates on his early professional teams. In these early scenes, John Goodman wears clothes that are too tight, emphasizing the Bambino's weight. The problem here is that, although most people think of Babe as being heavy throughout his life, his weight fluctuated during his career and he was seldom extremely obese during his playing days. In any event, Ruth's weight is hardly a sufficient theme for the movie, even though it comes up again at the end of the film.

Next, the film moves to Ruth's juvenile characteristics, such as farting in public and driving a motorcycle onto sidewalks. Then the film moves to his drinking and carousing, including his large appetite for both food and women. *The Babe* is more a character study of Ruth than a study of his baseball career, and that would be okay, except that the film only provides caricatures of Ruth, not a portrait of his real personality.

At the end of *The Babe*, the film has a new theme—Babe's desire to become a manager so that he can stay in the game he loves. Although this idea is mentioned early in the film, it only becomes the focus of the film near its conclusion, in order to gain some audience sympathy for Babe Ruth. How unfair is it to deny Babe Ruth the chance to manage in the majors after all that he has given the sport? The problem, however, is that the theme does not work, at least not for this film. The movie has spent so much time making Ruth into such a disagreeable character, cheating on his first wife, arguing with managers, umpires, and fans, not to mention his excessive drinking and boasting, that there is little sympathy left for Babe by the end of the film. It is hard to disagree with Colonel Ruppert, the owner of the Yankees, when he tells Ruth (based on a true incident), "How can you manage a team when you can't even manage yourself?"

Much like William Bendix in the earlier film, forty-year-old John Goodman must play a teenage Babe Ruth at St. Mary's where Ruth is first discovered by professional baseball. Goodman manages to get past that scene (and the tight clothing he has to wear) to give a good performance as the Babe, although not one that would convince anyone that he really is Babe Ruth. Fortunately, Goodman is not required to display any baseball skills, generally being limited to a few wild swings, many of which end up as home runs, and then a jog-walk around the bases.

The Babe cleverly uses his three-home-run game in Pittsburgh in May 1935 for the conclusion of the film, allowing Babe to walk off the field while he is on top, even though that part of the story is fictional, as discussed before with regard to The Babe Ruth Story. However, while that was the correct dramatic approach, once again the filmmakers blew this moment. Because the baseball scenes for the film were shot at Wrigley Field in Chicago, the enormity of Ruth hitting a ball over the right field roof of Forbes Field could not be shown in the film. Instead, when Ruth hits a ball over the low center-field fence of the playing field used in the film, the announcer incorrectly states that that was the first ball ever hit out of Forbes Field. (In addition, having Ruth call his home-run shot, one more time, on one of the pitches is surely overkill.)

More importantly, The Babe would have an audience believe that because Ruth was ailing at the time, the National League allowed Ruth a pinch runner at first base, who completed Babe's home-run trots, and then Ruth continued playing in the game in subsequent innings. Not only is this untrue (and something Major League Baseball would never do), it is unbelievable (how could Ruth play the outfield if he could not even walk around the bases?) and is, in fact, more humiliating to Ruth's legend than anything professional baseball may have done to Ruth at the end of his career.

The Babe is a very disappointing film. As famous as Babe Ruth was as a baseball player and as outrageous as many of the incidents in his private life may have been, it may be impossible to make a good film biography of the Sultan of Swat. It is unlikely, however, that filmmakers will stop trying.

The Jackie Robinson Story (1950)

Upon occasion, a sports figure will transcend his sport and become so famous, even to people who do not follow the sport, that even many years after his death people still remember him and what he accomplished. This is a rare situation and the list of such sportsmen is short, but it would surely include Babe Ruth, Jesse Owens, Muhammad Ali, and, of course, Jackie Robinson. As everyone knows, Jackie Robinson was the first African American to break the color barrier in Major League Baseball.

Jack Roosevelt Robinson was born on January 31, 1919, in Cairo, Georgia, a few miles north of the Florida state line. His parents, Mallie and Jerry Robinson, were poor sharecroppers on a large plantation. The father eventually deserted the family, and in 1920, Mallie decided to move to Southern California with her four sons and one daughter. The Robinson family settled in Pasadena, just outside of Los Angeles.

In 1939, after excelling in sports in high school and junior college, Robinson enrolled at UCLA. In his first year there, Robinson immediately became a star running back, punt returner, and defensive player on the football team. He also played basketball that school year, was a shortstop on UCLA's baseball team, and participated in track and field, lettering in all four sports. In his second year at UCLA, Robinson became the quarterback of the football team and competed in basketball. He then left school early, without a degree, thereby skipping his final season of baseball. After school, Robinson had a few jobs, some of which were sports-related, until he was drafted into the army in 1942. There he survived a court-martial proceeding against him and was honorably discharged in 1944. He never went overseas.

After his military service concluded, Robinson joined the Kansas City Monarchs, a team in the Negro National League. Playing shortstop for the Monarchs in 1945, Robinson had a good year, showing some power and hitting for a high batting average. During that season, Robinson was secretly contacted by the Brooklyn Dodgers about becoming a major leaguer. When Robinson first met Branch Rickey, the president and general manager of the club, Rickey made it clear to Robinson that in addition to playing well for his team, Rickey expected Robinson to have the courage not to fight back when he became the target of racial slurs and discrimination. Robinson agreed and on October 23, 1945, Robinson publicly signed a contract to play the following year for the Dodgers' top farm club, the Montreal Royals of the International League.

In 1946, Robinson attended spring training with the Dodgers in Daytona Beach, Florida. Robinson then made his debut with the Montreal Royals on April 18, 1946, in a game against the Jersey City Giants in Jersey City, New Jersey. The following year, on April 15, 1947, Robinson started the season playing first base for the Brooklyn Dodgers, thereby breaking Major League Baseball's color barrier, becoming the first African American to play major-league baseball in either the National or American Leagues. (There had been some black players in the nineteenth century in the major leagues that preceded the National and American Leagues.) Robinson had an excellent season that first year, becoming the first-ever Rookie of the Year in the big leagues. Robinson's success continued in subsequent years for the Dodgers. He was named the Most Valuable Player for the National League in 1949 and in that same year, made his first of six consecutive All-Star Game appearances. He appeared in several World Series with the Dodgers, including the one in the world-championship season of 1955. Robinson retired from baseball at the end of the 1956 series.

Once Jackie Robinson starting playing for the Brooklyn Dodgers and got past many of the racist elements in the sport, Robinson became a popular figure in America. Huge crowds attended his games. In addition to using his fame for charity work, Robinson decided to turn his popularity into compensation, endorsing various commercial products such as bread, milk, and cigarettes. In 1947, he even appeared in vaudeville for four weeks. Robinson wrote his autobiography (*Jackie Robinson: My Own Story*, published in 1948) and went on barnstorming baseball tours in several off-seasons. From time to time, he had his own radio program. In 1950, Robinson starred in the film version of his life, *The Jackie Robinson Story*.

The Jackie Robinson Story is typical of most baseball biography films. The movie hits some of the high points of Robinson's life in a generally accurate manner. It shows Robinson growing up in Pasadena, with a single mother and his big brother, Mack, playing several sports at Pasadena Junior College and UCLA, leaving UCLA before

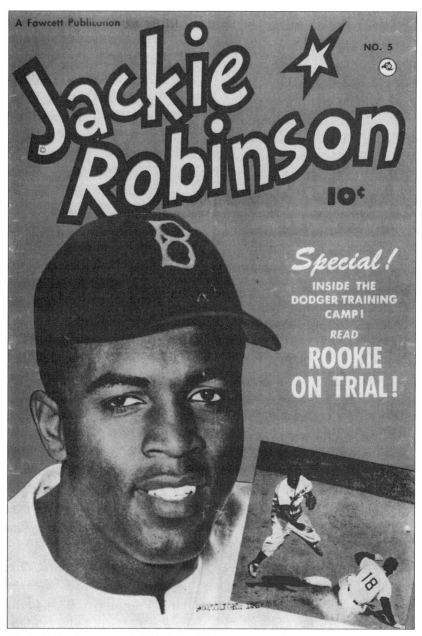

The Jackie Robinson Story (1950). Jackie Robinson eventually became a popular figure in America. Robinson turned that popularity toward commercial enterprises, including his own comic book, pictured here, circa 1951. *(Library of Congress, LC-USZC4-6144)*

obtaining a degree, being drafted into the army, and upon his discharge, playing for a team in the Negro Leagues, being approached by the Dodgers to play in the big leagues, spending a year in the minors, and then finally becoming a success in the majors. In addition to the big picture, some of the details in the film are also accurate. When Branch Rickey first meets with Robinson and explains the abuse he is guaranteed to receive if he joins the Dodgers, Robinson asks Rickey if he wants a player who is too afraid to fight back. Rickey famously responds, "I want a ballplayer with guts enough not to fight back." That is almost word for word what Rickey purportedly said to Robinson at their first meeting.

In other ways, *The Jackie Robinson Story* is inaccurate. Jackie did not make an error on the first ground ball hit to him in his first game with the Montreal Royals, and he did not bunt for a base hit in his first at bat for Montreal, although that did happen later in the first game. Robinson did not hit a triple in his first at bat with the Dodgers. In fact, his first major-league hit came the day after his major-league debut. The facts of these games were rearranged by the screenwriters for dramatic effect.

In the film, while Jackie's three other siblings are ignored, Jackie's older brother, Mack, is a key player in Jackie's life. In real life, Mack was only a minor figure in Jackie's life. Also, the film's portrayal of Jackie's wife, Rachel, is misleading. She has little personality and very little influence on Jackie in the film. Rachel was a much more important person in Jackie's real life, both personal and professional, than is shown in the movie.

The Jackie Robinson Story skips over some important events in Robinson's life, perhaps the most important being the moments in Robinson's military career in a segregated unit and particularly his court-martial in 1944. When Jackie starts to play in the Negro Leagues (although that name is surprisingly never used in the film), his cinematic team is the Black Panthers, not the Kansas City Monarchs as in real life. (The Black Panthers was actually the name of the segregated tank battalion that Robinson joined in the military at Fort Hood, Texas.) None of the teams the Dodgers play and none of the other Dodgers' players are identified by name in the film.

Then there are the completely made-up scenes in the film. For example, when Robinson is trying to decide whether or not to sign with the Dodgers (as if any African American ballplayer playing for low pay in the Negro Leagues, with lousy travel and awful eating and sleeping accommodations, would ever turn the opportunity down), Robinson goes to a minister in New York City to get some advice. The movie thus posits a moment in Robinson's life that when he has to make the most important decision of his life, he seeks the advice of a reverend he has never met in a city he is just visiting for the first time, not even knowing whether or not the reverend has ever seen a baseball game. The idea behind the scene is to demonstrate Robinson's strong religious faith, which was true in real life, but the scene only seems silly.

One of those made-up moments, however, is very effective. There is an avid Brooklyn Dodgers fan who is initially portrayed in the film as a man who hates Robinson because of his color, even agreeing with three other fans who threaten to physically abuse Robinson if he continues to play for the Dodgers. When Robinson first starts to play in the majors, the same fan shouts insults at Robinson. However, as the season goes along and Robinson turns out to be a great player, the fan starts to warm up to Robinson. By the end of the season, he is shouting for Robinson, not against him. This cinematic technique, while maybe not the cleverest ever employed in a film, works very well as a metaphor for all of the Brooklyn fans and fans around the country who started cheering for Robinson, black man or not, once Robinson was able to display his baseball skills at a major-league level.

The Jackie Robinson Story was probably a better film when it was released in 1950 than it is today. The movie had a very low budget, about $300,000, and had a short shooting schedule so that the film could open early in the 1950 baseball season. The low budget is readily apparent in the film, with tight shots of most of the batters, no location shooting, an almost nonexistent score, and a scene early on in the film where the story is told by monthly calendar sheets and pages of a calendar book floating on the screen. Low-budget films were not that unusual in 1950, but today's movie audience expects the big-budget, slick film production values that one can see in the other film biography of Jackie Robinson, *42* (2013).

The Jackie Robinson Story does have one distinction. While many baseball players have appeared as themselves in many films,

Jackie Robinson is the only one to star in a film biography about his life. (*Headin' Home* [1920], starring Babe Ruth, hardly counts.) Robinson received some good reviews for his performance when the film was released, but, in fact, his performance is awkward. He has difficulty speaking his lines with any conviction. Of course, his play on the baseball diamond is superb, so at least in that regard the movie is quite convincing. (While Robinson was the first African American to break baseball's color barrier, he was not the first to play himself in a movie. Larry Doby, the first black player in the American League, and Satchel Paige hold that distinction, playing themselves in *The Kid from Cleveland* [1949], although they only have small roles in the movie.)

The Jackie Robinson Story does not overlook the problems that Robinson had in becoming the first African American to play major-league baseball in quite some time. The film shows some nasty language or cracks directed at Robinson, including, on one surprising occasion, the use of the n-word. Three baseball fans accost Robinson outside a ballpark and threaten Robinson with injury if he continues to play; a group of teammates sign a petition asking the Dodgers to get rid of Robinson; a baseball game is canceled because a town does not permit white and black players on the same field; and Robinson is often booed when he comes out on the field. However, the film is never able to convey the alarming and outrageous nature of these activities. For example, the trio that threatens Robinson seem more like buffoons than frightening; the players who petition to have Robinson thrown off the Dodgers (an incident based on real life) quickly back down after Branch Rickey talks to them; and the remarks made by fans and other players to Robinson, with the exception of the use of the n-word, seem downright silly.

In other words, it was not enough for *The Jackie Robinson Story* to merely show the incidents. It was incumbent upon the filmmakers to ensure that the scenes were acted, directed, and staged in such a way as to make them outrageous and frightening, and in this regard, they dropped the ball. Little is shown of the pain and self-doubt that Robinson suffered throughout these attacks and, therefore, the difficulties that Robinson faced in cracking the color barrier seem somewhat muted in the film. (By contrast, see the scenes with Phillies manager Ben Chapman race-baiting Robinson in *42* [2013].) As a result, *The Jackie Robinson Story* suffers from the same faults as most film biographies. The movie consists of a number of chronological scenes thrown together, without any strong plot or theme tying them together. Robinson's real-life story had just such a strong plot and theme—the struggles of a black man to achieve equality—but by downplaying both the abuse thrown at Robinson and the enormity of Robinson's struggles and importance of those struggles, the film is just a series of incidents. Robinson's real-life story is better learned by reading a biography of Robinson than watching the film.

In fact, *The Jackie Robinson Story* actually misses the theme of Robinson's life. On several occasions, Branch Rickey explains that it is unfair to prevent any American such as Robinson from playing baseball, the American game, as if baseball is the most important aspect of American society. The true theme of Robinson's life, however, is that it is improper to prevent anyone from participating in any aspect of American life, not just a game, based on the color of that person's skin. Rickey's speeches in the film, while well intentioned, seem naïve, particularly when looking back from the perspective of many years.

The ending of the movie rings hollow for today's audience. Once Jackie Robinson has made it in his sport, he is called to Washington where he testifies to Congress about how great America is. As the film ends, patriotic music swells in the background, the Statue of Liberty is shown, and all is right with the world because, as the narrator states, this is America, a country that is truly free. However, many people probably knew in 1950, and surely all know today, that Robinson's ascension to big-league baseball was just the beginning of a long, difficult struggle, not the end. Despite the impression conveyed by the conclusion of *The Jackie Robinson Story*, the hardest fights of the civil rights movement were yet to come.

42 (2013)

On June 4, 1972, the Los Angeles Dodgers retired the number that Jackie Robinson wore on his back during his entire major-league career. On April 15, 1997, fifty years after Robinson first appeared in a game with the Brooklyn Dodgers, Major League Baseball retired Robinson's jersey number throughout the sport, the first time a major-league sport in North America had ever honored a player in such a manner. As a result, since 1997, except for a few players who were then wearing the same jersey number and were grandfathered in until their retirement, no other major-league ballplayer has worn Robinson's number on a regular basis. Sixteen years after that honor, Robinson's jersey number was still so famous that when a new motion picture about Robinson's life was released, his jersey number alone was sufficient to serve as the title of the film.

42 is not a film biography of Jackie Robinson. The film shows only three years of Robinson's life, 1945 (when he was playing in the Negro Leagues with the Kansas City Monarchs), 1946 (when he was playing in the International League with the Montreal Royals) and 1947 (when he was playing in the National League with the Brooklyn Dodgers). The film ends during the 1947 regular season, on the day that the Dodgers clinch the pennant. Because the filmmakers wanted to end the movie on a high note, they did not show that the Dodgers went on to lose the 1947 World Series to the New York Yankees.

The film does mention that Jackie was born in Cairo, Georgia; that his father deserted the family while Jackie was just a baby; that Jackie played sports at UCLA; and that Jackie was court-martialed in the army for refusing to move to the back of a bus. Other than those small mentions and a few personal matters, such as Jackie's wedding to Rachel and the birth of their first son, the film has a laser-like focus on Jackie's struggles to break the color barrier in Major League Baseball, the pain he suffers while doing so, and his ultimate triumphs on the baseball field through 1947. Later years are covered only by implication, as just before the final credits, the film notes that in 1962, Jackie was elected to the Hall of Fame.

As a result, 42 avoids the problems of most biographical films. By concentrating on a distinct time period in Robinson's life, a time period of inherent drama, 42 does not just consist of a number of scenes throughout Robinson's life put together in chronological order. Rather, the scenes in the film are chosen, almost exclusively, to dramatize Robinson's struggles to break Major League Baseball's color barrier. Thus, there is a unifying theme and dramatic purpose to the movie. It shows that, when properly done, movies can convey drama and conflict better than the written word, particularly better than a complete biographical work. 42 is no substitute for a book on the life of Jackie Robinson, but it does provide added value.

The difficulties that Robinson suffered as a black man in America are shown throughout the film, as he is denied the use of a bathroom while traveling in the Negro Leagues; his seats on an airplane are given to a white couple and the Robinsons bumped to a later flight; and he is shouted at and abused whenever he goes onto the field, including repetitive uses of the n-word. Many of these moments occur in the South, as might be expected, but the key scenes in the film that epitomize Robinson's struggles and his decision, at Branch Rickey's request, never to fight back occur in the North.

When the Philadelphia Phillies come to play the Dodgers at Ebbets Field on April 22, 1947, the Phillies manager, Ben Chapman, who was raised in Alabama, decides to make Robinson's race an issue. When Robinson comes to bat, he shouts things such as, "Hey, nigger, black nigger. Why don't you go back to the cotton fields where you come from?" and "Put on a little show, nigger, and do a shuffle," and "Who'd you put out of a job, nigger?" The insults seem unstoppable; the repetitive use of the n-word is infuriating. Most audience members would probably want to go right into the screen and punch out the Phillies manager. Robinson, however, remembering his promise to Branch Rickey, does nothing on the field. He does, however, go into the locker-room runway and relieve his anger by hitting a bat against the wall and screaming. The pressure that Robinson feels, both from the attacks upon him and his inability to respond, are excruciatingly depicted in this scene.

The problems with Philadelphia do not end there. When the Dodgers are about to leave Brooklyn and travel to Philadelphia for their first away series against the Phillies, Herb Pennock, the general manager of the Phillies, calls Rickey and asks him not to bring Robinson with the Dodgers because Philadelphia is not ready for that sort of thing. Rickey refuses, and when the Brooklyn Dodgers team bus arrives in Philadelphia at the Benjamin Franklin Hotel, the team's usual hotel, the entire team is refused accommodations because Robinson is one of the players.

These events in the film are based on true incidents (although the scene with Robinson in the clubhouse runway is fictional), and because they involve the North, and particularly because they involve Philadelphia, presumably a sophisticated East Coast city, they are all the more telling. After all, in 1947, Brooklyn Dodgers games were primarily played in the Northeast, and therefore, in theory, Robinson should have had an easy time acclimating to the game. That, of course, was not the case. While Northerners often feel superior to Southerners on race relations, 42 exposes the dark underside of rampant racism in the North at the time, and in a raw and telling way. The filmmakers could have gone the easy route and just shown racist attitudes against Robinson in the South or by Southerners. Instead, the filmmakers took the more challenging route, resulting in a special underlying theme of the movie—not that racism didn't exist in the South, which everyone knows it did, but there was also pervasive racism in the North, which appears to have been forgotten.

42 is generally accurate on the baseball facts of Robinson's career, including his hits, home runs, and stolen bases. For example, on the day that the Phillies manager, Ben Chapman, abuses Robinson with racial slurs, the movie accurately shows Robinson scoring the winning run for the Dodgers by hitting a single, stealing second, moving to third on the throwing error, and then scoring on a subsequent hit by Gene Hermanski.

The film also dramatizes some special moments that occurred during the 1947 season. When the Phillies return to Brooklyn later in the season, at the request of Ben Chapman and with the encouragement of Branch Rickey, Robinson poses for a picture with Chapman before a game, with both holding a bat. Pee Wee Reese, the Dodgers shortstop, puts his arm on Robinson's shoulder before a game to show his solidarity with Robinson. (Many baseball historians believe this event is apocryphal.) Teammate Ralph Branca prevents Robinson from falling into the dugout after the catch of a foul ball, resulting in the sight of a black man in a white man's arms, a first for many fans. Two of the most famous lines from the Robinson saga appear in the film. Branch Rickey tells Robinson, before he signs him, "I want a man with the guts not to fight back," and when Robinson is asked by sportswriters what will happen if a white pitcher throws at his head, Robinson says, "I'll duck."

On a few occasions, the facts are massaged for dramatic effect. In his first at bat in the big leagues, Robinson was thrown out on a close play at first base, although in the film version, he is shown as being safe, with the umpire inexplicably calling him out, presumably on racial grounds. The film ends at a game against the Pittsburgh Pirates on September 17, 1947, when, according to the film, the Dodgers won the pennant after winning the game on a late-inning home run by Robinson. In fact, but less dramatically, Robinson's home run came in the fourth inning on that day.

Of course, as always happens in a film biography, there are scenes inserted in the film that are fiction. At a game in Cincinnati in June 1947, a man takes his young son to the ballpark. Before the game, the father seems likable enough, talking about his memories of Honus Wagner with the young boy. However, as soon as the game starts, the father shouts a stream of abuse at Robinson,

This statue is located just outside MCU Park in Coney Island, Brooklyn, New York. It memorializes a moment (perhaps apocryphal) in Jackie Robinson's career when Pee Wee Reese put his arm around Robinson when a crowd was taunting him. The moment is depicted in *42* (2013). *(Emma Backer)*

including the n-word. The little boy is perplexed at first, but he eventually also starts shouting the n-word at Robinson. This scene was written to show that racism is not inherent in an individual; it is learned.

Then there is the scene of a young African American boy near the beginning of the film, who sees Robinson off on the train as Robinson heads north after spring training, receives a ball tossed by Robinson from the train, and even puts his ear to the rails so that he can feel the vibration of the train in the distance. According to the film, that young boy was Ed Charles, who became a major-league ballplayer and who played for the Mets in their world-championship season of 1969. The purpose of the scene is to show the positive effect of Robinson on black youth. (Ed Charles played third base for both the Kansas City Athletics and the New York Mets in a career that spanned eight years. While it is true that Charles grew up in Daytona Beach, Florida, watched the Dodgers in spring training the first year that Robinson played there, and was inspired by Robinson, the scene at the train station is not entirely based on fact.)

Much of the game action in the film is called by Red Barber, one of the most famous play-by-play radio announcers of all time. He broadcast baseball games for over four decades with several different teams, including the Brooklyn Dodgers from 1939 to 1953. Barber was born in Mississippi and was reluctant to call the Dodgers games with a black man on the team, but he came around, eventually becoming an ardent supporter of Robinson's. Barber was known for clever expressions and signature catchphrases, such as the ones that can be heard in the film. For example, Barber says that a pitcher is so fast that he "can toss a lamb chop past a hungry wolf," that Robinson on base "is just as restless as a cat with a hot foot," and that the "game is just as tight as a new pair of shoes on a rainy day." The character of Barber, as expertly portrayed by John C. McGinley, adds some background color for the movie, but it is still somewhat strange that a baseball film from 2013 uses a storytelling technique of baseball films from the 1930s and 1940s, i.e., having the action described and put into perspective by a radio announcer. It is not clear why clever filmmakers cannot tell the story of baseball games through cinematic techniques rather than by narration.

There is also an amusing aspect of the film, at least in retrospect. In the film, it seems that the punishment for Dodgers players who do not want to play with Robinson is a trade to the Pittsburgh Pirates. Later, in 1950, Branch Rickey had a dispute with the majority owner of the Dodgers, and Rickey left the organization. He then became the general manager of the lowly Pittsburgh Pirates, his personal banishment from the top tier of Major League Baseball.

Although 42 does not shy away from addressing important issues, the film still has to live and die on whether or not it is an entertaining film and, perhaps more importantly, whether or not it is an entertaining *baseball* film. 42 opened to somewhat mixed reviews, but most baseball fans will find the film quite satisfying. The action on the field is realistic; the actors always seem to be ballplayers, not actors pretending to be ballplayers. Through the magic of digital imagery, the games appear to take place in Ebbets Field, the Polo Grounds, Forbes Field, and Crosley Field, ballparks that have long ago been demolished. It is satisfying to observe great special effects in a film, particularly when they do not overwhelm the story.

In addition, the acting in 42 is excellent, from the not well-known Chadwick Boseman as Jackie Robinson to the very famous Harrison Ford as Branch Rickey through the smaller parts, with Alan Tudyk a particular standout as the film's primary villain, Phillies manager Ben Chapman. 42 delicately balances the issues of the day with the game of baseball, both on and off the field, making it an enjoyable film for baseball fans and non-baseball fans alike.

The Winning Team (1952)

Cy Young is the career leader in major-league wins by a pitcher, with 511 wins over his twenty-one-year Major League Baseball career. Next in line are Walter Johnson, with 417 career wins, and then Christy Mathewson and Grover Cleveland Alexander, each with 373. Yet out of all of those famous pitchers, only one has a biographical film made about him. The pitcher is Grover Cleveland Alexander and the film is *The Winning Team*, starring Ronald Reagan as the famous right-hander and Doris Day as his wife, Aimee. Perhaps the reason for this anomaly was best summed up by baseball historian Donald Honig, who once wrote, "Equal in glory with Mathewson and Johnson, [Alexander] outdid them in drama and tragedy."

The Winning Team commences with a young Grover Cleveland Alexander living in Elba, Nebraska, and working as a linesman for a telephone company. Baseball, however, is Alexander's primary interest and after a local game in which he pitches very well, a low-level professional team from Galesburg signs him to a professional contract. After having some success with the Galesburg team, an incident happens one afternoon that will affect the rest of Alexander's life. With Alexander on first base, the batter hits a ground ball to the shortstop, who tosses the ball to the second baseman. However, the throw to first from the second baseman hits Alexander in the head from close range, knocking Alexander out cold. When Alexander awakens after several days of unconsciousness, he finds that he has double vision.

That puts Alexander out of baseball for a while, but when his vision improves, Alexander goes back to the professional leagues, eventually ending up with the Philadelphia Phillies of the National League. Alexander has a very successful career in Philadelphia, but after the 1917 season, he is sold to the Chicago Cubs. Before Alexander can report to the Cubs, he is drafted into the army, where he serves overseas as a sergeant for a field artillery unit during World War I. There he suffers dizzy spells, possibly caused by the loud blasts of the artillery guns among which he must work. On his return to the States, Alexander begins to suffer from fainting spells, a result of the epilepsy he acquired either as a result of the baseball to the head in his early professional career or his war experiences. Alexander starts drinking to excess, affecting his pitching success and causing him to be thrown out of the major leagues. But, as the film ends, Alexander returns to the majors with the St. Louis Cardinals, becoming the hero of the 1926 World Series, winning three games and leading St. Louis to victory over the New York Yankees.

That set of facts about the life of Grover Cleveland Alexander from the film is essentially accurate, but it does not tell the whole story. What's missing is a sense of the baseball accomplishments of Alexander the Great. In addition to having 373 career wins, tied with Christy Mathewson for third all-time in Major League Baseball and for most in the National League, Alexander had 90 career shutouts, second only to Walter Johnson's 110, he won thirty or more games in three consecutive seasons (1915–1917), and he still holds the record for most wins by a rookie, twenty-eight, in 1911. The list could go on and on. Yet none of those feats really come through in *The Winning Season*. Most of Alexander's accomplishments are told through a montage of brief newspaper headlines, which do not succeed in bringing home the enormity of Alexander's baseball accomplishments.

Since *The Winning Season* never conveys the incredible pitching career of Alexander and the heights he reached, his fall from grace in the middle of the film is not as dramatic as it could have been. This is a significant missed opportunity for the film. In real life, Alexander's personal degradations after he left Major League Baseball in 1930,

The Winning Team (1952). This is a photo of Grover Cleveland Alexander pitching for the Philadelphia Phillies in 1913. *(Library of Congress, LC-DIG-ggbain-12276)*

and which continued to the end of his life in 1950, are as dramatic as one could imagine. That missed opportunity relates to the main problem with *The Winning Season*—the film operates on an even keel throughout, with no major dramatic moments. Newspaper headlines and archive footage are not sufficient to convey the true drama of a baseball game or a baseball career.

The film does cover in detail the most famous moment of Alexander's storied pitching career, his strikeout of Tony Lazzeri of the Yankees with the bases loaded and two men out in the seventh inning of the seventh game of the 1926 World Series, with St. Louis leading by just one run. Alexander was brought into the game in relief to face Lazzeri, even though Alexander had pitched a complete game the day before. Lazzeri, who was a rookie with the Yankees in 1926, drove in 114 runs that season. As a result of Alexander's pitching achievement in that seventh game, the Cardinals upset the Yankees for the 1926 world championship.

While *The Winning Team* covers the last three innings of that famous game in great detail, the film focuses on a fictional part of the story, whether Aimee, who has decided to forego watching the game because her husband is not pitching, will get to the ballpark in time to give her husband emotional support so that he can finish the game. That is the reason for the title of the film, *The Winning Team*, with Alexander apparently unable to pitch successfully in big games without his wife in the stands, making the couple a winning team. While this is complete fiction, it has an inspiration in a real-life situation with the Alexanders. As Grover's drinking became a bigger problem during his baseball life, Grover's teams often required Aimee (whose given name was Amy) to stay with Grover and travel with him on the road to prevent him from drinking so much. Aimee's influence on Grover was somewhat successful in that regard, making her part of a winning team.

By focusing on Aimee Alexander instead of Grover, the excitement of that seventh game of the 1926 World Series is muted in the movie. The tension in the game should have come from the game itself, not from the movements of Aimee. Also, most of the baseball scenes from that game, when they are not interrupted by Aimee's activities, are close-ups of the pitcher, then of the batter, and then usually a cut to long-distance archive footage of a game. There is no feeling that the game is taking place in front of a large crowd at Yankee Stadium or that the Yankees, with Ruth and Gehrig in the lineup, are an overpowering baseball team. In the seventh inning, there is never a sense that the bases are loaded (cuts to the base runners may have helped) or that the World Series is on the line. Even the close foul ball that Lazzeri hits has no excitement because of the quick cut to archive footage. Director Lewis Seiler simply blew the climax to *The Winning Team*, diffusing any tension that the scene should have had. This failure to create legitimate moments of tension and drama in *The Winning Team* is why the film, enjoyable though it may be at times, is easily forgettable.

In the real seventh game of the 1926 World Series, when Alexander came to the mound with the bases loaded and the game on the line, the tension was, as they say, palpable. Some people believe that Alexander was drunk when he was called into the game that day, but the better evidence and his pitching performance belie that assertion. (*The Winning Team* addresses that issue slightly, by showing Alexander with some double vision during the game, implying that his epilepsy may have been a factor in his demeanor on that day.) The first pitch to Lazzeri was a ball, the second a called strike, and the third was hit foul down the left-field side, close enough for many to believe that it could have been a hit. Lazzeri then swung and missed the last pitch, for the final out of the inning. (In the film, Alexander runs the count to 3–2 before he strikes out Lazzeri.) In the eighth inning, it was three up and three down for the Yankees. In the bottom of the ninth, Alexander got two quick outs but then he walked Babe Ruth. Then, in one of the most unusual endings ever to a World Series, Babe Ruth was thrown out trying to steal second base. This incredible finish is overlooked in *The Winning Team*.

In the film, Grover Cleveland Alexander is thrown out of baseball in the mid-1920s because of his alcoholism. He is then shown playing for a barnstorming professional team called the House of David, with all bearded players, and then working in a carnival in Coney Island, telling baseball yarns next to a fire-swallower and just before the headline act, which is a flea circus. All of this is based on fact, although those events occurred subsequent to Alexander leaving baseball in 1930. After his alcoholism ended his major-league career, Alexander kicked around with Minor League Baseball teams and barnstorming teams such as the House of David, which was a baseball team sponsored by a religious sect. Alexander also landed in jail on many occasions as a result of his drunkenness. Alexander hit rock bottom around 1939 when he performed at Hubert's Dime Museum and Flea Circus, a penny arcade located at Seventh Avenue and West 42nd Street in Times Square, New York. There, for a few bucks, the Hall of Fame baseball pitcher told stories about the early days of baseball, including his strikeout of Tony Lazzeri in the World Series.

According to the credits of *The Winning Team*, one of the technical advisors for the film was "Mrs. Grover Cleveland Alexander." Thus it is surprising that the portrayal of Aimee Alexander in the film is so inaccurate. Aimee was not a childhood sweetheart of Alexander's from back home who wanted him to become a farmer. Rather, the two met on a blind date in St. Paul, Minnesota, in 1918, and they married for the first time just before Alexander went overseas. In total, the two married and divorced on two occasions, and Aimee was often out of Grover's life for long periods of time. Of course, it must have been hard for Aimee to pass up the chance to have the blond-haired and very attractive Doris Day play her in a major motion picture, so Aimee may not have cared so much about the accuracy of the story line.

Then there is a scene with Alexander pitching for Philadelphia against St. Louis and rookie Rogers Hornsby at the plate. Since Philadelphia is far ahead in the score, Alexander, who does not know Hornsby, nevertheless throws a ball straight down the middle so that Hornsby can get a hit and not be sent back to the minors. The problem with the scene is that there is no historical evidence that the event actually occurred, and, more importantly, even though the event allegedly took place before the Black Sox scandal of 1919, it raises many legal and ethical issues, so why insert it in a baseball movie from 1952?

Although Grover Cleveland Alexander had a serious drinking problem during his lifetime, most people now believe that his epilepsy, not his alcoholism, caused some of his erratic behavior. Epilepsy was not well known during Alexander's lifetime, and he kept that disease hidden from the general public, perhaps believing that alcoholism was more socially acceptable than epilepsy. However, by 1952, that should not have been the case, and it seems inexplicable that *The Winning Team* and the physician portrayed in the film never mention the word "epilepsy" when describing Alexander's illness.

Ronald Reagan is believable as a major-league pitcher, employing a realistic pitching motion, if not the usual sidearm motion of the real Grover Cleveland Alexander. (Reagan's involvement in the film leads to the interesting fact that a future president of the United States is portraying a ballplayer named after a prior president of the United States.) Reagan had no significant baseball playing experiences in his life, but he did have one interesting connection to baseball. Reagan began his career in entertainment as a sports broadcaster for a Des Moines radio station, with one of his duties to re-create baseball games of the Chicago Cubs from telegraph reports. Doris Day, who has top billing in the film, is fine as Aimee Alexander, although the part is not very demanding. *The Winning Team* was an early film in Day's screen career and so it is hard to blame Warner Bros. for inserting a song in the film for Day to sing to highlight her talents, even though there is no indication that Aimee Alexander was an accomplished singer in real life.

Although *The Winning Team* commences with a slide that states,

"This is the true story of Grover Cleveland Alexander," it overlooks or is inaccurate on many aspects of Alexander's baseball career, and some of the scenes are pure inventions of the screenwriters. (It does not help that Ronald Reagan's face is shown on Alexander's Hall of Fame plaque at the beginning and conclusion of the film.) That is why, if a fan wants to learn about the career of a major-league ball-player (as well as any other real-life figure), books and articles are much better source materials than movies. *The Winning Team* is an okay film, but it is not a true portrayal of the life of Grover Cleveland Alexander, one of the greatest pitchers of all time.

Cobb (1994)

There comes a point in the baseball fantasy film *Field of Dreams* (1989) when Shoeless Joe Jackson (Ray Liotta) tells Ray Kinsella (Kevin Costner) that he invited other players to come to the corn-field to play and that he found a lot of interest from the old-timers. He then says, "Ty Cobb wanted to play. None of us could stand the son of a bitch when we were alive, so we told him to stick it." That line nicely sums up the reputation of Ty Cobb, certainly one of the greatest to ever play the game and just as certainly one of the mean-est player ever to lace up his spikes and proceed onto the diamond. Greatest and meanest would seem like good material for a feature film, and a biography of Ty Cobb, titled simply *Cobb*, made it to the big screen in 1994.

The overriding problem with *Cobb* is that it is not a biography of Ty Cobb, the player whose career lifetime batting average was .367, and who, when he retired, held the records for most career hits (4,191), most runs scored (2,246), and most stolen bases (892). Cobb batted over .400 on three occasions, and his batting average over one four-year period was .401. While many of Cobb's records have since been broken, no one has improved on his lifetime average or his twelve batting titles. (Some sources have slightly different statistics for Cobb than the ones set forth above.) There could have been a very good biographical film about that Ty Cobb. Instead, *Cobb* is about an old, sick man who used to be Ty Cobb.

The premise of the movie is that Tyrus Raymond Cobb, now in his seventies and with little time to live, hires sportswriter Al Stump to be the ghostwriter on his autobiography. Cobb has retained editorial control over the book, and he wants the book to be about baseball, the theory of the game, and his baseball achievements, with nothing about his personal life or bad reputation. Stump agrees to write such a book, but he also takes notes so that he can write a second book, which Stump believes would tell the true story of Ty Cobb. Much of the movie dwells on incidents in Ty Cobb's present-day life while he is meeting with Al Stump, including driving recklessly down a mountain road covered with snow; threatening people with his gun; shooting his gun off whenever he can; chasing after young women to get laid; spewing racial and religious epithets; being shunned by some of the Hall of Famers he meets at a reunion in Cooperstown; and later, being shunned by his daughter. It is all very dreary and depressing, and worse than that, these moments have little to do with baseball.

There is only one extended baseball scene in the movie. Cobb tells Stump about the time he came to bat against the Philadelphia Athletics, where, after a brushback pitch, Cobb hit a double deep into the outfield, stole third with spikes high into the fielder's crotch, and then stole home with his spikes high into the catcher's chest protector. The scene also shows Cobb's interactions with the fans and other players. It is an interesting scene, aided by the fact that Roger Clemens, a seven-time Cy Young Award winner, plays the pitcher in this scene. Clemens even has a few lines, trading barbs with Cobb.

The only other baseball shown in *Cobb* comes in a newsreel, titled "A Cavalcade of Heroes," that opens the movie. The newsreel is shot in the style of the newsreels from the 1930s, but it is only an imitation, as Tommy Lee Jones plays Cobb in the footage. (If the newsreel reminds viewers of the opening to *Citizen Kane* [1941], that is probably intentional. Cobb surely had the hubris of Charles Foster Kane, and Kane often displayed the meanness of Tyrus Raymond Cobb.) The purported impetus for the newsreel is Cobb's selection as the first member of the Baseball Hall of Fame in 1936. The newsreel is a clever device to provide important information about Cobb's playing days, such as some of his career statistics; his unique hands-apart grip on the bat; a 1926 scandal about throwing a game for which Cobb was found innocent; and his celebrity status, without taking too much time away from the rest of the film. The newsreel is about all there is in the film about the real Ty Cobb when he was still a star of the diamond.

In addition, the newsreel provides the setup for the best scene in the film, which takes place at a reunion dinner for Cobb and some other greats, such as Rogers Hornsby, Mickey Cochrane, and Pie Traynor, at the Baseball Hall of Fame in Cooperstown. As part of the tribute to Cobb at the festivities, a newsreel is played. It is the same as the one that opens the film, but in this case, as Cobb watches the newsreel, he imagines that it covers some of the more sordid moments in his life. As Cobb perceives the footage, he sees himself slapping his first wife around; running into

Cobb (1994). This is a photo taken on September 6, 1913, of Ty Cobb on the left and Shoeless Joe Jackson on the right. *(Library of Congress, LC-DIG-ppmsca-31945)*

the stands in 1912 to attack a heckler who, as it turned out, had no hands; as to the game-fixing claim, hearing that he once told friends that he had so much information on other players fixing games that Commissioner Landis had to acquit him; and seeing himself pistol-whip a man and leave him to die in a city alley.

Some of this surreal footage is based in fact. On May 15, 2012, in New York City, a man named Claude Lueker, who about a year earlier had lost all of one hand and three fingers on the other in an industrial accident, rained a ton of abuse at Cobb from his seat. As the game wore on, Cobb finally had enough. He jumped into the stands, knocked Lueker down, and started kicking and stomping him. Even when Cobb saw Lueker's disability, Cobb continued to beat him. Similarly, Cobb was once accused of throwing a baseball game and then subsequently acquitted by Landis. However, there is no evidence that Cobb blackmailed Landis into the decision. The remainder of the incidents in the imagined newsreel footage cannot be confirmed.

Although the title of the film would probably lead potential viewers to think otherwise, *Cobb* is essentially a character study of a former great, not a baseball movie. Tommy Lee Jones is excellent portraying the elderly ballplayer, dominating every scene in which he appears, even though he has so much pancake makeup on his face that he sometimes appears to be playing the Joker in a Batman movie. Robert Wuhl, who plays Al Stump, fades into the background whenever he appears in a scene with Jones. Jones convinces the audience that Cobb was mean and unfeeling very late in his life, but so are many other people. Moviegoers would rather learn about the real Ty Cobb, at a time when he was the best player in the game, not when he was near his death.

Baseball fans would even be interested in Cobb's personal life, his two marriages, and five children. Why does Cobb's daughter refuse to see him when he visits her home in Georgia? Once again, the viewer never finds out. Most importantly, the viewer never finds out why Ty Cobb played the game, throughout his career, so intensely, aggressively, and recklessly and why he deliberately injured so many players on the base paths. If *Cobb* is a character study of a great ballplayer, isn't that the minimum amount of information about Cobb's character that the film should disclose to the audience? Instead, *Cobb* spends most of its time developing the relationship between Cobb and Stump, which is of little interest to anyone. *Cobb* so overlooks the baseball aspects of the movie that after the film is over, if someone were to ask a non-baseball fan which position Cobb played in the field all those years in Detroit, he would have no answer. (Cobb was the center fielder). Interestingly, Cobb became the player-manager of the Tigers in his last six years in Detroit. No one viewing *Cobb* would ever learn that fact from the film.

When Al Stump argues with Cobb about the focus of Cobb's autobiography, Stump tells Cobb that he wants to write a book about the real Ty Cobb, not some sanitized version or some how-to baseball book. Stump believes that his readers will be more interested in Cobb's personal life than how to steal second base. After seeing this film, however, it is clear the viewers would be much more interested in Cobb's views on baseball, such as learning how Cobb managed to steal so many bases or maintain such a consistently high batting average throughout his long career, rather than this sordid picture of his last years.

In recent years, much of Al Stump's writings about Ty Cobb have been called into question. Was Ty Cobb a mean, crazy bigot in the months preceding his death? Few who know Cobb personally at the time support Stump's portrayal of Cobb during that time period, and the film simply does not ring true in that regard. The Cobb of the film seems like a caricature of a man, not a real person. In Charles C. Alexander's excellent and detailed biography of Cobb, titled *Ty Cobb*, there is a throwaway sentence near the end of the book that has significance on this issue. In detailing the last months of Cobb's life, Alexander mentions that toward the end of January 1960, just before Stump started meeting with Cobb, Cobb was honored by the B'nai B'rith of New York, a Jewish organization, as one of the "men of age in sports." If Cobb were truly a racist and anti-Semite at the end of his life, that award would never have happened.

Ty Cobb was a person of contradictions, the greatest player and the meanest player, perhaps the smartest player, but also perhaps the least-liked player by his fellow major leaguers. Surely there must be a good biographical film that could be made of Cobb's life. However, *Cobb*, a movie that focuses on the least interesting time period in Cobb's life, is not that film.

The Pride of St. Louis (1952)

On the surface, Dizzy Dean would seem to be an ideal candidate for a film biography. In the early 1930s, he was perhaps the most successful of all major-league pitchers. In his first full season with the St. Louis Cardinals in 1932, Dean won eighteen games and struck out 191 batters. In his first five full seasons in the majors, he averaged over twenty-four wins. In 1934, he had a record of 30–7, still the last National League pitcher to win thirty games in a season. He was the National League strikeout leader for four consecutive seasons, 1932–1935, and in 1936 he was the runner-up, second only to Van Mungo of the Brooklyn Dodgers. In a game in 1933 against the Chicago Cubs, he struck out seventeen batters, a major-league record at the time. Along with his brother Paul, he led the 1934 Cardinals, known as the Gashouse Gang, to the world championship. Dean was named the Most Valuable Player in the National League that year.

In addition, Dean was one of the most interesting characters ever to play the game. Dean was confident in his pitching abilities, an affable boaster of what he could do in a game and never afraid to compare himself favorably to other players. He reveled in his background of growing up poor in the South, his limited schooling, and his unusual use of the English language in his radio announcing days, such as a player "slud" into a base, or a batter was "throwed out" at first base, or the "runners are returning to their respectable bases." He was not above playing practical jokes, such as wrapping himself in a blanket and starting a bonfire in the dugout on a hundred-degree day in St. Louis. He once deliberately hit seven batters in a row in an exhibition game.

Yet, for all of that, every movie, even a biography, needs a plot. Where is the conflict in Dizzy Dean's life? Where are the serious illnesses or physical disabilities of Lou Gehrig and Monty Stratton, the personal demons of Grover Cleveland Alexander and Jimmy Piersall, or the fight against segregation by Jackie Robinson? Why did Dean deserve a film biography when other great stars such as Honus Wagner, Ted Williams, Stan Musial, and Willie Mays never had one? The unfortunate answer is: Dean did not deserve a film biography and *The Pride of St. Louis* is conclusive proof of that fact.

Without any true conflict in Dean's life, screenwriter Herman J. Mankiewicz had to create story arcs for the film to try to develop a plot and to hold the attention of viewers. For example, an early story arc consists of Dizzy meeting and quickly wooing Pat Nash, correctly indicating that Dean met her when she worked in a department store, but the rest of the vignette is fiction, and uninteresting fiction, at that, consisting mainly of boy meets girl, boy gets girl, but forgetting the middle part where boy loses girl. Another involves Dizzy and his brother Paul going on strike when they were fined for not staying with the team on a train ride (based on a true incident, but with the resolution completely fictionalized).

Perhaps because it has a strong basis in fact, the best story arc of the film comes in the last third of the movie. In real life, misfortune struck Dizzy during the 1937 All-Star Game. In the third inning, after Dizzy gave up a two-out, two-run homer to Lou Gehrig, Earl Averill of the Cleveland Indians hit a sharp line drive back at the mound. The ball hit Dizzy in the foot, fracturing Dizzy's big toe. (Dizzy allegedly told the doctor that his toe was not fractured, it was broke.) Dizzy came back to pitching too soon after the injury (even starting a game two weeks after his injury) and to compensate for the injury, changed his throwing motion, hurting his arm. His famous fastball was no more.

In 1938, St. Louis traded Dizzy to the Chicago Cubs, and Dizzy, with his 7–1 record in limited play, helped the Cubs win the National League pennant that year. In the World Series, Dizzy pitched Game 2 against the Yankees, and he was very good in the early innings, even without a fastball, but in the bottom of the eighth inning, with two men out, he gave up a two-run homer to Frank Crosetti, putting the Yankees ahead of the Cubs. Dean also gave up a two-run homer to Joe DiMaggio in the ninth inning. That effectively ended Dean's major-league pitching career. He pitched a few more games for the Cubs in the following years, but in 1940, he was sent to the minors, where he pitched in Tulsa for one year, achieving an 8–8 record, with the end of his regular pitching career coming soon thereafter.

The Pride of St. Louis covers most of these events in some detail, finally providing some drama for the film as Dizzy, who knows only baseball, loses his career at an early age. It is a personal tragedy for Dizzy. However, the film over-dramatizes the events, with Dizzy chasing Crosetti around the bases after that World Series home run, telling him that a year ago he could not have hit him, and Crosetti agreeing (in real life, Dean shouted at the runner, receiving a similar response); Dizzy turning to drink and gambling; and Dizzy temporarily losing Pat. This situation is resolved when Dizzy gets into radio broadcasting, but then one more story arc is added to the movie, with school teachers upset with Dizzy's misuse of the English language and its effect on children, causing him to quit his broadcasting career (based on fact except that Dean never quit his job). The whole vignette seems like an add-on to the movie just to extend the length of the film after the loss of a career has been resolved, with next to no drama in the new situation.

The Pride of St. Louis does not work as a film drama, because it consists of a number of events from Dizzy's life thrown together in chronological order and then embellished for Hollywood purposes. The film does, however, provide some value for those interested in the life of Dizzy Dean. Broadly speaking, the film is accurate with regard to the major events in Dean's life, from his being discovered by a scout, starting his career in the minors, finally playing in the majors and winning a World Series, and then the unfortunate ending to his career. However, and as is always the case, a written biography is a far better way of learning about Dean's life and career, since a book would be more detailed and more accurate than a biographical film.

In fact, much of *The Pride of St. Louis* is fiction, in whole or in part. The young, disabled businessman, Johnny Kendall, who provides inspiration to Dizzy during his career and gives him a start in broadcasting after his baseball career is over, appears to be imagined. There is no evidence that Dizzy and Paul sold tickets at the ballpark before some of the Cardinals games in which they played, worked as ushers in the stands before those games, or that Dizzy sang and led a band in the grandstand to entertain the fans. Then there is the moment in the film when Dean is struggling on the mound in his first game back after suffering an injury, and the opposing manager from the Pirates calls time and comes out to the mound to give Dizzy some advice about his injury. These and some of the other made-up instances are so ridiculous, in the context of Major League Baseball, that fans of the game who view the film must be flabbergasted.

Some of the smaller moments in the film are based on fact. Dizzy did want his marriage ceremony to take place at home plate of a minor-league game, but Pat, his bride-to-be, put her foot down. They were married in a church. Dizzy did once give three different dates of birth and three different cities of birth to three different sportswriters in quick succession, purportedly because he wanted to give each of them an exclusive story. While in the minors, Dizzy did successfully pitch in an exhibition game against a major-league team, the Chicago White Sox. One version of how Dean received his nickname, as shown in the movie, comes from that game. Dean threw so many fastballs past the White Sox batters that their coach told the players that the kid was making them look dizzy, a nickname that was then picked up by a local sportswriter.

The production of the film is disappointing. Much of the baseball information in *The Pride of St. Louis* is conveyed through newspaper headlines and, of course, the ubiquitous radio announcer that seems to be a necessity in Hollywood baseball films. These are un-cinematic methods of telling a story, although many baseball films display these same deficiencies. To add to the problem, when baseball moments are actually shown in the film, they are dissatisfying. They consist generally of Dizzy or Paul starting their pitching motion in a close-up and then a long shot from behind the catcher when the pitch is actually delivered. Except for his pitching loss to the Yankees in the 1938 World Series, the only interesting game footage in the film, the score of the games, the innings, the opponents, and the significance of the games are seldom provided. As a result, the viewer is not invested in any of the games.

For baseball fans, the most significant baseball defect in the film is that the viewer never gains an understanding of just how dominating a pitcher Dizzy Dean was in the 1930s. Viewers of *The Pride of St. Louis* would only come away with the notion that Dean was a likable, slightly crazy man, who once pitched well for St. Louis. This makes the film very disappointing for baseball fans, and who else would ever want to watch the film?

Dizzy Dean's life obviously did not end with the release of *The Pride of St. Louis* in 1952. The next year, Dean was elected to the Hall of Fame. In the 1950s, Dizzy made the transition to television broadcasting, even providing color for the national *Game of the Week* on CBS for many years. Dean retired from broadcasting in the late 1960s. He passed away in 1974 at the age of sixty-four.

The Stratton Story (1949)

Baseball film biographies have generally been about famous ballplayers and future Hall of Famers, such as Lou Gehrig, Babe Ruth, Jackie Robinson, and Grover Cleveland Alexander. Presumably the filmmakers hoped that famous names would make for large box office returns. The rare exception to the rule applies to players with disabilities, such as the mental disability suffered by Jimmy Piersall and dramatized in *Fear Strikes Out* (1957) and the physical disability suffered by Monty Stratton and dramatized in *The Stratton Story* (1949).

Monty Stratton was a right-handed pitcher for the Chicago White Sox from 1934 to 1938. He became a starting pitcher in 1937, going 15–5 during the season, with an ERA of 2.40. He was chosen for the American League All-Star team that year, although he did not get to pitch in the game. In 1938, Stratton had another fifteen-win season. At the time, the White Sox believed that Stratton had a promising future with the team.

All of that ended in late November 1938 when Stratton went hunting on his mother's farm near Greenville, Texas. He was alone when the gun in his holster went off, shooting him in the leg. He managed to crawl down a private road from the scene of the accident and get his wife's attention. Stratton was rushed to the hospital, but when gangrene set in, his right leg had to be amputated above the knee. That ended Stratton's major-league pitching career. The White Sox then offered him a lifetime job with the organization. Stratton was equipped with a wooden leg, and starting in 1939, he pitched batting practice each day for the White Sox and usually coached first base.

In 1941, Stratton asked for a release from his Chicago White Sox contract so that he could become the manager of the Lubbock, Texas team in the New Mexico League. However, Stratton quit after only ten days on the job, finding the constant bus travel too difficult on his leg. Having given up managing, Stratton became determined to become a pitcher once again. He went back to his farm, drew the figure of a batter on the side of a barn, and during the subsequent two years, pitched baseballs against the barn, with his two sons retrieving the balls. In 1945, Stratton made a comeback as a pitcher, playing for semi-pro teams in Texas, until he was offered a job as a pitcher for the Sherman Twins of the East Texas League, a Class C league. This return to professional baseball was a success for Stratton. His record for the Sherman Twins in 1946 was eighteen wins and eight losses.

According to an article in *The Sporting News* from 1947, when Stratton, who was a good hitting pitcher in the major leagues, hit the ball well for the Sherman club, he had to hippety-hop to first base, taking two steps with the good leg and one with the wooden one. As a result, he sometimes got thrown out at first base on hits to the outfield. If Stratton made it to first base safely, he was given a pinch-runner and then allowed to remain in the game, through a

In this photo from *The Stratton Story* (1948) before Monty Stratton suffered his debilitating injury, from left to right in the foreground are Barney Wile (Frank Morgan), the major-league scout who discovered Stratton; Chicago White Sox manager Jimmy Dykes, who played himself in the film; and Monty Stratton, played by Jimmy Stewart.

special rule of the league. Despite his disability, Stratton was able to field bunts, preventing batters from taking a cheap means of getting on base against him.

Stratton's activities came to the attention of Hollywood, and in 1947, Stratton quit baseball to become an advisor on the film story of his life. That film, titled *The Stratton Story*, starring Jimmy Stewart as Monty Stratton and June Allyson as his wife, Ethel, was released in 1949. Sam Wood, who had previously directed two other baseball films, the forgotten *They Learned About Women* (1930) and the well-respected *The Pride of the Yankees* (1942), was the director. The credits listed Monty Stratton as a technical advisor.

The Stratton Story is a fictionalized account of Monty Stratton's personal and professional life. According to the film, an ex-major-league catcher and now train-riding hobo, Barney Wile, discovers Stratton in Texas pitching for a local team and brings him to a White Sox training camp in California, where, after some initial reluctance, manager Jimmy Dykes agrees to take Stratton onto the team. Forgoing any minor-league seasoning and after a long time riding the bench, Dykes puts Stratton into pitch in a regular season game against the New York Yankees. Stratton is clobbered in his major-league pitching debut. He is sent down to Chicago's minor-league team in Omaha, which is convenient because Ethel, the woman Stratton met in Chicago and with whom he has fallen in love, lives in Omaha. Monty is finally called back to the big leagues, where he has a very successful season, even making the All-Star team. Monty and Ethel marry.

Tragedy then occurs back in Texas on the family farm. While out hunting one day, Stratton falls and his rifle discharges, shooting him in the right leg. The leg has to be amputated above the knee. Stratton is understandably despondent after the accident, and it takes him quite some time to want to become active again. Stratton is fitted with a prosthetic leg, and after some encouragement from his wife, Stratton starts to pitch into a bucket nailed onto the wall of a barn. His favorite dog, Happy, retrieves the balls for him. In the climax to the film, Stratton surprises everyone by agreeing to pitch in a minor-league All-Star Game, where, after some initial difficulties, he is successful in his pitching, fielding, hitting, and base running, winning the game for his team, the Southern All-Stars.

The Stratton Story was a great financial success in its day, and writer Douglas Morrow won the Academy Award for Best Story. Unfortunately, the film has not held up well over the past sixty years. Part of the problem is that for at least half of the film, *The Stratton Story* is a love story, not a drama, and it is a sappy love story at that. There is a little bit about baseball in these early moments in the film, but not very much. It is true that in order to properly set up the tragedy to come, the film has to make Stratton personally likable to the audience, and in addition, has to emphasize his baseball skills, amplifying the importance of his leg to him. One can even argue that the story arc where Stratton secretly takes dancing lessons so that he can dance with his wife sets up the tragedy of the loss of a leg even more. While the filmmakers did succeed in making Stratton and his family into very likable characters, it takes them way too long to do so. Stratton's hunting accident does not occur until about an hour into the film, and it is only then that the film finally has a dramatic story line. Prior to that, the movie is just a collection of vignettes haphazardly thrown together.

While the accidental shooting of Stratton is handled somewhat off-screen, and the scope of Stratton's injuries is not fully disclosed to the viewer, the film effectively conveys the extent of Stratton's personal tragedy and the effect of that tragedy on his family. It is a rare viewer who will not be emotionally affected by Stratton's misfortune. However, the story then falters again, by showing little of Stratton's rehabilitation process. Once Stratton overcomes his despondency, he straps on his wooden leg, throws some balls against the barn wall, and is almost immediately pitching professionally once again. *The Stratton Story* spends so much time setting up Stratton's life before his injury that it did not have the time to adequately explore his life after the injury.

In some of the major-league games shown in the film, it is clear that Jimmy Stewart is pitching in front of a projection screen. Contemporaneous reports indicate that filming was done in several American League ballparks, so the footage used is not technically archive footage. The footage is not as grainy as one sees in archive footage in baseball films from the 1930s, and most of the footage is shot closer to the field than the typical newsreel footage. Unlike many baseball films of prior years, the background footage blends well with the new footage, making it all somewhat realistic.

The Stratton Story hits its stride in the final sequence of the movie, which involves Stratton's pitching, hitting, and fielding performance in the All-Star Game. The scene is enhanced by the fact that Jimmy Stewart is clearly out on a real mound, with real players behind him on a real field. The scene has its intrinsic interest, because everyone wants to know if a pitcher with a wooden leg can be successful in a professional game. That interest is intensified for most viewers because they have come to like Stratton, his wife, and mother, and they sympathize with them.

Jimmy Stewart has a realistic pitching motion, but it is difficult to totally suspend disbelief when some of the actor-batters appear to be deliberately missing the fairly slow balls thrown to them. The film and the Western All-Stars could have used some better batters in the lineup. It is hard not to appreciate the callous but baseball-correct decision of the opposition to walk a batter to load the bases, knowing that Stratton would be coming up to the plate, with his distinctive difficulty of making it to first base safely, even on a ball hit to the outfield. It is just as hard not to cheer along with the crowd when Stratton hits a ball to the outfield, makes it safely to first base, thereby knocking in two runs, and eventually winning the game for his team.

The climactic baseball game has some true-to-life moments in it. The Western All-Stars try to bunt to get base hits, believing that a one-legged pitcher could not have the speed or dexterity to field the balls and throw them to first base. That was a common method that opponents used against Stratton in real life after his accident, and in real life, Stratton learned to field bunts successfully, although he often toppled over while doing so. In the film, Stratton is eventually successful in fielding bunts. Then there is the scene where Stratton hits a ball to left field but falls on the way to first base, resulting in an out. That happened at least once to Stratton in real life, when he was playing in the East Texas League. With a man on first base, Stratton hit a ball into center field. The center fielder started to make the customary throw to second base, but when he saw that Stratton had fallen about two-thirds of the way to first base, the center fielder threw to first. Stratton attempted to crawl to first base, but the throw just beat him. The film also shows Stratton's hippety-hop style of running to first base.

The final baseball scene in *The Stratton Story* runs about fifteen minutes, a long time for even the most baseball-oriented of baseball films. It is the highlight of the movie and goes a long way to ameliorating the disappointing nature of the rest of the movie.

Nevertheless, much of the film is pure fiction. The tramp-turned-major-league-scout, Barney Wile, is a made-up character and not a very believable one at that. Presumably, all of the events in the courtship of Monty and Ethel are fictional; they seem like Hollywood concoctions. The time line of events in Stratton's life is truncated, and important events, such as becoming a coach for the White Sox after his accident, are eliminated. Of course, the highlight of Stratton's post-injury career was his 1946 season with the Sherman Twins. The All-Star Game in the film is fictional. However, movies have to tell a story; they are not a substitute for a true biography of a ballplayer. A story needs a climax, and for a film, an entire season of pitching cannot be a climax. The fictional All-Star Game was a reasonable substitute for Stratton's season in the sun.

Jimmy Stewart is good as Monty Stratton, although he was too old for the part. Jimmy Stewart was over forty years old when this movie was released; the real Monty Stratton was in his twenties for most of the film's early action. Nevertheless, Stewart's performance works in *The Stratton Story* because Stewart was always good when playing a common man. Monty Stratton is the baseball version of George Bailey from *It's a Wonderful Life* (1946). June Allyson plays Ethel Stratton, and she is very likable in the role. Stewart and Allyson were such a success in this film that they appeared together as husband and wife in two more films, *The Glenn Miller Story* (1954) and *Strategic Air Command* (1955). In the latter film, Stewart also plays a professional baseball player.

There are several real-life ballplayers in the film. Bill Dickey, the Yankees catcher for many years and a Hall of Famer, gets a big hit against Stratton when he first bats against him but strikes out against Stratton on a later at bat. Dickey also has a few lines of dialogue. The pitcher whom Stratton beats in the All-Star Game is Gene Bearden, a pitcher for several American League teams over a seven-year career. Jimmy Dykes, the manager of the White Sox when Stratton played for the team, plays himself in the film. The part is fairly significant, with several lines of dialogue, so it is unclear why an actor was not brought in for the role. (A character actor, Cliff Clark, plays Stratton's manager in the All-Star Game.) Nevertheless, Dykes is not bad in the role. There is also background footage of Joe DiMaggio hitting a home run for the Yankees.

Monty Stratton received a huge payday for *The Stratton Story*, a sum estimated at $100,000. After the release of the film, Stratton made sporadic appearances pitching in the minor leagues, worked with Little League teams back home in Texas, and participated in baseball training schools and camps. Monty Stratton died in 1982 at the age of seventy.

Fear Strikes Out (1957)

The movie *Fear Strikes Out* is based on Jim Piersall's autobiography of the same name, published in 1955 and written with the assistance of Al Hirshberg, a sportswriter from Boston who also wrote books about Carl Yastrzremski, Frank Howard, and Bob Cousy, among others. Although Piersall had a long and successful baseball career, he would be an unknown figure today if not for his autobiography and, more importantly, for the movie that it inspired.

According to Piersall's autobiography, Piersall was born in Waterbury, Connecticut, on November 14, 1929. His father was a housepainter who worked only sporadically during the Depression years. His mother suffered from mental illness, often leaving the family for extended stays at the Norwich State Hospital. His only sibling, a substantially older brother, was not a factor in his life. The family lived close to poverty for many years, and Jim was forced to work at odd jobs at a young age.

Piersall acquired an early interest in baseball, and his father pushed him in that regard, never allowing him to play football because he might get seriously injured. Piersall did play basketball, however, leading his team to the New England championship in his senior year, also making the All-State and All New England teams that year. While Piersall always enjoyed playing basketball, his main career interest was professional baseball and, particularly, his dream of becoming an outfielder with his beloved Boston Red Sox. Boston eventually signed Piersall to a contract, and from 1948 to 1950, Piersall played in the minor leagues with a Boston affiliate. Piersall was a September call-up for the Red Sox in 1950, and in 1951, Piersall started the season in Boston.

After the 1951 season, Piersall read a story in *The Sporting News* that the new Boston manager, Lou Boudreau, wanted to move Piersall to shortstop and that he would receive special training for that position the following year at Boston's winter instructional school, which was to take place in Sarasota, Florida, just before regular spring training. That newspaper article set Piersall off, with all of his anxieties and self-doubts coming to the surface. He did not want to go to the instructional school; his friends and family had to talk him into leaving. When Piersall finally agreed to go, he intentionally forgot his infielder's mitt at home so that he did not have to learn the shortstop position at the Red Sox camp.

Piersall boarded a plane to Sarasota, took a limousine to his hotel, paid the driver, and walked into the hotel lobby. The next conscious thing he remembered was waking up in the violent room in West-

High school ballplayer, Jimmy Piersall (Anthony Perkins), on the left, is concerned about a leg injury before a game in which professional scouts will be watching him, as Jimmy's coach (Howard Price), center, and Jimmy's father (Karl Malden) look on, in *Fear Strikes Out* (1957).

borough State Hospital, a mental institution, more than six months later. Piersall had had a nervous breakdown, and the ensuing electroshock therapy had wiped out most of his memory of events that occurred earlier that year. After therapy, Piersall recovered from his illness, learning to reduce his worrying about events he could not control, to relax and to enjoy his life inside and outside of sports.

At the point in the book when Piersall walks into the hotel lobby in Florida, the style of *Fear Strikes Out* becomes a bit unusual, at least for an autobiography. Because Piersall had lost much of his memory of 1952, he has to learn about what happened in his life from his wife and from copies of contemporaneous sports stories that are provided to him. In a sense, the reader learns about Piersall's activities at the same time that Piersall does. It turns out that while Piersall adjusted exceptionally well to the shortstop position and started the regular season at shortstop with the Red Sox, his emotional problems became steadily worse. He fought with umpires, opposing players, and teammates. He often acted immaturely on the field as, for example, walking behind center fielder Dom DiMaggio as the two returned to the dugout after an inning and imitating his walk, garnering laughs from the fans. In one notable game, while Piersall was batting and running the bases, he taunted the legendary pitcher Satchel Paige, at one point flapping his arms like a chicken and squealing like a pig.

Despite playing well for the Red Sox, Piersall was demoted to the minor leagues, but even there, he kept up his antics, mocking his manager and umpires and even, on one occasion, stealing the game ball from the pitcher's mound as he was walking to the outfield and refusing to give it up. Upon returning to Boston, Piersall was finally convinced to see a doctor and stay in a rest home for a while. It was there that Piersall had his massive nervous breakdown, eventually leading to his memory loss. Luckily, this also led to his cure, and Piersall was back playing for Boston at the beginning of the 1953 season.

The movie *Fear Strikes Out*, with Anthony Perkins as Jim Piersall and Karl Malden as his father, is generally based upon Piersall's autobiography. The film shows Jim's early days growing up in Waterbury, Connecticut, his being signed by the Red Sox, his days in the minors, where he meets and then marries Mary Teevan, and his eventual debut in a Red Sox uniform. As in real life, Piersall's mental problems eventually overwhelm him, leading to a spectacular nervous breakdown.

The primary difference between the film and real life, as described in Piersall's autobiography, is the purported cause of Piersall's mental illness. In the film, the blame is put squarely on the father, who dreams of his son's professional baseball career, dominating every aspect of his son's life in order to achieve that goal. Mr. Piersall finds mistakes in Jim's play even when Jim has a great game. He will not let Jim have fun with his friends, insisting that Jim return home immediately after games and work. He always talks about himself and his son as one unit, in phrasing such as "We're on our way, Jim" when the Red Sox show an interest in Piersall, or "We finally made it" when Jim is told he will play for the Red Sox. The pressure on Piersall from his father in the film becomes too much, leading to his spectacular mental breakdown.

In the book, the characterization of the father is much more subdued. Early on in the narrative, Jim writes that while he often loved and always respected his father, he was also afraid of him. When he was angry, Jim's father's dark eyes would bore through Jim, his face and gleaming head would redden, and he would bellow at Jim in a voice that was so deep and raucous that it would make the windows rattle. Sometimes, when Jim did not do what he was told, his father would kick him with a heavy shoe that tapered to a point at the toe. If Jim came home late, there was a strapping waiting for him.

Jim lived in fear of his father's wrath. He never wanted to disobey his father's rules; he always searched for his father's approval. However, while Jim's father wanted Jim to become a major leaguer in real life, it was not an all-consuming passion for him, as portrayed in the film. In fact, Jim's father discouraged Jim from signing with the Red Sox at age seventeen, encouraging him to work for a year before becoming a major-league ballplayer, believing he was then too young to start a professional career.

This characterization of Jim's father in the book is told in just a few paragraphs. Jim's father is not the focal point of Jim's life story. In *The Truth Hurts*, a later book written by Jim Piersall, he writes about the film as follows, "They made my father out to be a real bastard, one who was trying to drive me to a mental breakdown. Well, he wasn't. I have never blamed my father for that breakdown" (Chapter 2: "Good Times in Boston"). In fact, it was Jim's mother who was in and out of institutions during much of Jim's early life. (This is only hinted at in the movie.) Jim worried about everything during his youth, including how to support his parents and whether or not he was good enough to play in the big leagues. Even as a teenager, he constantly yelled at his teammates, telling them what to do in practices and in games. Jim had almost constant headaches from the age of fifteen.

As a result, the true cause of Jim's mental illness is much more complex than portrayed in the film. Clearly, some of the problems were inherited, as Jim's mother also had mental issues. Other causes or symptoms involve his constant worrying, an inability to sit still and relax, and just an overall lack of confidence. The book does not go into many details of Piersall's psychiatric analysis and therefore does not detail how he was cured. Other than a mention of electroshock therapy in the book and some talks with a psychiatrist, Piersall just seems to have suddenly become better. This makes the book slightly disappointing. Most readers probably yearn for a better description of the causes and cure of Jim's mental illness.

In addition to being disappointing in the book, this approach to storytelling would never have worked for the film. Cinema, by its nature, requires drama and a dramatic conclusion. By focusing on the father as the sole cause of Jim's mental illness, *Fear Strikes Out* becomes more dramatic than real life and, in the process, provides a real villain for the audience. It also provides a basis for the cure of Piersall's illness—obvious villain, easy cure. Thus, while the film may be inaccurate in portraying the causes and cure of Piersall's illness, it is far more compelling than the true story.

In real life, Piersall's illness manifested itself in Piersall's strange conduct over many months, both in the major and minor leagues. Once again, that slowly developing story line would not work well for the movies. The cinema requires a dramatic, even if fictional, manifestation of the mental breakdown, not one that occurs gradually over many months. The screenwriters obviously recognized this issue, cleverly devising a dramatic scene that would capsulize many months of incidents into one memorable moment.

In a night game at Fenway Park, on the day Piersall returns to action after a multi-game suspension for fighting with a teammate, Piersall comes to bat, spots his father in the stands behind home plate, and after two swinging strikes, hits a long ball to the outfield. As Piersall runs the bases, he keeps shouting, "All the way!" After he crosses the plate with an inside-the-park home run, Piersall runs toward the stands, shouting at his father, "How was that? Was it good enough? Did I show them?" As the Red Sox players grab Piersall and try to force him back to the dugout, Piersall breaks loose and climbs the netting behind home plate. As his father is shouting and his wife is screaming, Piersall is pulled down by his teammates, with the camera focusing on his fingers being yanked from the netting of the fence. Piersall is dragged to the dugout, but he gets loose again, swinging a bat back and forth, until he is subdued by the police. As the scene reaches its conclusion, Mary is shouting, "Don't hurt him."

Critical opinion is mixed about *Fear Strikes Out*, but the scene of Jim Piersall's mental breakdown and his climbing the fence at Fenway Park is always included on any list of greatest baseball cinematic moments of all time. The decision to have the incident occur at a night game was fortuitous, providing the scene with a surreal back-drop of shadows and lights. Elmer Bernstein's score is excellent, un-heard while Piersall is batting so that the crowd noise becomes the score, and then suddenly bursting onto the scene as Piersall rounds the bases, pounding and pulsing as Piersall climbs the fence, em-phasizing the surprising and terrifying events that are unfolding. An-thony Perkins is excellent in the role, with his wide, unseeing eyes as he is batting, then becoming convincingly hysterical after he crosses home plate. Over fifty years since the film was released, those who saw *Fear Strikes Out* when it was first released or when the film was shown a few years later on television have never forgotten this scene.

In *The Truth Hurts*, Jim Piersall wrote that while he liked An-thony Perkins on a personal basis, he was upset that Perkins played him in the movie. "I mean, he threw a baseball like a girl, and he couldn't catch one with a bushel basket. He danced around the outfield like a ballerina, and he was supposed to be depicting me, a Major League Baseball player" (Chapter 2: "Good Times in Boston"). While perhaps overstating the matter a little bit, Piersall is accurate about Perkins's baseball skills or lack thereof. Perkins throws the ball weakly, and it would be a miracle if that swing of his ever hit a pitch thrown hard by a real pitcher. Much of the problem here is that Perkins was a left-hander, who had to adapt to playing Piersall, a right-hander, and while Perkins makes a great effort in that regard, his baseball performance is unconvincing.

By the time of the film's production in 1956, Jim was back playing for Boston. He made the American League All-Star teams in 1954 and 1956. While his hitting was variable, he always made spectacu-lar plays in the outfield. Thus, as of the release of *Fear Strikes Out* in 1957, Piersall had turned his life around. The film, however, does not show this, once again going for the more dramatic but also more effective ending. As Piersall returns for his first game after his illness is cured, Mary goes to the locker room to talk to him. After asking him not to play, she understands that he has to go out on the field. Mary leaves and as the film ends, Piersall walks down the excep-tionally long hall of the locker room with his back to the audience, pauses on the steps to the field, and then goes out to play. As he does so, the film fades to black. Piersall's triumphant return to the game is left unspoken, but the audience is confident that he will succeed.

The release of *Fear Strikes Out* did not end the story of Jim Piersall's baseball career. Although he was traded from Boston to Cleveland after the 1958 season, Piersall continued to play baseball until 1967 with several different teams. He was a Gold Glove winner in 1958 and 1961. (The award was not given out until 1957). In all, he played in 1,734 games, with a lifetime batting average of .272. According to Piersall, his lifetime fielding percentage was .997. Piersall prefers not to include his games at shortstop, which cause his fielding percentage to drop to below .990.

After his retirement from playing baseball, Piersall stayed involved in the game, in ticket sales, as an instructor, and as a baseball broadcaster, among other non-baseball pursuits. He had nine children with his first wife, Mary. They divorced in 1968.

5

FANTASY BASEBALL

Field of Dreams (1989)

Field of Dreams is considered by many to be the best baseball film of all time. "Best of all time," of course, is always a matter of opinion, discussion, and argument, but it is difficult to dispute the opinion that *Field of Dreams* is, at least, the best fantasy baseball film ever made.

Field of Dreams tells the story of Iowa farmer Ray Kinsella, who hears an enigmatic voice in his cornfield, which causes him to build a baseball field in the middle of his farm. The result is the appearance of Shoeless Joe Jackson, played by Ray Liotta, and some of his contemporaries, ready to play ball on the new field. The voice also causes Ray to bring Terence Mann, played by James Earl Jones, a reclusive writer who is a baseball fan, and Moonlight Graham, a doctor who played in only one Major League Baseball game, back to Iowa so that the sport of baseball can provide closure to Ray and the other two with regard to some unfulfilled aspects of their respective lives.

The strength of *Field of Dreams* is its evocation of baseball in its glory days, a nostalgic trip back to the time when baseball was still America's national pastime, when players did not jump from team to team for a few dollars more, when World Series games were played at a time of day when people could actually watch, and when a catch with your father in the backyard was something very special. While the film takes place in the present day of the 1980s, there are apparitions from the past—Shoeless Joe Jackson playing once again as if it were the 1920s, the Moonlight Graham of the 1920s finally getting a chance to bat in a major-league game, and Ray's father getting a chance to play in the big leagues for the first time. There was a time in America when many young boys imagined playing for their favorite Major League Baseball team when they grew up. This movie captures the sentiment behind those dreams and the lure that the game was to many youngsters in a bygone era.

Terence Mann speaks the most quoted lines from the film. He says:

> The one constant through all the years, Ray, has been base-ball. America has rolled by like an army of steamrollers. It has been erased like a blackboard, rebuilt, and erased again. Baseball has marked the time. This field, this game—it's a part of our past, Ray. It reminds of us of all that once was good and it could be again.

Mann is talking about the baseball of another day, and it is for that reason that, while *Field of Dreams* appeals to older baseball fans, many younger fans find it difficult to fathom what all the fuss is about.

Field of Dreams glorifies baseball as the quintessential American sport, part of the fabric of American life. Thus, it is surprising to find that a Canadian, W. P. Kinsella, wrote *Shoeless Joe*, the book upon which the film is based. Kinsella was born in 1935 in Edmonton, Alberta. He received most of his schooling in Canada, although he did complete a master of fine arts degree at the University of Iowa. Of course, Iowa is the location where most of the action of the book and movie unfolds.

Three real-life people are portrayed in *Field of Dreams*. One is Shoeless Joe Jackson, the most famous member of the Chicago Black Sox, one of eight players who were accused of throwing the 1919 World Series, paid to do so by gamblers. (See *Eight Men Out* [1988] in chapter one of this book.) Jackson played very well in the 1919 World Series, so although Jackson did receive some money from the gamblers, it is still a matter of controversy as to the extent of Jackson's involvement in actually throwing the games. What is not a matter of controversy are Shoeless Joe's skills as a baseball player, a sport he played during thirteen seasons, until he was banned from the game after the 1920 season. Jackson was an excellent outfielder, but his greatest fame today is as a hitter. Jackson batted .408 in his rookie season in 1911, and his career batting average of .356 is still the third-best lifetime batting average in the major leagues.

In both the film and the book, when the voice first speaks to Ray Kinsella, it says, "If you build it, he will come." Ray instinctively knows that the voice is talking about Shoeless Joe. When Ray finally builds the baseball field in the book—initially consisting only of left field, a left field wall, and just fair approximations of the remainder of the field—and turns on the lights, Shoeless Joe Jackson is out in left, fielding fly balls. In the film, Shoeless Joe does not appear until several months after Ray builds the entire field. In

Field of Dreams (1989). Burt Lancaster as an older Moonlight Graham, who only played in one game in the big leagues.

both formats, Jackson is excited to be back playing baseball again after so many years, and in both formats, Shoeless Joe provides the connection between the fantasy players on the field of dreams and Ray Kinsella.

While most baseball fans and many non-fans have at least heard of Shoeless Joe Jackson, the other real baseball player in the film, Moonlight Graham, was virtually unknown until *Field of Dreams* was released. Archibald Wright "Moonlight" Graham, or often just "Doc" Graham, appeared in one Major League Baseball game in his entire career. It occurred on June 29, 1905, in a game between the New York Giants and the Brooklyn Superbas (another name for the Brooklyn Dodgers) in Washington Park in Brooklyn. In the bottom of the eighth inning, with the Giants leading by ten runs, Graham was inserted into right field. No balls were hit in his direction. In the top of the ninth, Graham was in the on-deck circle when the last out was made. Graham then played right field in the bottom of the ninth, but, once again, he had no putouts. About a week later, the Giants sold Graham's contract to the Scranton Miners, a minor-league team in the New York State League. Graham never made it back to the big leagues.

After playing in the minor leagues through 1908, Graham left the sport and enrolled at the University of Maryland, where he earned his medical degree. He then traveled to Chisholm, Minnesota, where he practiced medicine for over fifty years. By all accounts, he was an excellent doctor and his patients loved him. Doc Graham died on August 25, 1965. The obituary of Graham that is read in the movie by the Chisholm newspaper publisher is the same obituary that was published upon Graham's death in *The Chisholm Free Press and Tribune*. However, some of the facts of Graham's life and careers were altered for both the book and the movie.

In *Field of Dreams*, Graham finally comes to bat and in his only plate appearance hits a sacrifice fly. That is very satisfying to Graham, as he is credited with an RBI, but his plate appearance would not be considered an official at bat in baseball's scoring system. Burt Lancaster plays Moonlight Graham.

In the book, Ray Kinsella seeks out the famous author J. D. Salinger, after instructions from the voice saying, "Ease his pain." Salinger was the author of several works, the most famous of which is *The Catcher in the Rye*, first published in 1951. Salinger was a famous recluse. Two years after *The Catcher in the Rye* was published, Salinger moved from New York City to a secluded site in Cornish, New Hampshire, refusing all interviews and most visitors. Subsequent to that time, very few works of his were published. Salinger died in 2010.

Salinger was upset to find that his name was used in *Shoeless Joe*. He threatened to sue W. P. Kinsella over that use, presumably for breach of his right of publicity. Many states recognize an individual's right of publicity, that a person's name cannot be appropriated for commercial purposes. The right of publicity applies even if the celebrity's name is not used, but there are enough facts set forth that a reader or viewer could determine who the character is supposed to be. Salinger may have had a cause of action against Kinsella, but he never brought suit, perhaps because Kinsella was a Canadian citizen, perhaps because *Shoeless Joe* was not a well-known book, perhaps because of the clear legal difficulties with the case, or perhaps because Salinger would have had to appear in public for depositions and trial.

For the movie, however, with a star cast and a large budget, Salinger's name would have been placed before an immense audience very quickly, and therefore, Salinger may have been more likely to sue if his name were used in the film. Recognizing that possibility, the name of the character was changed to Terence Mann for the film. He became an African American who was somewhat overweight; he lived in Boston, not on a farm in New Hampshire; and although he was still a writer and a recluse, he had a background in the civil rights movement and the antiwar movement of the 1960s. Indeed, Salinger is a figure of the 1950s; the fictional Terence Mann is an icon of the 1960s. As a result of these modifications when the novel was adapted for the cinema, no one could confuse Mann with Salinger and litigation was avoided.

Actually, there are more than three real-life people portrayed in *Field of Dreams*. Moonlight Graham identifies three players on the opposing team: Smoky Joe Wood (a pitcher and outfielder for the Boston Red Sox and the Cleveland Indians from 1908 to 1922), Mel Ott (a right fielder for the New York Giants from 1926 to 1947), and Gil Hodges (a first baseman in the major leagues from 1943 to 1963, primarily with the Dodgers, both in Brooklyn and Los Angeles, and then the manager of the Mets, leading them to the 1969 World Series). Shoeless Joe's teammates on the field of dreams are the other seven members of the Black Sox, six of whom no one disputes threw the 1919 World Series for money. (Buck Weaver's involvement in the conspiracy is still controversial.) This results in a true anomaly for the film. *Field of Dreams* paints a mythic image of baseball at a time in the not-so-distant past, when people played for the love of the game, not just for the money. As Shoeless Joe says to Ray:

> Man, I did love this game. I'd have played for food money. It was a game. The sounds, the smells . . . did you ever hold a ball or a glove to your face? I used to love traveling on the trains from town to town, the hotels, brass spittoons in the lobbies, brass beds in the rooms. It was the crowd rising to their feet when the ball was hit deep. Shoot, I'd have played for nothing.

Yet, the film brings back the worst baseball players of all time, when it comes to taking a dive for money and selling out to some lowlife gamblers. Shoeless Joe Jackson has become a legendary figure over time, and his apparition in the film is understandable. Since he played with the Black Sox, the inclusion of the other players in the film makes sense. And yet, given a little thought on the matter, the presence of the rest of the Black Sox in *Field of Dreams* is somewhat out of place with the tone and theme of the film.

As much as the film extolls the game of baseball, there are a few lines of dialogue that do bring matters into perspective. When Ray meets Moonlight Graham in Chisholm, Minnesota, and talks to him in his doctor's office about the one inning in which he played in the major leagues but never got to bat, the following dialogue ensues:

> **KINSELLA:** "Fifty years ago for five minutes, you came this close. I mean, it would kill some men to get that close to their dream and not touch it. They'd consider it a tragedy."
> **GRAHAM:** "Son, if I'd only gotten to be a doctor for five minutes, now that would have been a tragedy."

For a movie that extolls baseball as if it were a religion, Graham's line of dialogue puts it all in perspective. Baseball is, after all, just a game.

The plot of *Field of Dreams* is actually quite absurd. One of the ways that the filmmakers make it more convincing to the audience is to insert humor into the film, most of which does not come from the novel. It is easier to entice the audience into suspending its disbelief when the characters do not take themselves too seriously. For example, when Ray tells his wife, Annie, that Terence Mann had a considerable interest in baseball, she looks at Ray's notes and feigns mock surprise to discover that when Mann was a small boy, he had a bat named Rosebud. When Ray starts on his trip to find Terence Mann, and his wife asks what she should do if the voice calls, he tells her to take a message. When one of the players disappears into the cornfield, he yells in a squeaky voice, "I'm melting. I'm melting," like the Wicked Witch of the West. *Field of Dreams* never takes itself too seriously, paradoxically adding to its credibility.

The film does seem to have a problem, though, with its time

line. It is hard to understand how young Archie
Graham, playing in the
early 1920s, would have
any idea who Gil Hodges
was, since Hodges did not
start playing baseball until 1943. It is even more
surprising to see a 1919
Black Sox player quoting
dialogue from the 1939
film *The Wizard of Oz*.
But since the audience
has to suspend its disbe-
lief in any event, a few
more times are of little
matter.

There are a number
of excellent performanc-
es in the film, including
Kevin Costner as Ray
Kinsella, Amy Madigan
as Annie, and James Earl
Jones as Terence Mann.
However, the unforgetta-
ble performance comes

Shoeless Joe Jackson, c. 1920, who is played by Ray Liotta in *Field of Dreams* (1989) *(Library of Congress, LC-USZ62-78070).*

from Burt Lancaster as Moonlight Graham, the baseball player
turned doctor. As Graham talks to Ray about baseball in general,
the one game in which he appeared, his dream to bat one time
in the majors, and his work as a physician in a small town, Lancaster makes the part come alive, the magnificent dialogue rolling
off his tongue, convincingly portraying the multiple emotions that
the character feels. Lancaster is in the movie for only about five
minutes, but in many ways it is the best five minutes of the film.
Field of Dreams was one of the last films in which Burt Lancaster
appeared, in a career that stretched back to 1946. Even though he
was nominated for an Academy Award four times, including a win
in the Best Actor category for *Elmer Gantry* (1960), Lancaster's

performance in *Field of Dreams*, brief as it is, may be his best film performance ever.

Field of Dreams is a marvelous film, and not just because of its baseball story and evocation of another time. It is also because the film is about family, dedication, literature, and dreams. It also has a strong plot, with the threat of foreclosure always hanging over Ray, his family, and his baseball field, a real-world story line that is re-solved, perhaps in a fanciful way, but resolved to the satisfaction of the audience. It has an incredible climax, with Ray's daughter falling off the bleachers and almost choking to death, and young Archie Graham coming off the field of dreams, morphing into Doc Gra-ham, and then saving the young girl's life. At least Moonlight had that one chance to finally bat in a major-league game.

Field of Dreams is not just a great baseball movie. It is a great film.

It Happens Every Spring (1949)

While baseball has been the subject of fantasy films from time to time (e.g., *Field of Dreams* [1989]), science fiction and baseball have seldom mixed. One exception is the well-remembered episode of *The Twilight Zone* television series titled "The Mighty Casey," which first aired in 1960. It details the story of a robot pitcher named Casey and what happens when he receives a heart. The only other signifi-cant example is the 1949 film *It Happens Every Spring*, which is so lighthearted in tone that it is easy to forget that the film is at its foun-dation a work of science fiction.

Vernon K. Simpson, a university chemistry professor, accidentally discovers a substance that when rubbed on a baseball, causes the baseball to be repelled by wood, including wooden baseball bats. Recognizing that he now has a chance to earn significant money, Simpson tries out with the St. Louis baseball team as its new pitcher. Using the pseudonym King Kelly, Vernon becomes an overnight sensation because the batters cannot seem to hit his "hop" ball. The ball hops because Vernon puts his compound on a cloth inside his glove and then, through a hole in his glove, rubs the secret substance on the ball. When the batter swings, the ball hops over the batter's bat, resulting in a swinging strike. Vernon is so effective that he leads the St. Louis team into the World Series, and in the deciding game, even though Vernon is short on his compound, he manages to win the game for his team. However, Vernon catches the last out with his bare hand, resulting in several fractures, permanently ending his baseball career.

What a disappointing film! From the very beginning, things go wrong with *It Happens Every Spring*. Over the opening credits, an insipid song, presumably titled "It Happens Every Spring," is sung, as drawings of male animals chasing female animals of the same species with amorous intent are shown with the credits. Apparently, in the spring a man's thoughts turn not just to baseball, they also turn to love. While that may be true, what does that have to do with a baseball film? Needless to day, there was no Academy Award nomination for this silly theme song.

Another problem with *It Happens Every Spring* is that Ray Milland was too old to play the part of Vernon K. Simpson/King Kelly. The other baseball characters constantly refer to Vernon as "kid" or "young man," but Ray Milland was born on January 3, 1907, making him forty-two years old at the time of the film's production. It does not help that Milland's character is dating a college student named Debbie Greenleaf, who is played by twenty-three-year-old Jean Peters. Peters is the right age for her part in the movie, making Milland seem even older than he actually is. If Milland were a good baseball player, his age may not have stood out so much, but Milland is not much of an athlete. Milland is severely miscast in this film.

As the film proceeds, a knowledgeable baseball movie fan will gradually realize that there is something slightly wrong with the film. While the players' uniforms have the name of their baseball cities lettered on the shirts, the team nicknames are not on the uniforms and are never mentioned in the film. For example, Vernon pitches for St. Louis, but is it the St. Louis Cardinals of the National League or the St. Louis Browns of the American League? The film does not say. (Evidence in the film indicates that Vernon pitches for the St. Louis Cardinals.) Another deficiency in *It Happens Every Spring* is the lack of real-life baseball players appearing in the film. It was common in baseball films of the 1940s, and continuing to the present day, for current major-league players or former major-league stars to appear in movies, even if they were just in cameo roles. None of that occurs in *It Happens Every Spring*, depriving the film of some verisimilitude.

The reason for all of these anomalies, according to the Turner Classic Movies website, is the then-commissioner of baseball, Albert B. "Happy" Chandler, would not grant permission to the filmmakers to use actual team names or professional players in the film, as he believed that the film was the story of a cheat who violated Major League Baseball rules and stole a pennant and a World Series. As a result, the most the filmmakers could do to create some authenticity for the movie was to use the names of real sportswriters in the newspaper columns shown in a montage of Vernon's successful pitching performances, a very disappointing substitution.

Of course, Commissioner Chandler was correct when he stated that Vernon was a cheat. Section 8.02 of the current Major League Baseball rules provides that a pitcher may not rub the ball on his glove, clothing, or person, or apply a foreign substance of any kind to the ball, nor have any foreign substance on his person or in his possession. Violation of these rules can result in a balk, a ball being called on the batter, ejectment from the game, and/or a ten-day suspension. The spitball has been banned from Major League Baseball since at least the 1920s, so Vernon was in violation of the rules in 1949.

Vernon's cheating is one of the reasons that *It Happens Every Spring* is so hard to like. It is hard to root for a dishonest person and it is difficult to enjoy his exploits, no matter how lighthearted in tone the movie is. Indeed, the supposed lightheartedness of the film is another one of its problems. The film purports to be a comedy, but it has almost no laughs. Also, some of the purported comedy is unfunny, low humor. When Vernon pitches a ball and it hops over the batter's bat, a silly sound effect is heard. When some of the characters mistakenly use Vernon's compound as hair tonic, there is a clattering sound when their hair comes near wood.

Those, however, are not all of the problems with the film. The story line simply makes no sense. At one point in the film, Vernon is shown completing a no-hit, no-run game, which is presumably a perfect game. The announcer is incredibly excited about the event. Yet, if Vernon had been using his substance at every game, there could not possibly have been any hits against him in any of his games. The only base runners would have been players who walked, were hit by a pitch or struck out with the catcher dropping the ball. All of Vernon's games would have been no-hit games, and probably no-run games. Given that Vernon would therefore have been the greatest pitcher who ever played the game, wouldn't someone check out his history, question his lack of pitching experience, and, more importantly, investigate the hop that all of his pitches take?

It Happens Every Spring has so little natural conflict in its story line that the writers had to create an unconvincing one. Since Vernon never told his fiancée, Debbie Greenleaf, or the president of the university, Professor Greenleaf, that he needed a leave of absence from teaching to play baseball, Vernon believes he has to conceal his true identity from everyone. He wears glasses as a teacher but none as a baseball player, thereby becoming the Clark Kent/Superman of baseball. He uses a pseudonym, King Kelly, avoids newspaper photographers, and leaves one game in the middle when he spots Professor Greenleaf in the stands. Debbie Greenleaf believes that Vernon has joined the mob. It is all pretty ridiculous. Then, at the end if the film, everything falls together—Vernon wins the World Series, his broken hand gives him an excuse for never pitching again, everybody from the University is thrilled by Vernon's success, and Vernon becomes the director of the University's research laboratory. It is all somewhat hard to swallow.

In a film that is science fiction and fancy, there is a stark dose of realism at the end of the movie. Vernon and his catcher, Monk, are talking about things that do not make sense. Vernon tells Monk, "I was a chemistry teacher. I can tell you that now. And the sum of money I received for teaching science to the youth of this state for an entire year was a little less than I got in a single afternoon for tossing a five-ounce sphere past a young man holding a wooden stick." That is a significant point to consider, but it is lost in the frivolity of *It Happens Every Spring*.

Of course, it may not be fair to *It Happens Every Spring* to overanalyze the movie. It is only intended as a fluff piece, to provide some light entertainment for the moviegoing public. So for the general public, *It Happens Every Spring* may be worth a view. But for a real baseball fan, the film is hard to watch, much less enjoy.

√ *Angels in the Outfield* (1951)

In 1951, when MGM had to decide which Major League Baseball team most needed the help of angels to compete, the choice of the

Pittsburgh Pirates must have been easy. While the team had the presence of Ralph Kiner, the National League leader in home runs for seven consecutive seasons, 1946 through 1952, not much else was going well for the team after the end of World War II. In fact, from 1946 to 1957, the Pirates finished in the top half of the National League in only one year, and that was a fourth-place finish in 1948. In 1950, the year before *Angels in the Outfield* was made, the Pirates finished in last place in the National League, 33 1/2 games out of first place. The Pirates would go on to lose over 100 games in 1952, 1953, and 1954. In two of those years, the team finished more than 50 games out of first place. From 1950 through 1955, the Pirates finished in last place, except for 1951, the year *Angels in the Outfield* was released. In that year, they managed to improve to seventh place out of eight slots.

Of course, as bad as they were, the 1950s Pirates were never as bad as they are characterized in *Angels in the Outfield*. If the film were to be believed, there was an occasion in the 1950s when a Pirates player rounded second and then decided to go back to first, causing a head-on collision with another runner; a fielder got hit in the head by a pop-up; three Pirates runners ended up on third base at the same time; and Pittsburgh lost a game to Cincinnati, 21–2. All of those incidents are examples of cinema exaggeration for the sake of comedy. Nevertheless, the travails of the 1950s Pirates were so well known at the time that in the classic 1954 film *On the Waterfront*, a character complains that his coat is full of more holes than the Pittsburgh infield. Clearly, divine intervention was needed for the 1950s Pirates.

Luckily for the team, an eight-year-old orphan, Bridget White, has been praying for the Pirates and their manager, Guffy McGovern, and so the Archangel Gabriel has sent an aide, along with his heavenly choir of former baseball players (the Heavenly Choir Nine), to assist the Pirates during their games, but only so long as McGovern improves his language, treats others with kindness, and stays out of fights. McGovern hews to that promise, and with the assistance of the angels, the Pirates start winning, rising out of the cellar and finally playing for the National League pennant on the last day of the season. Along the way, McGovern falls in love with newspaper reporter, Jennifer Paige, and starts to take steps to adopt Bridget. Un-

Manager Guffy McGovern (Paul Douglas), second from the left, has an argument with pitcher Saul Hellman (Bruce Bennett) after another Pirates' loss, early in *Angels in the Outfield* (1951).

fortunately, just before the championship game, McGovern breaks his promise to the angels and gets into a fracas with a sports broad-caster, Fred Bayles. Thus, in the last game of the season, the Pirates must go it alone, without divine intervention.

Angels in the Outfield is a marvelous fantasy film, with some com-edy, charm, and romance thrown into the mix. The film is legiti-mately funny in spots, such as McGovern arguing with an umpire and making his point by quoting from Shakespeare; McGovern ru-ining Jennifer's shoes, which he was supposed to place below the oven to clean off some mud, not in it; an ominous clap of thunder signaling that it is raining, not that the angels are angry; and a nun questioning why McGovern did not call for a suicide squeeze in the seventh inning of the prior day's game.

The comedy element could only have succeeded with an excel-lent performance in the role of Guffy McGovern, and Paul Doug-las is equal to the task. He is aggravating early in the film when he fights with umpires, yells at his players, and engages in fisticuffs with Fred Bayles. He is endearingly perplexed when the angels first make contact with him, and finally likable when his rough edges fall away and he acquires an interest in Bridget and Jennifer. The filmmakers cleverly handled the issue of how to address his obscenity-laced dialogue early in the film by playing back the dialogue in such a way that it is both gibberish to the audience but also very clear as to the type of language he is using. This enabled the film to meet censorship requirements of the day (and even requirements of family movies of the current day) without, on the one hand, turning the character off for the audience and, on the other hand, without neutering the character so much that he would have been unconvincing.

The charm of *Angels in the Outfield* lies in Bridget, the cute orphan girl who is the only one who can see the angels on the field. Donna Corcoran (the sister of Kevin Corcoran, who played Moochie of the Little League), who was about the same age as her character at the time the movie was produced, is excellent in the role. She is not cloying or sappy. She is convincingly likable and sincere, making an unbelievable part in an unbelievable story into a very believable character.

The similarities between *Angels in the Outfield* (1951) and the Christmas classic *Miracle on 34th Street* (1947) are patent. Both involve an adult's belief in a religious symbol or being (whether angels or Santa Claus), a little girl who provides them with support, a hearing to resolve the issue, and vindication on the side of the divine. Both films derive much of their charm from that story template. However, there is a significant difference between the two movies, arising from the fact that *Angels in the Outfield* is, at its core and despite its other elements, a baseball film. The climax of *Angels in the Outfield* is not a trial; it is the final-day-of-the-season game with the National League pennant at stake.

The championship game in *Angels in the Outfield* does not disappoint, partially because it has several different subplots. The Pirates are on their own, without any expectation of divine intervention. The Pirates' pitcher is Saul Hellman, who once pitched a two-hitter in the World Series, but is now tired after sixteen years of professional ball. Saul used to be friends with McGovern, but their friendship went awry once McGovern started to treat his players, including Saul, in a demeaning manner. McGovern has learned from the angels that Saul is set to die early the next year, so this is Saul's last season in baseball.

The footage of the game is convincing, with real action intercut with close-ups of Bruce Bennett, playing Saul, winding up and then throwing to the plate. There is some projection-screen footage that may not be that convincing, but it is kept to a minimum. One of the most important factors in the effectiveness of the game footage is that it is quite extensive, showing the game from its beginning through the final inning (although some of the baseball in the middle innings is shown by way of the requisite montage). *Angels in the Outfield* takes the necessary time to tell the story of the final game just as a game, interesting on its own, but also with the story of the game enriched by Saul Hellman's personal story.

Saul appears to be tiring as the game progresses, but he keeps pitching. In the ninth inning, with the Pirates ahead by one run, Saul starts to rub his aching shoulder and then hits a batter. When the New York Giants get two men on with two men out, the crowd yells for McGovern to take Saul out for a relief pitcher. Guffy sticks with his aging right-hander, even when the Giants load the bases for the next batter. Fortunately, Saul strikes out the next batter on three pitches and the Pirates win the pennant.

Because the film has so many other interesting facets, the baseball aspects of *Angels in the Outfield* are often overlooked. That is unfortunate because the championship game is enthralling throughout, with its story-within-a-story about the team's aging pitcher, extensive baseball action that includes outs along with hits, and a great performance by Bruce Bennett in the role of Saul Hellman. In real life, Bruce Bennett won a silver medal for the shot put in the 1928 Olympic games and also played Tarzan in the movies. By 1951, Bennett was an aging athlete himself, perfect for the role of Saul Hellman.

For baseball fans, there are some special delights in *Angels in the Outfield*. Much of the film was shot in Pittsburgh and particularly at Old Forbes Field (as it is often called in Pittsburgh these days). Forbes Field was the home of the Pirates from 1909 to 1970, until the Pirates moved into Three Rivers Stadium and began to share a multi-sports field with the Pittsburgh Steelers. Although the lack of color in the film prevents the viewer from appreciating the deep green of the outfield grass and the ivy-covered walls in left and center fields, the beauty of Forbes Field does come through, with the old-fashion scoreboard in left field where the runs had to be placed into their slot by hand, a field that was so deep to center field that the batting cage was stored there during the game, the roof of the Carnegie Library and Carnegie Museum that can be seen beyond the left field wall, and the University of Pittsburgh's tall Cathedral of Learning looking down on the field.

For the discerning baseball fan, the film does raise an interesting question concerning Forbes Field. At one point in the championship game, a player for the Pirates hits a ball off the left field scoreboard, for a two-run home run. Now, most Pittsburghers know that a ball hit off the scoreboard was not a home run at Forbes Field. Rather, the ball was still in play. Thus, this game incident appears to constitute a blatant error on the part of the filmmakers. Yet surprisingly, *Angels in the Outfield* is accurate in this regard. For the 1947 season, the Pirates bought the contract of slugger Hank Greenberg from the Detroit Tigers, and in order to assist the right-handed hitter's home-run prowess, the team shortened left field by moving the bullpens from foul territory to left field and erecting a wall from the foul line to left-center field. Balls landing over the inner wall or off the scoreboard were now home runs. The approximate thirty-foot area between the new wall and scoreboard was called "Greenberg Gardens."

Hank Greenberg retired after one year, and the area was then renamed Kiner's Korner, for the Pirates' right-handed hitting home-run sensation of the era. (After Ralph Kiner's retirement from baseball, *Kiner's Korner* became the name of Ralph Kiner's long-running postgame television show for New York Mets baseball games, for which Kiner was an announcer.) After Kiner was traded to the Cubs during the 1953 season, the inner wall of Forbes Field came down. However, in 1951, the inner wall was in existence, and it can be seen in the film. Thus, in 1951, when *Angels in the Outfield* was produced, a ball hit off the scoreboard was a home run even though throughout most of Forbes Field's existence, it was not.

It is always nice to see some major leaguers or former major leaguers in a baseball movie. In that regard, *Angels in the Outfield* does not disappoint. In the final game, Pie Traynor, the Pirates' Hall of Fame third baseman and former manager, plays a coach who is asked by McGovern to take care of the bullpen during the game. When news of the angels in Pittsburgh's outfield becomes public, there are news-reel interviews with Joe DiMaggio and Ty Cobb, two of the most famous and successful ballplayers of all time. Of the two pseudo interviews, the Ty Cobb segment is the most striking. For current baseball fans, Cobb always seems like a legendary figure who played so long ago, with such incredible career statistics and unique personality, that he never seems quite real. Yet here he is, in a 1951 film, at the age of 64, saying, "Well, all I can say is, that this game of baseball has certainly changed." Cobb seems amiable enough. Is he really the man who deliberately slid into bases with his spikes high, trying to injure opposing infielders?

Angels in the Outfield (1994)

For the 1951 film version of *Angels in the Outfield*, the writers chose the worst team in baseball, the Pittsburgh Pirates, as the Major League Baseball team most in need of assistance from the angels. For the 1994 film, different considerations resulted in using the California Angels as the foils for the story.

That is not to say that the California Angels were a great team in 1994. Fans would have to go back five years to 1989 to find a season in which the Angels had a winning record, although they finished exactly at .500 in 1991. Fans would have to go back to 1986 to find a year in which the Angels were in the postseason.

Nevertheless, in the two years before *Angels in the Outfield* was released, there were several major-league teams that had worst records than the Angels, even some teams in the same division as the Angels. Presumably, the deciding factors in using the Angels in 1994 was the fortuitous situation of a team actually having the name Angels, the proximity of the team to Hollywood, and the fact that Walt Disney, the company that produced *Angels in the Outfield*, had a partial ownership interest in the California Angels at the time. Of course, the California Angels could not have been used in the 1951 movie of the same name, because the Angels, originally known as the Los Angeles Angels, first played in the major leagues in 1961 as an expansion team.

Angels in the Outfield (1994) is, well, the Disney version of the 1951 film, which, in effect, makes them two completely different movies, even though they have the same basic plot. In the newer film, the manager of the California Angels, George Knox, has no contact with the angels. Instead, the film is told solely from the perspective of two foster children, Roger and J.P., with Roger the only one who can see the angels. Unlike the prior film, the audience can see the angels assisting the players on the field, and when the boss angel, Al, talks to Roger, the audience can see him too. The romantic subplot of the earlier film (thankfully) has been eliminated.

Adults will probably prefer the 1951 version of the story because it is adult-oriented. The angels are not actually shown on-screen during that film, perhaps for budgetary reasons, but the result is that the film never becomes too silly for an older audience. Even though the original film has a fantasy premise, it still seems to take place in the real world with, for example, McGovern's use of street language when arguing in the film and McGovern realizing he could never adopt a child while he was unmarried. Since the newer film is not directed to an adult audience, these niceties of the real world can be avoided. For example, at the end of the film, the single Knox, with no parenting experience, decides to adopt both Roger and J.P., even though as a baseball manager, he will be on the road for half of each year. *Angels in the Outfield* (1994) has a happy ending, at least temporarily, but one has to wonder what the situation will be like ten years hence.

The adoption of the foster children is not the only happy ending for the movie. Angels' dead-tired pitcher Mel Clark is able to get the final out in the championship game solely on the belief that the angels are behind him; Knox has changed from a hot-tempered manager into a caring person and a lover of children; J.P., who once was afraid to talk to strangers, is now comfortable enough to talk to anyone; and paper villain Ranch Wilder, the Angels' pompous and aggravating broadcaster, gets his comeuppance when the owner of the Angels, Hank Murphy, fires him. Admittedly, these are the types of multiple happy climaxes that kids expect when going to the cinema, particularly in a film from Disney, but it would have been nice if Disney had changed its formula just a little bit. How often has this type of ending been seen before?

While one can argue over whether or not it was appropriate to show the angels to the viewing audience, it is hard to deny that the special effects are special, for example, with Al suddenly appearing and disappearing as if by magic and the angels physically lifting a player in the outfield to make a leaping circus catch. Also, this is a kids' movie and kids will enjoy actually seeing angels on the field. Unfortunately, the film sometimes goes overboard, as when, at the suggestion of Roger, Knox brings in a utility infielder, Danny Hemmerling, to pinch-hit for a better batter. To assist Danny, the angels stop a pitch in midair on the way to the plate. The pitch then comes in very slowly. Danny manages to hit the ball, and the ball then keeps bouncing around the infield, doing loops, going off at strange angles, and hitting fielders until Danny scores on his inside-the-infield home run. In a scene such as this, the effects make the film into a cartoon, undercutting their effectiveness.

Character actor Ben Johnson plays Hank Murphy, the owner of the Angels. Johnson wears a cowboy hat throughout most of the film, an indication that he is actually playing former cowboy star Gene Autry, who was the original owner of the Angels and was still a majority owner of the team when the film was released. It would have been special seeing Gene Autry actually play the part of the owner in the 1994 film, although Autry's last significant performing work before 1994 was in 1950s television.

Unexpectedly, *Angels in the Outfield* (1994) has one of the same strengths as the 1951 film. Baseball games are long (perhaps overly long according to many outside observers), and they have an ebb and flow that make each game unique. *Angels in the Outfield* (1994) does an excellent job of re-creating that atmosphere in the concluding game, with action shown in the first and middle innings, such as runners on base, some slick fielding plays, and only a few runs scored by either team. Clark is often struggling, getting out of jams with the aid of the excellent play by his team in the field. In the bottom of the eighth inning, a suicide squeeze puts the Angels ahead by one run. Clark comes out in the top of the ninth to face the heart of the White Sox lineup. There is a bloop single, a call to the bullpen, a sacrifice bunt, an infield hit, a circus catch in the outfield, and a hit batter. The bases are loaded with two out, and the top RBI producer on the White Sox at bat.

Clark runs the count to three and two, saved at the last second by a home-run ball that just goes foul. Then, after Knox comes to the mound, Clark, with the encouragement of the fans and some faith in himself, throws as hard as he can to the plate. The batter smacks a line drive back to the mound, which Clark catches on a diving stab. The Angels win!

The footage of the championship game lasts for over sixteen minutes, long for any baseball film. Unlike most baseball films, any viewer watching the championship game will have the feeling that he has watched a real nine-inning game, not just a highlight reel.

Despite its attributes, the 1994 version of the final game is not as effective as the final game shown in the 1951 film. In the newer film, Al the angel only tells young Roger that Mel Clark will become an angel after the end of the season. Manager George Knox is unaware of that fact. Thus, why does Knox keep Clark in the game when he is clearly tiring? While the earlier film told the story of pitcher Saul Hellman, and part of the story of the final game was about Hellman proving that he could still pitch, that is not really the case with Mel Clark in the newer film because since July, Clark had recaptured his pitching touch after an old injury, so he has little to prove on the last day of the season. In fact, Clark appears to want out of the game in the ninth inning. Perhaps most importantly, it was much more common for a pitcher in the 1950s to throw a complete game. By 1994, that was no longer the case. (According to the book *Baseball Between the Numbers*, the percentage of complete games out of games started in 1954 was 34 percent; by 1994, the percentage had dropped to 8 percent.) Thus, it would have been no shame for Clark to be replaced by a relief pitcher with the game on the line. From a baseball perspective, it is hard to understand why Knox leaves Clark in the game with the bases loaded and two men out.

From a movie perspective, that decision by Knox fits into the theme of *Angels in the Outfield* (1994). While the earlier film had no overriding idea behind the story, the latter film is about faith, not necessarily about religious faith, but faith in oneself and the faith to accomplish big things. That is a worthwhile topic, of course, but for true baseball fans, winning a pennant is more important. Knox should have brought the Angels' closer in with the bases loaded, if not before, to complete the game.

All of that said, *Angels in the Outfield* (1994) is a very good film. It may come in second in a comparison with the 1951 version, but it is surely better than most baseball movies.

The Kid from Left Field (1953)

The Kid from Left Field relates the story of the Bisons, a major-league team from an unnamed city. The Bisons are the worst team in baseball, so much so that in their latest game, they draw only 123 fans to the park, a major-league record of dubious distinction. Much like the Bisons, Larry "Coop" Cooper, a former player for the Bisons, is not doing well. After a fairly successful career in the big leagues, he is now a peanut vendor at the Bisons' ballpark. Coop is a widower who has a nine-year-old son, Christy, a baseball fanatic. Christy is named for Christy Mathewson, the famous pitcher for the New York Giants.

One day, Christy becomes a batboy for the Bisons and in that capacity, gives hitting tips to several of the struggling Bisons' players. With the players using Christy's advice, most of which he learned from his father, the Bisons start to turn their season around. When the owner of the club fires the manager, Christy becomes the new manager. The team's success continues under Christy, but as the team draws close to winning the pennant, Christy is hospitalized with pneumonia. Luckily, his father takes over as manager of the Bisons and leads the team into the World Series.

The title of the film, *The Kid from Left Field*, is unusual. After all, Christy never plays left field for the Bisons. The title is actually a play on words, using the words "left field" to indicate the movie is about baseball but also using a common expression, "from left field" or "out of left field," meaning something that it is unexpected, out of the blue, or without warning. A nine-year-old manager for a Major League Baseball team clearly fits that definition. The origin of the saying is unknown, but everyone agrees that the expression derives from some aspect of baseball.

The Kid from Left Field is not well known today, but it is a surprisingly enjoyable film. It is more serious than expected, with its emphasis on the father-son relationship, the humiliations in Coop Cooper's life, the difficulties in developing a winning baseball team, and the authenticity of the baseball, with some interesting strategic moves and playing tips discussed or shown in detail. There are also some funny baseball moments, such as the left fielder going back to catch a fly ball and running into the wall; a ground ball going through the shortstop's legs; a pop-up falling right behind an infield-

The owner of the Bisons, Fred Whacker (Ray Collins), expresses his amazement to team secretary Marion Foley (Anne Bancroft) that the Bisons have made the World Series in *The Kid from Left Field* (1953).

er; a fly ball hitting an outfielder in the head; and Christy cleverly managing to sneak into the ballpark on a few occasions. Low humor though it may be, it is hard not to laugh at a fly ball hitting an outfielder in the head.

For those who like "inside baseball," *The Kid from Left Field* has several interesting moments. In his first managerial game, Coop Cooper pinch-hits for a good hitter, Olsen, by replacing him with Pierce, a mediocre batter. Fortunately, Pierce gets a hit, knocking in a run for the Bisons. The reason for Coop's unexpected but successful decision, as explained by Christy, is that Pierce historically hits this particular pitcher better than Olsen. Given baseball's current reliance on sabermetrics, that reasoning for a substitution is common today. It is interesting to see that the same thought process was in use as far back as the 1950s.

In that same game, Cooper brings in Slater, a relief pitcher, for Bermudes, the starting pitcher, but instead of taking Bermudes out of the game, Cooper moves Bermudes to third base. After Slater gets a tough batter out, Slater is taken out of the game and Bermudes returns to the mound, to pitch the rest of the game. The television announcer is surprised by these moves, but while this type of switch is a rare occurrence in baseball, it does occur from time to time. The game ends with another infrequent occurrence, a successful steal of home plate, resulting in the Bisons winning the game. While stealing home plate is a very rare occurrence in baseball today, it is not as rare historically as one might expect. Ty Cobb stole home more than any other player, with fifty-four successful steals in his career, a number that seems unbelievable for current baseball fans.

The hospitalized Christy is forced to watch his father's first game as manager on television from his hospital room. Of course, by 1953, watching baseball games on television had become the norm, even though the sets were small and the pictures were in black and white. What is not the norm is how the director, Harmon Jones, chose to shoot these scenes. While there are a few shots with the camera situated within the ballpark, pointed toward the dugout as Coop Cooper makes his managerial decisions, all of the game action is shown from Christy's hospital room, on television. In other words, the moviegoer is also watching the Bisons' game on television rather than being outdoors at the ballpark.

This is a very strange directorial decision. Perhaps the reason was to show events from Christy's limited viewpoint, since he is so invested in each managerial decision his father makes. The effect, however, is to place the viewer far removed from the events of the game, lessening the audience's involvement in the game. How many moviegoers who went to the theater to see this movie in 1953 expected to watch the most important game in the film on television?

✓ *Little Big League* (1994)

Little Big League is the story of Billy Heywood, a twelve-year-old who inherits the Minnesota Twins after his wealthy grandfather suddenly passes away. As the new owner of the ball club, Billy instantly gets into a dispute with the manager, who is not very happy working for a young boy. Billy fires the manager, and when no one else will take the job, Billy names himself the new manager. After a rocky start, the Twins start playing well for Billy, eventually tying the Seattle Mariners for the last wild card playoff spot, leading, at the conclusion of the film, to an exciting one-game playoff.

Little Big League falls into the broad category of family film, and for that reason, baseball fans may overlook the movie, believing that it will be clichéd, puerile, and routine. If baseball fans forgo the movie for those reasons, it would be a shame because the film sets itself apart from most family-oriented sports films in significant ways. For example, while always light in nature, *Little Big League* has a bit of a theme to it, one that can also be seen in the non-sports film *Big* (1988). As much fun as Billy has managing a major-league team, he eventually misses his friends and the simple pleasures of playing stickball or going fishing. Billy finally tells his mother, "I'm tired of being a grown-up." Being a kid is an important part of life, and Billy finally understands that, but only when his season in the sun is about to come to its conclusion.

While *Little Big League* is not above employing some schoolboy comedy, particularly in Billy's scenes with his two young friends or the tossing of water balloons out of a hotel window by the supposedly adult ballplayers, there are also some funny lines in the film that knowledgeable baseball fans will appreciate. When Billy's friend first suggests that Billy should manage the Twins, Billy demurs, saying it is too hard to be a baseball manager. The friend responds, "It's the American League. They've got the DH. How hard can it be?" Also, the Twins baseball announcer is full of those perplexing (and meaningless) statistics that only baseball can produce, such as describing a batter as "sixth in the American League in hitting right-handers he was facing for the first time after the seventh inning at home."

Even though *Little Big League* involves the movie cliché of an underdog team trying to make it to the top against incredible odds, the film's ending is not the cliché one might expect in a family-oriented sports film. In the usual family film, everyone knows that the underdog team will somehow put it all together and defeat the big, bad opponents, surprising everyone. This can be seen in *The Mighty Ducks* (1992) (ice hockey) and *The Big Green* (1995) (soccer).

In a more adult-oriented sports film, that type of ending is generally unacceptable, because it is too unbelievable. Instead, the protagonist sets a goal that is just short of winning an important game or championship, i.e., a goal that is believable. Thus, in *Rocky* (1976), Rocky Balboa sets a goal of making it through all fifteen rounds in his boxing match with Apollo Creed, thus seeming to be a winner at the end, even though he loses the title fight. In *Tin Cup* (1996), washed-up golfer Roy McAvoy is actually tied for the lead on the eighteenth hole of the final round of the US Open when he attempts

In this publicity photo for *Little Big League* (1994), twelve-year-old Billy Heywood (Luke Edwards), right, talks to his grandfather (Jason Robards), from whom Billy will soon inherit the Minnesota Twins baseball club.

a long shot over a pond, instead of laying up, resulting in his ball going into the water. This happens several times until, on Roy's last attempt, his shot clears the water and the ball rolls into the hole. Roy loses the tournament, but by making a nearly impossible shot, Roy seems like a winner.

Similarly, in *Little Big League*, the Twins do not go on to win the American League pennant and then the World Series, a true fantasy. Instead, they almost become the wild card team in the playoffs, losing the play-in game in extra innings and only after being robbed by a circus catch in the outfield, thereby preventing a home run. That is enough for the Twins to seem like winners, at least according to the fans who remain in the Metrodome to cheer their team long after the game is over, even though the Twins, in fact, are losers on that day. This is a trademark of an adult sports film, not a family film.

A good baseball film will provide the viewer with intriguing baseball moments and in that regard, *Little Big League* does not disappoint. *Little Big League* opens with Billy playing Little League Baseball and three of Billy's teammates ending up at third base at the same time. The umpire asks Billy what to do, and Billy advises him that the lead runner is safe and the other two are out, recalling the incident that occurred at Ebbets Field on August 15, 1926, in a game between the Brooklyn Dodgers and the Boston Braves. With the bases loaded and no one out, Babe Herman, the Dodgers right fielder, hit a line drive to right field. The runner on third scored. Then through a strange set of running miscues, the runners who were originally on second (Dazzy Vance) and first (Chuck Fewster) and the batter, Babe Herman, all ended up on third base at the same time. All three runners were tagged by the third baseman (although in some versions of the story, Herman is tagged out on his way back to second base), putting out Fewster and Herman but not Vance, who was entitled to third base as the lead runner (and not forced to advance from there). Many people believe the story of three men on third base is apocryphal, but it really did happen in a major-league game.

Another intriguing baseball moment occurs at the end of the one-game playoff between the Twins and the Mariners. Billy instructs his team to use a trick play that Billy invented and the team has been practicing. With Ken Griffey Jr. on first, the pitcher appears to throw the ball to first in a pickoff attempt. It then appears that the throw was wild and the ball has rolled to the fence by the stands. While the first baseman, the right fielder, and even a security guard start looking for the ball, Griffey runs to second base. He is thrown out when the pitcher, who never actually threw the ball to first base, calmly throws the ball to the second baseman.

This is a fun moment in *Little Big League*, but upon further reflection, the scene does not work. The problem is that the trick play could never have been successful in a real baseball game. Rule 6.02 of the Major League Baseball rules provides that if there is a runner on base, it is a balk when the "pitcher, while touching his plate [the pitching rubber] feints a throw to first or third base and fails to complete the throw." Thus, in *Little Big League*, the umpire should have called a balk and Ken Griffey awarded second base automatically. While *Little Big League* is surprisingly accurate in most of its depictions of baseball games, the film comes up short with this incident.

There are a number of famous ballplayers who make appearances in the film, particularly near the end during the playoff game between the Twins and the Mariners. Lou Piniella, who managed several teams in the major leagues, including the 1990 world champion Cincinnati Reds, plays himself as the then-manager of the Seattle Mariners. Randy Johnson, a five-time Cy Young Award winner and strikeout king for many years, pitches in relief for the Mariners in the eleventh inning of the playoff game. Johnson was a starting pitcher during most of his career, although he did make a surprise relief appearance on behalf of Seattle in 1995 in the deciding game of a division championship series against the New York Yankees. Indeed, his relief appearance in *Little Big League* presages that memorable relief appearance in that 1995 game. Ken Griffey Jr., a home-run hitter both for the Seattle Mariners and the Cincinnati Reds during his long career, hits a prodigious home run for Seattle in this film. Seven years later, in *Summer Catch* (2001), Griffey would hit another cinematic home run, that time while he was playing for Cincinnati.

Little Big League starts to drag near the end, as Billy becomes disenchanted and bored with managing a big-league team. The audience similarly becomes bored and disenchanted, as the fantasy of a boy owner, particularly one who is only twelve years old and has so much knowledge about baseball, starts to wear a little thin. Fortunately, once Billy regains his interest in managing the Twins, *Little Big League* comes alive, leading to the film's exciting conclusion. Family film though it may be, *Little Big League* has its interest for sports fans. It is a film that should not be overlooked by any of them.

Roogie's Bump (1954)

Roogie's Bump was made in 1954 at John Bash Productions, an independent film company. There are no stars in the cast; the film appears to have a minimal budget. Extensive archival footage of the Brooklyn Dodgers is inserted throughout the film, but even with this padding, the film runs only about seventy-one minutes. Anyone choosing to view *Roogie's Bump* today, and who does a little research before doing so, will have low expectations about the quality of the movie.

Sad to say, those low expectations are justified. Adults will be bored by the puerile story lines of the film. While youngsters from the 1950s may have enjoyed the film back then, today's kids will have little interest in a movie made in black and white, with embarrassing special effects and little baseball of significance.

Nor does *Roogie's Bump* have much of a plot. Remington "Roogie" Rigsby has just moved from Ohio to Brooklyn, and while Roogie loves to play baseball, the neighborhood kids have no interest in playing with the newcomer. When Roogie's grandmother gives Roogie a signed baseball card from former Dodgers great Red O'Malley, Roogie tries to trade it to the leader of the gang for a chance to play for the neighborhood team. Unfortunately, the card is torn in half and Roogie does not play. As a disappointed Roogie walks away from the game, the deceased Red O'Malley magically appears and talks with Roogie. After O'Malley rubs Roogie's upper arm, a bump appears. That bump gives Roogie incredible strength in his pitching arm. Then, through an unusual set of circumstances, Roogie pitches on behalf of the Dodgers in an exhibition game. Roogie is so successful in his first major-league appearance that he is brought into the final game of the season, late in the game, with the National League pennant on the line. Can Roogie save the Dodgers?

As unfocused as *Roogie's Bump* is, the film does try to develop some themes that could have had significance in a better production. Echoing an idea from *Little Big League* (1994), Roogie's bump has caused Roogie to grow up too fast, being snatched out of normal childhood experiences and becoming a big leaguer overnight, probably not a good idea for any youngster. At least O'Malley seems to realize the predicament he has put Roogie in with his good intentions, so he does not allow Roogie to pitch well in the season-ending game, putting an end to Roogie's short career. As Red O'Malley tells Roogie after Roogie walks back to the locker room, "I didn't think ahead. I didn't realize all the things that could happen when I arranged that bump of yours."

This relates to the other theme of the movie — the exploitation of athletes and performers for commercial use, particularly young ones. Roogie makes personal appearances on behalf of the Dodgers and even endorses commercial products, such as cereal. He makes the cover of *Time* magazine and appears on radio and television. Although Roogie will see some money from these endeavors, in a college trust fund, the main purpose of these activities is to improve the bottom line of the Dodgers. With the exception of Doug Boxi, the manager of the Dodgers, no one on the baseball side of the film has an interest in the well-being of Roogie. *Roogie's Bump* demonstrates that even back in the 1950s, baseball was foremost a business. That is not a more recent phenomenon, as some may believe.

If *Roogie's Bump* had concentrated on these themes, it might have been a good film, poor production values and all. Instead, the film is all over the place on story lines, first with the neighborhood kids unwilling to play with Roogie (an issue never resolved in the film), the problems of a single mother raising a child on a limited budget, and a potential romance between Boxi and Roogie's mother. There is no overriding theme or story line to the film.

What is truly disappointing, however, are the special effects, consisting of Roogie winding up in his double-pump pitching motion and then when he throws, the ball becoming a cartoon ball which, on one occasion, explodes through a brick wall and on another occasion, flies across the East River and knocks down part of a smoke stack in Manhattan. At one point in the exhibition game, Roogie hangs on to a ball he is pitching, his entire body becomes a cartoon, speeds through the air, and then is caught by the catcher. It is hard to suspend disbelief with these unconvincing effects.

Baseball fans will find joy in the fact that the film does have a feel of the borough of Brooklyn. Some of the outdoors scenes appear to have been shot on location in Brooklyn, as some of the publicity of the day asserts. It also appears that the "live" scenes in Ebbets Field were actually shot in Ebbets Field. The only part of the outfield shown in "live" action is right field (and right field is never shown in the stock footage), but the right field in the movie, with no seats behind the fence and advertising on the wall, such as "Gem" and "Esquire Boot," approximates photos of the ballpark from the 1950s.

Several Dodgers from 1954 appear in the film as themselves. The two most famous are Carl Erskine, who pitched two no-hitters for the Dodgers in his eleven-year career with the team, and Roy Campanella, the Dodgers Hall of Fame catcher, who played for the team for ten years, starting in 1948. Campanella's career tragically ended after an automobile accident in 1958, from which Campanella became paralyzed. Today, most people remember Campanella from his years in a wheelchair, so the movie provides a good opportunity

Catcher Roy Campanella of the Brooklyn Dodgers places a bat in the lap of Roogie (Robert Marriot), as other Dodgers look on, in *Roogie's Bump* (1954).

to see Campanella in his playing days. Campanella is shorter and stockier than one might expect.

For baseball fans, *Roogie's Bump* provides the scenes in Ebbets Field and some real-life Dodgers. That is about all. Since baseball fans can see Ebbets Fields and some real-life Dodgers of the 1940s in *Whistling in Brooklyn* (1943), a slightly better film, there is really no reason to spend time on *Roogie's Bump*.

Rookie of the Year (1993)

It is hard not to like a film that has the following dialogue:

> CHICAGO CUBS EXECUTIVE: Hey, kid. How would you like to pitch for the Chicago Cubs?
> KID: Great! But I got to ask my mom first.

The kid is Henry Rowengartner, a Little Leaguer who loves baseball but who is not very good at the game. One day, while playing in the outfield, Henry slips on a ball lying on the grass, flips high in the air, and breaks his arm when he falls. Henry is rushed to the hospital, his arm is placed in a cast, and weeks later when the cast is removed, the doctor realizes that Henry's tendons have healed a little too tight. As a result of this medical phenomenon, Henry can now throw a baseball at an incredible speed. That leads to a stint as a pitcher for the Chicago Cubs, where Henry's throwing skills are so good that perhaps he could win Rookie of the Year honors. Unfortunately, in the last inning of the division championship game, Henry slips on another baseball and hits his arm, causing him to lose his incredible pitching skills. Is there some way Henry can get through the last inning and get the Cubs into the World Series?

The answer to that last question is obviously "no," but this is Hollywood and this is fantasy and so, unsurprisingly, the answer to that question is actually "yes." That leads to the low point of the film, the top of the ninth inning of a game between the Cubs and the Mets for the division championship. The Cubs are ahead by one run. Because Henry can barely reach home plate with pitches using his normal arm, Henry intentionally walks the first batter. He then essentially picks off the runner, with the old hidden-ball trick. Henry then intentionally walks the second batter, and then goads him into trying to steal second base while Henry has the ball in his hand. That leads to the second out.

The third batter, Heddo, however, is not going to be such a patsy. Heddo is a huge, monstrous ballplayer with a large tongue, who hit a home run against Henry earlier in the year and intends to do so again. Instead of intentionally walking him, Henry decides to pitch to him. Henry's first pitch, with his normal arm, is so slow that Heddo misses it. Heddo hits the second pitch a long way, but it curves foul just at the end. For his third pitch, Henry lobs the ball underhand, as it if were a softball, and Heddo misses it with a big swing. The Chicago Cubs are off to the World Series!

It is not a good situation for a baseball film when its climax at the championship game is disappointing or, in this case, disappointing and ridiculous, but that is the problem with Rookie of the Year. It is true that Rookie of the Year is a kids-oriented fantasy film, but that does not excuse the way the film insults the national pastime in this last sequence. Only in a young kid's dreams would a major-league ballplayer be fooled by the hidden ball trick. Only in a Hollywood film would a major-league ballplayer try to steal second base when the pitcher is holding the ball. Only in a young kid's dreams in a Hollywood film would a major leaguer swing at, much less miss, a ball lobbed underhand high in the air. Equating a division championship game with a youth pickup game or a Sunday-morning adult softball game is demeaning to the game and insulting to the viewer.

After the division championship game, Henry can no longer pitch for the Cubs, and so none of the World Series action is shown in the movie. However, at the end of the film, Henry is shown wearing a World Series ring, so the Cubs must have won the World Series that year. If anyone has any doubt that *Rookie of the Year* is a fantasy film, that moment will confirm it, at least until 2016.

The ending of *Rookie of the Year* is particularly dissatisfying because there is a lot to like in the earlier parts of the movie. For example, there are some truly humorous moments in *Rookie of the Year*. When Henry first pitches for the Cubs, he has some difficulty with the resin bag, causing him to sneeze. When the owner of the Cubs, Bob Carson, learns that his nephew, Larry (Fish) Fisher, who appears to be the general manager of the Cubs, is trying to sell Henry to the Yankees, Fisher is next seen selling hot dogs in the stands.

Because of his small stature and tiny strike zone, when Henry first comes to bat in a game, he is walked. (This brings back memories of Bill Veeck inserting Eddie Gaedel, a midget, into the batting order of the St. Louis Browns on August 19, 1951. Gaedel promptly walked on four straight pitches.) Then Henry, still just a young boy, invokes his young boy experiences and personality and starts taunting the pitcher, dancing off first base and shouting comments such as, "Hey, pitcher, you have something hanging out of your nose," or "We want a pitcher, not an underwear snitcher." Henry survives a pickoff throw and then mocks the first baseman by stepping on and off first base quickly. When another batter hits a ball into the outfield, Henry runs so much slower than the adult base runner behind him that the two reach home plate at almost the same time.

Unlike the end of the movie, this sequence is funny because it does not insult major-league ballplayers. Assuming a twelve-year-old could ever play in a major-league game, he would probably act in the same silly way that most twelve-year-old boys do. The scene ties in to a moment after Henry pitches in a Cubs game, when the stands are empty and Henry and his two friends play a pretend game of

Barry Bonds, then an outfielder for the Pittsburgh Pirates, goes up against twelve-year-old pitching phenom Henry Rowengartner in *Rookie of the Year* (1993). Just like most other batters Henry faces, Bonds strikes out.

baseball in Wrigley Field. That is just what many twelve-year-old boys would do, given the opportunity, and since all major-league ballplayers were twelve-year-old boys at one time, when one of the Cubs players sees the pretend game, he asks another player, "Think they'll let us play?"

Rookie of the Year contains a nice montage sequence that shows how effective Henry's fastball truly is. In quick succession, Bobby Bonilla, who, after being in the majors for many years with Pittsburgh, played in his first season for the Mets in 1992 (the year the movie was filmed); Pedro Guerrero, who played his last season of baseball for St. Louis in 1992 after a long career in the majors; and Barry Bonds, still an outfielder for the Pirates in 1992, each swing and miss one of Henry's pitches. All three of them were excellent hitters during their careers. They were good sports for appearing in a film that shows them failing against a youngster.

There are many other films that have baseball scenes that occur in Wrigley Field in Chicago, but none do the historic ballpark as much justice as *Rookie of the Year*. Wrigley Field is the oldest active ballpark in the National League, second only to Fenway Park in all of Major League Baseball. *Rookie of the Year* shows Cubs fans coming to the stadium before the game, the field staff preparing the playing surface, long action sequences on the diamond, and, of course, fans watching the games from the roofs of the buildings across the street. Wrigley Field is still in use today, so a movie is not needed to memorialize the field in viewers' minds, but there were substantial renovations made to Wrigley Field before the 2015 season. Wrigley Field no longer looks like it did in *Rookie of the Year*, and so the movie does etch in stone some memories of the ballpark as it once was, which adds value.

The plot of *Rookie of the Year* is obviously very similar to that of *Roogie's Bump* (1954), with Roogie mystically receiving a bump on his arm that allows him to pitch for the Brooklyn Dodgers. *Roogie's Bump* is a low-budget film; *Rookie of the Year* has a high budget. Yet *Roogie's Bump*, while not much of a film, is better than *Rookie of the Year* in several regards. *Roogie's* has two themes. One is the exploitation of athletes for commercial use. By contrast, while *Rookie of the Year* does show Henry making commercials and endorsements, those scenes are used for comedy, not for thematic purposes. The other theme of *Roogie's Bump* is that kids should not grow up too fast. That idea is hardly touched upon in *Rookie of the Year*, as Henry decides to quit baseball, probably more because he is about to be traded to the Yankees than for any other reason. There are many missed opportunities in *Rookie of the Year*.

Rookie of the Year was a box office hit in 1993, leading directly to two other youth fantasy films about baseball, *Angels in the Outfield* (1994) and *Little Big League* (1994). If *Rookie of the Year* is not quite as good as its progeny, it is still worth viewing, particularly for young baseball fans (and others who can suspend disbelief), who will enjoy the sight of a twelve-year-old pitching in the major leagues.

6

YOUNG FANS AND REAL PLAYERS

The Kid from Cleveland (1949)

For the average filmgoer, *The Kid from Cleveland* is not much of a movie, and for baseball fans it provides an additional disappointment. While promoted as a baseball film, *The Kid from Cleveland* is more about juvenile delinquency than baseball. Nevertheless, because of the real-life sports figures who appear in the film, *The Kid from Cleveland* has some interest for fans of the summer game.

The plot revolves around juvenile delinquent Johnny Barrow, who sneaks into Cleveland Municipal Stadium the day before the fifth game of the 1948 World Series. Instead of being immediately thrown out of the park, the Indians radio broadcaster, Mike Jackson, invites Johnny home for dinner, allows him to stay the night at his house, and also gets him a seat for the next day's game. Jackson continues his interest in Johnny, despite Johnny stealing money and an autographed baseball and lying to Jackson about being an orphan. After a series of small crimes, Johnny is sent to juvenile hall. Jackson then decides to adopt Johnny, despite Jackson having two young girls at home, but at the hearing in juvenile court, matters resolve into a happy ending. Johnny stays with his mother and begins to appreciate and understand his stepfather.

The Kid from Cleveland was produced by Republic Studios, an independent company that is most famous for its serials and B Westerns. While Republic usually made low-budget films, it was still a step above the poverty-row studios, such as Monogram Pictures, which produced the very low-budget *East Side Kids* films. However, in its scenes involving Johnny and his delinquency and his relationship with his stepfather, *The Kid from Cleveland* could be another entry in the *East Side Kids* series. *The Kid from Cleveland's* treatment of juvenile delinquency and personal relationships is itself juvenile and obvious, and its psychological underpinnings are suspect. The saccharine-sweet ending is hard to take.

By contrast, the baseball scenes are well handled. The filmmakers use archive or newsreel footage, interspersed with some new footage and narration from radio broadcasts, to provide a continuity of the story line of the games. Since newsreel footage of games from that era was usually shot from high above the seats with very few cameras, it can be difficult to appreciate major-league games through newsreel footage alone. However, with the new footage and the voice-over radio narration of Mike Jackson, the viewer can become engaged in the ball games in *The Kid from Cleveland*. In its baseball moments, *The Kid from Cleveland* rises above the constraints of its low budget.

Russ Tamblyn, in only his second screen appearance, plays Johnny Barrow. It is highly doubtful that his performance in *The Kid from Cleveland* had anything to do with it, but Tamblyn's best known role in his long screen and television career was playing another young delinquent, Riff, the leader of the Jets, in *West Side Story* (1961). Coincidentally, both roles involve misunderstood young men, with untapped good inside, who never had the love every child ought to get.

A number of famous ballplayers appear in *The Kid from Cleveland*. Just sticking with the Hall of Famers (and excluding those who appear only in archive footage), there is Hank Greenberg (the famous outfielder, first baseman, and slugger for the Detroit Tigers, who, in 1949, was an executive with the Indians); Tris Speaker (an outfielder and player-manager for the Indians, who, in 1949, was an advisor and scout for the Indians); Satchel Paige (the great Negro League pitcher, who debuted as a pitcher for the Cleveland Indians in 1948, at the age of forty-two); Bob Feller (the great strikeout pitcher, who won 266 games in his career, all with the Cleveland Indians); Lou Boudreau (the player-manager of the Indians, who led the team to the 1948 world championship); Joe Gordon (second baseman for the New York Yankees and Cleveland Indians, who was the Most Valuable Player in the American League in 1942); Bob Lemon (Cleveland Indians pitcher, who won over 200 games for the team); and Larry Doby (discussed below).

Surprisingly, the real-life personality with the most screen time is not a baseball player. It is Bill Veeck, the owner of the Cleveland Indians from 1946 to 1949. Veeck also owned several other major-league teams during his life in baseball. Always an innovator and promoter, Veeck is most remembered today for one of his stunts, sending a midget to the plate for the St. Louis Browns in 1951, but he should be better remembered today for his success in breaking the color barrier in the American League. Bill Veeck was also elected to the Hall of Fame as an owner, not a player.

In a flashback, Bill Veeck tells Johnny a story about Larry Doby, the first black player to play in the American League. According to Veeck, when Doby came to bat for the first time in his career, with all of the pressure on him, he struck out swinging on three straight pitches. Doby then walked back to the Indians dugout and sat by himself at the end of the bench with his head in his hands. The next batter, Joe Gordon, then deliberately struck out, or so Veeck implies, so that Doby did not feel so bad. Gordon then went to sit with Doby at the end of the bench, where both sat with their heads in their hands.

It is a great story. Unfortunately, it is not true. Doby's first plate appearance occurred on July 5, 1947, when he pinch-hit for the Indians pitcher Bryan Stephens in the seventh inning. While Doby struck out, he did not miss all of the pitches. Doby fouled off the second pitch he swung at. Also, the box score and game summary clearly show that Joe Gordon was on third base when Doby came to bat, so he could hardly have batted right after Doby. Nevertheless, the real Larry Doby and the real Joe Gordon actually act the scene out in *The Kid from Cleveland*, just as Veeck tells it. It is unclear why they were willing to re-create a baseball incident for the film that was not true.

Doby went on to an excellent career in baseball, appearing in seven straight All-Star Games beginning in 1949. Although not mentioned in the movie, in Game 4 of the 1948 World Series, Doby hit a home run, becoming the first black player to do so in a World Series game.

The Kid from Cleveland was inspired by a momentous season in Cleveland baseball history. The Cleveland Indians was one of the eight original teams in the American League when it was first established as a major league in 1901. However, it was not until 1920 that the team won its first World Series. Under player-manager Tris Speaker, the Indians beat the Brooklyn Robins (soon to be known as the Brooklyn Dodgers), five games to two. (The 1903 and 1919–1921 World Series were best-of-nine series.)

Although Cleveland dominated the 1920 World Series, it took another twenty-eight years before the Indians returned to the Fall Classic. In 1948, the Cleveland Indians defeated the Boston Braves, four games to two. Newsreel footage of part of Game 5, which the Boston Braves won, 11–5, is shown in *The Kid from Cleveland.* As mentioned in the film, that game, which was played at Cleveland Stadium, also the home of the Cleveland Browns football team, set an attendance record for a Major League Baseball game: 86,288 fans attended the game. That record was not broken until 1959, when over 92,500 people attended a World Series game between the Los Angeles Dodgers and the Chicago White Sox at the Los Angeles Coliseum, another football field.

Game 6, a part of which is also shown in the film, was played at Braves Field in Boston, Massachusetts. Cleveland won, 4–3, becoming the World Series champions. The film then shows a portion of the subsequent ticker-tape parade for the team in Cleveland, when a purported 200,000 fans lined the streets of the city to cheer their team.

From the perspective of over sixty-five years later, there is an ironic moment in the film, which takes place during spring training the year after the Indians won the World Series. Mike Jackson asks manager Lou Boudreau if he thinks Cleveland is headed to another pennant. Boudreau replies, "Barring injuries, we should make it." In fact, Boudreau's prediction was wrong. The Cleveland Indians did not win the pennant that year, and although they have appeared in the World Series on four additional occasions (1954, 1995, 1997, and 2016), they have yet to win another world championship. Boudreau's prognosticating was about as far off as anyone can get.

Safe at Home! (1962)

In 1961, Roger Maris and Mickey Mantle were the most famous duo in professional sports. Playing for the New York Yankees, Maris hit sixty-one home runs, besting Babe Ruth's thirty-four-year-old record of sixty home runs in a season. Mantle also had a great season, hitting fifty-four home runs. Mantle and Maris were chosen for the 1961 All-Star Games. In the Fall Classic that year, the Yankees beat the Cincinnati Reds, four games to one, with Maris hitting one home run in the series.

Given how famous the two ballplayers were at the end of 1961, it was natural that Hollywood would come calling, just as it did many years before for another Yankees home-run-hitting sensation, Babe Ruth. Given their fame, however, the film in which Mantle and Maris chose to appear seems surprising. While *Safe at Home!* is a film about baseball, it is a low-budget enterprise, hardly befitting the duo's superstar status. However, Mantle and Maris had little time to star in a film between the end of the World Series in 1961 and the start of the regular season in 1962. *Safe at Home!* was therefore the perfect film for the two, because it could be partly filmed in Fort Lauderdale, the spring-training home of the Yankees in 1962.

The film involves Hutch Lawton, a Little League ballplayer in northern Florida, who is goaded into telling his teammates that his father is a good friend of Mickey Mantle's and Roger Maris's and that he can get the two to attend the following week's Little League banquet. When Hutch has to make good on his promise, he decides to contact Mantle and Maris personally by hiding in the back of a truck that is on its way to Fort Lauderdale. Once in Fort Lauderdale, Hutch finally meets Mantle and Maris, and after Hutch apologizes to his teammates for his lies and wrongful conduct, the Yankees invite the entire team to Fort Lauderdale for a day at spring training, providing the film with its expected happy ending.

In fact, there is very little that is unexpected in the film. Everyone knows that Hutch will make it to Fort Lauderdale on his own, even though he is only ten years old, that he will meet Mantle and Maris, and that matters will turn out satisfactorily. Even better for Hutch, the experience may lead Hutch's single father to reconsider his unmarried lifestyle and propose marriage to a woman that Hutch knows and adores.

The faults of *Safe at Home!* are patent, and yet despite all of them, the film is still entertaining. *Safe at Home!* is actually quite amusing in parts, in moments such as fish and fish spray falling on Hutch on his long trip to Fort Lauderdale in the back of a truck carrying fish; the odor Hutch then carries with him to the Yankees facility; Hutch sneaking into the Yankees' hotel just after the doorman brags that no kid has ever sneaked into the hotel before and none ever will while he is the doorman; and a gruff William Frawley, playing a Yankees coach, interacting with the very young Hutch, often mimicking his naïve expressions. There are no belly laughs in the film but there are lots of smiles.

Another reason for the success of the film is the location shooting, particularly the scenes at the Yankees training camp, which were shot on location in Fort Lauderdale Stadium, then the spring-training grounds of the Yankees. Indeed, it is the scenes at the Yankees training facilities that provide much of the film's enjoyment for baseball fans. Every year in the spring, thousands of fans trek to Florida and other warm areas to visit the spring-training camps of their favorite teams. Even though there are no games of importance being played at the time, the fans are happy just to see practices and an exhibition game or two. They savor the chance to be close to the players. In *Safe at Home!* the weather is great, the practice routines are fun to watch, the style of the ballplayers on the field is graceful, and the fans get up close and personal with the players. Spring training is a special time of the year for baseball; no other sport has anything like it. *Safe at Home!* recaptures the special feeling of spring training, even for a fan watching the film in a theater or on television.

Then there is the fun of seeing Hutch explore the Yankees facilities, including the Yankees locker rooms, giving baseball fans a look at the inner sanctum of the ballplayers. When no one is around, Hutch pretends he is playing baseball on the Yankees ball field, bringing back memories of Buster Keaton doing the same in *The Cameraman* (1928).

The strengths of the film outweigh its negatives, but there are several. In addition to the unoriginal story line, Mickey Mantle and Roger Maris, not unexpectedly, fail miserably at the acting game. Although the two play off one of the great character actors of the cinema, William Frawley, who was such a great asset to Joe E. Brown in *Alibi Ike* (1935), even William Frawley cannot help Mantle and Maris, both of whom deliver lines in an unconvincing fashion. Of the two, Mantle is the better performer, because he has much more natural personality than the placid Roger Maris, but it is not surprising that even Mantle did not have much of a screen career after this film. Whitey Ford, the great Yankees pitcher of the era, has a brief moment in the film, which is a nice surprise. Also, Yankees manager

Ralph Houk has several lines in the movie. He gives a surprisingly good performance for an amateur actor.

Safe at Home! contains William Frawley's last movie appearance in a career that stretched back to 1933 (for sound films) and consisted of over one hundred films. For baseball movie fans, Frawley is a significant performer. In an unscientific survey, it appears that Frawley appeared in more baseball movies than any other actor. He started with Joe E. Brown in *Alibi Ike* (1935), appeared in two films about baseball in Brooklyn, appeared with a fictional Babe Ruth, a cat, a real Mickey Mantle, and a real Roger Maris, and also ran a cinematic umpire's school. Frawley passed away in 1966.

It should be noted that *Safe at Home!* was not the only film appearance for Mickey Mantle and Roger Maris in 1962. The two of them, along with Yogi Berra, had a cameo role in *That Touch of Mink*, starring Cary Grant and Doris Day. The film was a typical Doris Day light romantic comedy of the era. Day's character is allowed to sit in the Yankees dugout one night and berate the home-plate umpire. As a result, all three Yankees stars are thrown out of the game.

The baseball scene in *That Touch of Mink* is very short, as contrasted with the emphasis on Mantle and Maris in *Safe at Home!* While most moviegoers, baseball fans or not, will probably have low expectations about *Safe at Home!*, those who decide to see it may be quite surprised to find out how entertaining the film actually is.

Chasing 3000 (2007)

It is one of the most famous photographs in all of Pittsburgh Pirates history. The moment occurred on September 30, 1972, at Three Rivers Stadium in Pittsburgh, Pennsylvania, during a game between the Pirates and the Mets. In the bottom of the fourth inning, Roberto Clemente, in his second at bat of the day, smacked a line drive to left-center field. The ball hit off the wall on one bounce. Clemente ended up on second base with a double. It was Clemente's 3,000th career hit, and as the scoreboard flashed on that day, "Roberto is now one of 11 players in major league history to get 3000 or more hits."

At that point, Clemente waved his cap to his fans. The photograph freezes that moment in time. Clemente stands at second base, his left foot on the bag and his right foot on the ground. Cle-

Chasing 3000 (2007). This is the statue of Roberto Clemente in Roberto Clemente State Park in the Bronx, New York City. It commemorates Clemente's pose on second base in Three Rivers Stadium in Pittsburgh, Pennsylvania, on September 30, 1972, after getting his 3,000th career hit. *(Emma Backer)*

mente is holding his cap high off his head to acknowledge the cheers of the fans. Some have described Clemente's bearing on that day as regal. Perhaps that is so. Clemente is not smiling in the picture; he is staring directly at his fans. It is not an expression of jubilation but rather one of accomplishment. The picture epitomizes the skills of the Great One, of course, but also his attitude and earnestness about baseball and life, as well as his respect for his fans and the game he had played for eighteen years in the major leagues. The image of Roberto Clemente in that photograph endures to this day.

On June 27, 2013, a life-size statue of Clemente, in bronze, as he stood on second base that day in 1972 in Pittsburgh, Pennsylvania, was unveiled in Roberto Clemente State Park in the Bronx, New York City, New York. Now the figure of the man will also endure forever.

Clemente's 3,000th hit was the last one he ever had in a regular-season Major League Baseball game. Manager Bill Virdon removed Clemente from the game before his next at bat. Virdon intended to take Clemente completely out of the lineup for the final three games of the season, so that the thirty-eight-year-old ballplayer would be rested for the upcoming playoffs. However, in the penultimate game of the season, Virdon sent Clemente to right field for one inning so that he could break Honus Wagner's record for most games played by a Pirate.

The famous photograph of Clemente on second base in Three Rivers Stadium has even more significance in retrospect. Roberto Clemente spent his entire major-league career with the Pittsburgh Pirates, winning two world championships (1960 and 1971), being voted Most Valuable Player in the National League in 1966 and Most Valuable Player for the 1971 World Series, and winning four National League batting titles and twelve Gold Glove Awards for his play as the Pirates right fielder. Although the Pirates lost to the Cincinnati Reds in the playoffs in 1972, Clemente intended to come back for at least one more season with the Pirates.

That was not to be. Clemente's life was struck tragically short on New Year's Eve in 1972, when a plane with Clemente on board crashed into the ocean just after leaving San Juan, Puerto Rico. Clemente was on a relief mission for earthquake victims in Nicaragua. His body was never found.

Chasing 3000 is about that last week in September 1972 when the baseball world was abuzz with the possibility that Clemente would achieve the 3,000-hit mark. Two teenage Pittsburgh natives, Mickey and Roger, are huge Roberto Clemente fans. They often talk about the way Clemente walked to the plate, his batting ritual, his basket catches in right field, and his spin throws to third base. Mickey is a fine athlete and a good baseball player; Roger has been stricken with muscular dystrophy and can only participate in baseball games vicariously. During 1972, Marilyn, the mother of the brothers, moves the family to California as a result of Roger's health problems. When Marilyn goes out of town on a business trip, Mickey, even though he only has his learner's permit, decides to drive the family car back to Pittsburgh to see, in person, Clemente reach the 3,000-hit plateau. Mickey reluctantly agrees to bring Roger along with him, not realizing that Roger, along with his other medical issues, is contending with a severe bout of bronchitis.

The bulk of *Chasing 3000* is taken up with the unlikely road trip of the two young brothers, the people they meet, and the trouble they encounter along the way. This section of the film varies substantially in quality, with some nice moments, such as when they meet a pretty young girl in the boxcar of a freight train, who is a runaway herself, and a farmer in Alabama who still has a ball he was given by Clemente many years before. Then there are other moments that strain credulity, such as a short-order cook who tries to kidnap the brothers to obtain a nonexistent reward and an intimidating motorcycle gang that helps the two brothers out. Coincidences abound; people's motivations are unconvincing. At times, *Chasing 3000* seems more like a variation on films such as *It's a Mad, Mad, Mad, Mad World* (1963) than anything else.

However, *Chasing 3000* is far different from chase comedy films that have been popular from time to time, primarily because *Chasing 3000* is a personal story about the relationship of two brothers, who have always been close but in their journey learn about the strengths and limitations of each other, thereby becoming even closer. If Mickey seems unlikable throughout much of the movie, he does grow into the person who takes care of his brother when he becomes sick, carries him from place to place when he cannot walk, and is unwilling to abandon him, even when he has the chance to see the big game without his brother. Roger, who is initially reluctant to go on the trip, finally becomes more enthusiastic about it than his brother. Recognizing that he is unlikely to live long past his teenage years, Roger understands that the cross-country trip may be the last, or perhaps only, great adventure of his life.

Chasing 3000 is purportedly based upon a true story, but while screenwriter Bill Mikita and his younger brother, Stephen, who is afflicted with muscular dystrophy, were great Pirates fans, they grew up in Steubenville, Ohio, not Pittsburgh, Pennsylvania, although Steubenville is only about thirty-nine miles from Pittsburgh. The brothers never traveled cross-country to see a Pirates game. However, while fictional, the film is set in the context of true events, thereby making it difficult for the filmmakers to create tension for the viewers. Most of the audience for *Chasing 3000* will know, well in advance of the ending, that Roberto Clemente did reach his goal of 3,000 hits that week. What does create interest, however, is the question of whether or not Mickey and Roger will actually see the event in person.

According to Mickey, when the two brothers set out on their journey, Clemente already has 2,997 hits. Then, while the brothers are on their cross-country journey and the Pirates are still in Philadelphia, Clemente hits his 2,999th. Mickey and Roger worry that Clemente could get his 3,000th before the team and the brothers get back to Pittsburgh. All seems lost until Mickey and Roger learn that manager Bill Virdon removed Clemente from the lineup once he hit number 2,999, so that Clemente could try to get his 3,000th hit before a home crowd in Three Rivers Stadium in Pittsburgh. The brothers still have a chance.

Mickey and Roger push on, but they are waylaid in Steubenville when Roger must go to a hospital. That night, the Pirates are back in Pittsburgh, and the brothers can only witness the game on television from Roger's hospital room. There they witness a play that is controversial to this day. In the first inning, Clemente hit a ball off pitcher Tom Seaver of the Mets that bounded high above Seaver and then skipped off the glove of second baseman Ken Boswell. Clemente reached first safely and the scoreboard flashed an "H" for hit. People in the stands and those watching on television believed that Clemente had reached 3,000 hits. However, the official scorekeeper ruled it an error on the second baseman, the scoreboard was corrected, and Clemente still had only 2,999 hits. Clemente had no other hits that day. (The footage actually shown in the film is of a different play, as footage of the real error on that day was unavailable.)

Nevertheless, Mickey and Roger believe that Clemente got his 3,000th hit and while excited for the Pirates right fielder, they also believe they missed the chance to see the event in person. It is only by accident that they learn what actually happened, resulting in the brothers making it to Three Rivers Stadium the next day to see their hero reach the 3,000-hit plateau. By incorporating a real-life incident into the film, the controversy on September 29, 1972, the filmmakers cleverly added some needed suspense to the film.

It may be that Pittsburghers will enjoy *Chasing 3000* more than other baseball fans. There are complimentary expressions about Pittsburgh throughout the film, shots of interesting parts of Pittsburgh to admire, including the downtown area and the new PNC Park, and Pittsburgh references, such as Isaly's chipped-ham sandwiches, Clark candy bars, and a hot-dog shop affectionately referred to as the "Dirty O." The film avoids an embarrassing fact for Pittsburgh, that there were only 13,117 people in attendance on the historic occasion of Clemente's double, and also avoids the undeniable fact that before his death, Clemente was unappreciated by a number of fans in Pittsburgh. *Chasing 3000* only emphasizes the positives of the city while celebrating the legend that Clemente has become.

An older Mickey tells the story of *Chasing 3000* in a flashback. At the beginning of the film, Mickey is driving his two children to Roberto Clemente Day in Pittsburgh, when a policeman stops Mickey for speeding. Mickey and the policeman start talking about their memories of Clemente, leading the policeman to crumple the ticket he was writing for Mickey. The policeman also appears to be tearing up from his memories of Clemente. As Mickey pulls away, Mickey's young son asks, "Dad, was he crying?" Mickey's two children do not understand why the Pittsburgh policeman is crying; perhaps baseball fans around the country will not understand. Pittsburgh Pirates fans, however, who remember how well Clemente played and how short he lived, do understand.

Everyone's Hero (2006)

There have been cartoons about baseball from the beginning of cinema's silent era, into the early days of the sound era, and continuing to the present day. Whether starring Felix the Cat, Popeye, Woody Woodpecker, Bugs Bunny, or other famous or non-famous characters, these cartoons were always short, usually running no more than ten minutes.

Everyone's Hero is different. It is a full-length cartoon, running almost ninety minutes. It employs computer-generated animation, which gives the film a 3-D effect, a much different look than that of earlier baseball cartoons.

Everyone's Hero tells the story of Yankee Irving, obviously a Yankees fan but whose closest association with baseball is his father, who works as a janitor at Yankee Stadium. One night during the ongoing World Series between the Yankees and the Cubs, Yankee brings dinner to his father while his father is working at a deserted Yankee Stadium. Yankee's father then gives Yankee the opportunity to look around the Yankees locker room, including viewing Babe Ruth's famous bat that the Babe has named "Darlin'." Many people, including Napoleon Cross, the owner of the Cubs, believe that Darlin' is the secret to Ruth's hitting success.

While Yankee is in the locker room, the bat is stolen by Lefty Maginnis, a pitcher for the Chicago Cubs, at the direction of Napoleon Cross. As a result of the theft, Yankee's father loses his job. Believing that the situation is partly his fault, Yankee sets off to retrieve the bat. Yankee is accompanied on his road adventure by a talking baseball named Screwie and, for much of his trip, the talking bat named Darlin'.

Everyone's Hero is a family movie, oriented to young children. The film has slapstick humor, a few good jokes, a talking baseball, a talking bat, a child hero, and a happy ending. The villain, Napoleon Cross, is overly villainous; his assistant in crime, Lefty Maginnis, is overly clumsy. What is not to enjoy, at least for children?

For adults, the movie is tougher going, because of its unexceptional plot, several anachronisms, and the hard-to-believe ending. Nevertheless, there is also much for grown-ups to like in the movie. Rob Reiner provides the voice of Screwie, and Whoopi Goldberg provides the voice of Darlin'. They are very funny at times, particularly when they argue with each other or make sarcastic comments.

Also, some of the drawings of the settings in the cartoon are appealing, such as the primitive sandlot on which the kids play early in the film, with a broken jalopy in the outfield; Penn Station in New York, with its high pillars outside, old-fashioned yellow cabs on the street, and a high glass roof on the inside; the noirish streets of the Bronx; and the streets of Chicago at nighttime bathed in lights. The cartoon image of Babe Ruth is spot-on, as it does not try to caricature him but rather tries to create a reasonable replica of his visage. There is clever animated newsreel footage, made to look grainy just like the newsreel footage of yesteryear.

Of course, *Everyone's Hero* is hardly accurate on its baseball facts. The movie appears to be set in 1932, a year in which the Yankees swept the Cubs, 4–0, in the World Series. In the film, the Yankees also win that World Series but only after a come-from-behind victory in the seventh game. The drawing of Yankee Stadium early in the movie shows a completely enclosed ballpark with consistent seating creating a half-circle behind the outfield, when, in fact, the outfield of Yankee Stadium never looked like that in the 1930s. Similar errors are made in the drawings of Wrigley Field, from its incorrect outfield seats to the misplacement of the support beams in the infield stands. Obviously, many baseball films are shot in locations other than the true settings of the story, but how hard would it to have been to draw accurate representations of two iconic ballparks for a cartoon?

Somewhat surprisingly, *Everyone's Hero* may have been inspired by a true event, although it happened to Joe DiMaggio in 1941, not to Babe Ruth in 1932. In 1941, Joe DiMaggio set the record (56) for most consecutive games with a hit, breaking the previous records of George Sisler (41, then the modern record) and Wee Willie Keeler (44, then the all-time record). During the streak, an unusual incident occurred. On June 29, 1941, between games of a double-header in Washington, D.C., DiMaggio's favorite bat, "Betsy Ann," went missing, even though a batboy had been ordered to guard the bat rack. DiMaggio had to borrow other bats for the second game, making outs in his first three at bats before finally getting a hit after borrowing a bat from Tommy Henrich. The bat was actually one that DiMaggio had lent to Henrich earlier in the month. DiMaggio broke George Sisler's record that day with that hit off Henrich's bat.

About a week later, Betsy Ann was returned to DiMaggio by an unknown courier in a plain brown envelope. It turns out that the bat was stolen in Washington by a small-time hood who lived in Newark, New Jersey. While there are many different versions of how Betsy Ann got back to DiMaggio, the most important aspect of this story is that DiMaggio did keep his streak alive while Betsy Ann was gone. So perhaps Babe Ruth is right in *Everyone's Hero*, when he tells Yankee Irving, "It's not really the bat; it's the batter."

Baseball films, even cartoons, need a great championship game at the end of the film for it to be a success. *Everyone's Hero* meets that challenge, at least for kids. Yankee finally delivers Darlin' to the Babe in the ninth inning of the seventh game of the World Series in Wrigley Field in Chicago, but Babe has already struck out that inning. With two men out, the Yankees need a batter, and whom do they call on—none other than Yankee Irving. Yankee takes the first two pitches down the middle for called strikes, but then he remembers all that he has learned about baseball on his road trip, from Screwie, Darlin', a team of Negro League players, and the daughter of a Negro League player. Yankee swings at the next pitch and hits the ball! Unfortunately, it is a high pop-up in the infield. Fortunately, the Cubs let it drop, and then, with skills reminiscent of the Bad News Bears, the Cubs throw the ball all around the infield, resulting in Yankee hitting an inside-the-infield home run, starting a rally that leads the team to victory.

Of course, a film that allows a youngster to pinch-hit in the seventh game of the World Series and then hit a home run does not make a lot of sense, but then *Everyone's Hero* does include a talking ball and talking bat, so who can complain? For baseball fans, it seems more important to notice that even though the Yankees have a manager during the seventh game of the World Series, it is Babe Ruth who decides to pinch-hit young Irving, which somehow turns out to be a good mana-

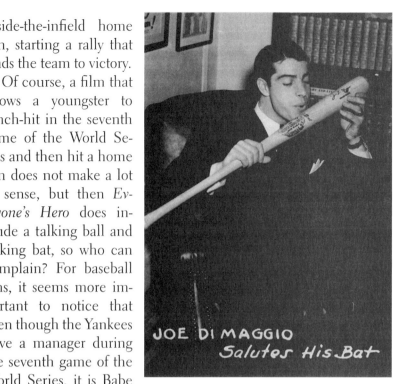

Joe DiMaggio in 1941 kissing his bat, perhaps the bat that may have been the inspiration for the story line of *Everyone's Hero* (2006). *(Library of Congress, LC-DIG-ppmsca-18794)*

gerial decision. Thus, *Everyone's Hero* gives Babe Ruth the chance to finally manage the Yankees, something he always wanted to do in real life but was never given the chance.

7

BASEBALL ROMANCES

Fever Pitch (2005)

Most baseball films are about the players, with the fans incidental participants in the story. *Fever Pitch* is different, with the main story line being about the fans and, in particular, some of those crazy, obsessive Red Sox fans from Boston. The Boston Red Sox were a good choice for the subject matter of the film because if a film is going to be about a fan's obsession with a sports team, that obsession should be about a losing team (to provide some empathy for the characters and some extra excitement if the team finally wins), and the Boston Red Sox surely fit that description, at least until 2004. Who knew while *Fever Pitch* was being filmed during 2004 that the Boston Red Sox would pull off one of the biggest surprises ever in baseball, winning their first World Series in eighty-six years and providing a great finish for the film?

Even though baseball is the backdrop for the film, *Fever Pitch* is primarily a love story. It tells the tale of schoolteacher Ben Wrightman and his pursuit of businesswoman Lindsey Meeks. Opposites do seem to attract, and after some early difficulties, the two get together. Ben, however, has one significant weakness that causes problems with women. Ben is a die-hard, obsessive Boston Red Sox fan. Ben first went to a game at the age of seven with his uncle Carl and was immediately hooked. When Uncle Carl died several years ago, Ben inherited his two season tickets. Ben never misses a home game; he goes every year to spring training in Florida. Lindsey, who is not a baseball fan, nevertheless attends many Red Sox games with Ben in an attempt to gain an interest in Ben's personal pastime.

However, when Ben refuses to go with Lindsey to Paris and when Ben becomes upset after going to a party with Lindsey, all caused by Boston Red Sox games, there is a strain in their relationship. They break up. Ben, in order to prove his love for Lindsey, then decides to sell his season tickets. Lindsey is upset about Ben's decision, and during a Red Sox–Yankees playoff game, Lindsey runs out onto the field and convinces Ben not to take that drastic step. The two reconcile and finally marry, making 2004 a banner year for Ben, since the Red Sox win the World Series that year with Ben and Lindsey in attendance at all of the World Series games.

The title of *Fever Pitch* is based upon a common expression that means a high level of excitement among a group of people, such as in the phrase "The excitement in Boston about the upcoming series between the Boston Red Sox and the New York Yankees has reached a fever pitch." In the book *Fever Pitch* by Nick Hornby, the credited source material for the 2005 baseball film, the word "pitch" has a double meaning. The book is about English football (soccer), and the term "pitch" in the title also refers to the playing field for soccer. When the book was adapted into the American film, *Fever Pitch*, the title remained the same even though the story was changed from soccer to baseball. Obviously, the word "pitch" also has a special meaning in baseball and so the title of the film works for both sports.

Fever Pitch has an abundance of baseball references that are interesting to all baseball fans, not just those from Boston. The overriding one is the Curse of the Bambino, the Bostonian explanation for the failure of the Red Sox to win the World Series since 1918. Babe Ruth, of course, originally played for the Red Sox and pitched for them in the 1918 World Series. Ruth was sold to the Yankees after the 1919 season, sparking the Yankees into becoming the greatest baseball team of all time and causing, or so it is said in Boston, the World Series drought for the Red Sox. In *Fever Pitch*, Ben and the adjoining season ticket holders relate some of the manifestations of the Curse to Lindsey. They include, according to these fans, the 1978 season where the Red Sox led the Yankees by fourteen games on July 19, lost the lead, and then lost a one-game playoff when Bucky Dent, the shortstop of the Yankees, hit a pop fly, three-run homer over Fenway Park's short left field wall known as the Green Monster; the 1986 World Series, which the Red Sox lost after leading the New York Mets, three games to two, and also leading in the tenth inning of the sixth game, 5–3, when the Mets came from behind and scored the winning run on a ground-ball error by Bill Buckner; and the 2003 American League Championship Series, with the Red

Sox leading the Yankees, 5–2, in the eighth inning of the final game, when manager Grady Little left pitcher Pedro Martinez in the game for a few batters too many, allowing a Yankees rally that led to a Yankees win in that series.

Of course, if there truly was a Curse of the Bambino, the 2004 season is hard to explain. On August 15, 2004, the Red Sox were ten and a half games behind the first-place Yankees and not playing very well. Then, in a little over three weeks, the Red Sox were only two and a half games behind. Although the Red Sox were unable to overcome the Yankees and win the division, they made it to the playoffs as a wild card team. In their first series, they swept the Anaheim Angels, but in the championship series with the Yankees, they lost the first three games. No team in Major League Baseball history had ever come back from a three-game deficit in a postseason series. Not only that, the Red Sox were behind, 4–3, in the bottom of the ninth inning of the fourth game. Yet the Red Sox came back to win that game in extra innings, win the next three playoff games against the Yankees, and defeat the St. Louis Cardinals, four games to none, in the World Series. To which legendary figure do the Boston fans attribute this type of luck?

With its extensive use of archive footage as a background to the story, *Fever Pitch* returns to the storytelling style of baseball films from the 1930s and 1940s. There is, however, a significant difference. In *Fever Pitch*, the archive footage comes from television, not newsreels. Thus, the images are cleaner (and in color) and also contain close shots of the action, as contrasted with newsreel footage from the earlier decades of baseball that often used just one camera angle high above the field. Also, at the climax of *Fever Pitch*, the archive footage, which only comes from the 2004 season, is telling a separate story—the Red Sox world-championship season of 2004. Since the actors are, for the most part, actually sitting in Fenway Park for the games, the archive footage easily blends with the new footage, making it seem as if all of the footage in the film is new.

Fever Pitch is not the first cinematic love story that is set in the world of baseball. An obvious film of contrast is *For Love of the Game*, a disappointing movie from 1999 that stars Kevin Costner and Kelly Preston. In *For Love of the Game*, the love story is intrusive to the baseball story and has little interest on its own. In *Fever Pitch*, the love story complements the baseball story and the two are integrated, with the problems between Lindsey and Ben arising primarily as a result of baseball and with the love story climaxing at the same time as, and in the setting of, the baseball story. Also, the love story in *Fever Pitch* is told with a genuine sense of humor, making Jimmy Fallon and Drew Barrymore into much more likable performers than Kevin Costner and Kelly Preston.

Over the years, there have been several movies about baseball that have also been love stories. Although some of them are pretty good, if baseball fans have time to view only one, *Fever Pitch* is the film they should choose.

For Love of the Game (1999)

Kevin Costner starred in three baseball films in the 1980s and 1990s, *Bull Durham* (1988), *Field of Dreams* (1989), and then a decade later, *For Love of the Game*. The first two films are among the best baseball films ever made. *For Love of the Game*, based on a short novel with the same title written by Michael Shaara, is clearly the weakest of the three.

There are two separate story lines in *For Love of the Game*. One involves the summer game, with Billy Chapel of the Detroit Tigers pitching against the New York Yankees on the next-to-last day of the season. The Tigers are long out of the pennant race, but the game is important to the Yankees, who are in a battle for first place with the Boston Red Sox. Just before the game, the owner of the Tigers tells Billy that he has sold the team to a group of investors and that the new owners intend to trade Billy to the Giants at the end of the season. It is now up to Billy, a twenty-year veteran of the Tigers and a future Hall of Famer, to decide whether he wants to retire at the end of the season. Recognizing that this may be his last major-league game ever, Billy has an added incentive to pitch well that day, and despite some physical handicaps, he throws a perfect game against the Yankees.

It is somewhat incredible that a forty-year-old ballplayer is still good enough to pitch a perfect game, especially against one of the best teams in baseball and on the road. What makes the feat even more amazing is that Billy has trouble concentrating on the game that day. He spends most of the afternoon on the mound daydreaming about his five-year relationship with his girlfriend, Jane, the ups and downs of their love affair, and whether or not Billy can really commit to her. This is the other story line of the film, shown mostly in flashbacks, and it takes up more than half of the running time of the movie. It is a rare baseball film that is, in reality, a chick flick, but *For Love of the Game* clearly fits that description.

The baseball scenes in *For Love of the Game* are wonderfully filmed. They were shot at Yankee Stadium in New York City, and although

Billy Chapel (Kevin Costner) on the mound at Yankee Stadium, pitching for the Detroit Tigers, in *For Love of the Game* (1999).

there were undoubtedly some special effects employed in the filming of the game, they are invisible on the screen. The Tigers and the Yankees legitimately appear to be playing in front of a huge crowd in the real House That Ruth Built. Kevin Costner is convincing as a major-league pitcher, and if there was a double used for some of his pitches to the plate, that trick is invisible also. In addition, there is a unique baseball aspect to the film (and one that comes from Shaara's novel), as the viewer gets into the mind of Billy as he pitches to each batter, tunes out the noise and jeers from the crowd, comments on the batters as he pitches to them, decides on the type of pitch to throw, and on one occasion, decides to deliberately knock down a batter who crowds the plate. Billy's thought processes are interesting and provide a revealing slant on an important aspect of the game.

Some of the baseball scenes in *For Love of the Game* are shown as if the game were on television, with many of the shots of the batters on the pretend television broadcast of the game, coming from behind the pitcher and focusing on the batter and the catcher. The film also uses instant replays and television commentary from the pretend broadcast of the game. These types of shots are mixed in with a variety of other views of the action, adding to the reality of the game. The only things that seem amiss in the baseball scenes are the enhanced sound effects to create the illusion of speed in Billy's pitches.

For Love of the Game manages to create some legitimate tension at the end of the ball game. Will Billy actually be able to throw a perfect game or will he fall just short of that lofty goal? As the game reaches the late innings, Billy seems to be running out of steam and his shoulder appears to be injured. In the last couple of innings, the perfect game is saved by some slick plays in the infield; some hard hit balls landing in foul territory; an outfielder robbing a Yankees player of a home run, catching a ball just above the fence; and even Billy making a great defensive play. Then there is a clever twist at the end as the Yankees send in Ken Strout, a young player who has just been called up to the big leagues, who has his first major-league at bat with two outs in the ninth inning. Strout is a former batboy of Billy's and the son of a former teammate of Billy's. It would be ironic if Strout got the first hit off of Billy, breaking up the perfect game. For a second it looks like Strout will, but his high chopper is cleanly fielded by the shortstop and the throw to first base clearly beats the runner for the last out of the game.

While hardly a theme of *For Love of the Game*, the film does touch on some of the disappointing aspects of the modern game. The owner of the Tigers, Mr. Wheeler, laments to Billy that everything has changed in baseball, including the players, the fans, TV rights, and arbitration. He says, "It isn't the same; the game stinks." In a flashback, Billy's best friend on the Detroit Tigers, Davis Birch, leaves the Tigers to join the Yankees for more money, to the disappointment of Billy, who asks him, "How much money do we have to make?" Billy, however, is truly unfazed by the changes in the economics of the game. He tells the owner, "The game doesn't stink, Mr. Wheeler; it's a great game." This dialogue relates to the title of the film, as Billy does not play for the money. He plays for the love of the game.

As to the believability of a forty-year-old player pitching a perfect game on the road against one of the best teams in baseball, that is not unprecedented in baseball history, although it did not occur until after the release of this film. On May 18, 2004, Randy Johnson, at the age of forty, threw a perfect game against the Atlanta Braves at Turner Field in Atlanta, with the Arizona Diamondbacks beating the Braves, 2–0. The Atlanta Braves was one of the best teams in baseball that year, winning ninety-six games and becoming the Eastern Division champions of the National League. Presumably, Randy Johnson was not daydreaming about his love life while throwing his perfect game.

The play-by-play announcer in the pretend broadcast in the film is Vin Scully, one of the most recognizable voices in the history of baseball broadcasting. Vin Scully had been broadcasting Dodgers baseball games since 1950, first with the Dodgers in Brooklyn and then for many years in their new home in Los Angeles. Scully was on hand and called many famous baseball events, including Don Larsen's perfect game in Game 5 of the 1956 World Series.

In the film, Vin Scully mentions calling Don Larsen's perfect game over forty years before and then says, "I never thought I would be able to see another one." That is a puzzling statement, because Scully actually called two other perfect games — Sandy Koufax's perfect game on September 9, 1965 (the Dodgers beat the Cubs, 1–0, in Dodger Stadium), and Dennis Martinez's perfect game against the Dodgers on July 28, 1991 (the Montreal Expos beat the Dodgers, 2–0 in Dodger Stadium). If one includes Billy Chapel's perfect game against the Yankees, Scully called four perfect games in his storied broadcast career, an amazing total even though only three of them are real.

While the baseball aspects of *For Love of the Game* are fine, the love story is disappointing, mundane, and intrusive. *For Love of the Game* is unique for a sports film, as it covers just one game in the life of its star player. That may not have been enough to fill the running time of a feature film, but the insertion of the love story is not helpful (and results in the film running to an inordinate length, in excess of two hours and fifteen minutes, making the love story all the more tedious). If baseball fans can somehow ignore the remainder of the film, the story of Billy's last game in the major leagues is worth a view, but overall, the film is severely flawed. Put simply, while the baseball scenes are outstanding, the rest of the story sinks the film. If someone wants to see Kevin Costner in a baseball film, they should try *Bull Durham* or *Field of Dreams* before watching *For Love of the Game*.

It Happened in Flatbush (1942)

It Happened in Flatbush is set in the early 1940s in Brooklyn, New York, described in the opening frames of the film as a strange island just off the eastern coast of the United States. While the film is clearly about the Brooklyn Dodgers, the name "Dodgers" is not written on any of the uniforms. The team's name is never mentioned in the film, and there are no real-life Dodgers appearing in the movie.

As *It Happened in Flatbush* commences, that unnamed baseball club from Brooklyn has just lost its manager in the middle of the season. The owner of the team, Mrs. "Mac" McAvoy, decides to bring back a former Brooklyn player, Frank Maguire, as the team's new manager. Maguire was run out of town about seven years earlier as a result of a fielding error he made, an error that cost the team the pennant. Maguire agrees to take the job, but when Mac dies shortly thereafter, Maguire must convince the heirs of the team, who are not baseball fans, to keep the team and invest in new players. Maguire accomplishes this task by romancing pretty Kathryn Baker, now a majority owner of the team, and trying to convince her that baseball is a worthwhile investment.

While a romance, *It Happened in Flatbush* is actually more fantasy than fact, seeming to take place outside the real world. Despite the fact that World War II was then ongoing, all of the front-page newspaper headlines are about the baseball team. When the team returns from a successful road trip, Brooklyn schools close and there is a parade down the main street of the Borough. At one point, an upset fan comes down from the stands and slugs an umpire over a close call. The very adult Maguire lives with his mother and father in Brooklyn. All of this is set up with the whimsical opening frames of the movie: "This story is fictional—but anything might happen—and usually does."

Non-baseball fans may find some interest in *It Happened in Flatbush*. The romance between Maguire and Kathryn has some appeal, particularly in Maguire's bold advances to Kathryn, a wealthy sophisticate who is not used to such a direct approach. Unfortunately, the tension between sophisticated and unsophisticated is not well developed in the film, leaving the evening Maguire unwittingly stood Baker up on a date as the main strain between the two, hardly the weighty matter of a feature film.

The film is funny in spots, such as when Mac goes into the players' locker room of a minor-league team to chase down Maguire, sending the half-dressed players into a tizzy; a friendly dispute between neighbors over missing milk or pop bottles worth 2¢ a piece; one of the owners asking why pitchers cannot bat well and Maguire not having a good answer; and Maguire's mother hitting a fan on the head at a game, when the fan criticizes one of the players.

For baseball fans, however, *It Happened in Flatbush* is a loser. The direction of the baseball scenes by Ray McCarey is aggravating. While there is plenty of second-unit footage of Ebbets Field inserted into the movie, the "live" baseball action was filmed elsewhere, at a field that was hardly a look-alike for Ebbets Field. Ebbets Field had such a distinctive outfield, with the signs on the walls, that the true outfield where the game action was shot could not be shown in the movie, or the audience would have discovered the deception. Thus, all of the action in the film occurs in the infield, primarily pitching, catching, a few swings, a few grounders, and some base runners. Relief pitchers allegedly come out of the bullpens, but there are no bullpens ever shown. It is as if Brooklyn has only six players on the field. This style of filmmaking dissipates any suspense the baseball scenes might otherwise have had.

Then there is the moment in the film when, for reasons hard to understand, the Brooklyn players sign a petition requesting that Maguire be relieved of his duties as manager. While this is an unbelievable moment in a not very believable film, it may have actually been inspired by a true incident. Ossie Vitt, the manager of the Cleveland Indians from 1938 to 1940, was an acerbic coach, often clashing with his players and criticizing them for their laziness. The players despised him. Matters came to a head in June 1940, when the players had had enough. They petitioned the Indians owner to have Vitt removed as manager because of his insincerity, ridiculing of players, and caustic criticism. When the story came out, the Cleveland team became known as the "Cleveland Crybabies."

When Maguire learns of the petition against him in *It Happened in Flatbush*, he also calls his team "crybabies," hearkening back to the Cleveland situation from a few years before. Nevertheless, the whole situation makes little sense in the movie. Under Maguire's brief stint as manager, the Brooklyn team has gone from the cellar to just one game away from winning the pennant. Unlike Vitt, Maguire does not have a bad history with the team. Most of the players seem to like him. The catalyst for the petition, two straight losses, is not sufficient reason to cause such a strange reaction in the team. Whether inspired by a real event or not, it is totally unbelievable in the movie, just an obvious attempt to create a climax for the film because the final baseball game was not believed to be sufficiently interesting on its own by the filmmakers.

While *Whistling in Brooklyn* (1943) and *Roogie's Bump* (1954) are not very good films either, they do contain "live" action sequences shot on location at Ebbets Field and some real Brooklyn Dodgers of their respective decades, thus providing baseball fans with some special joys. There is none of that in *It Happened in Flatbush*. Indeed, amid all the fantasy, comedy, and romance, there is little that baseball fans can take from the film, except perhaps the realization that while Maguire may be a good manager, the Brooklyn team does not improve until the owners spend lots of money on better ballplayers. That is a harsh dose of baseball reality that is applicable to all generations of the game.

Ladies' Day (1943)

There is a subset of baseball movies that promotes a strange theory on how best to play the game. According to *The Winning Team* (1952), Grover Cleveland Alexander was unable to pitch well late in his career unless his wife, Aimee, was in the stands. In *The Slugger's Wife* (1985), home-run hitter Darryl Palmer can no longer smack the long ball when his wife, Debby, refuses to attend his games. In *They Learned About Women* (1930), pitcher Jack Glennon has two bad outings in the World Series, but once he learns that his girlfriend, Mary, still loves him and will marry him, his pitching suddenly improves. Other than movie fans, who knew that love is such an important factor in playing the summer game?

Ladies' Day fits squarely within that subgenre of baseball movies.

The premise of the film is that Sox pitcher Wacky Waters (Eddie Albert) does not pitch well whenever he falls in love. Unfortunately for Waters's pitching skills, Waters is young and handsome and falls in love on a regular basis. This situation obviously causes much consternation in the team's manager, but it also worries the wives of the other players, who have their sights set on the additional cash each will receive if the Sox can win the championship that season.

Early on in *Ladies' Day*, Wacky meets actress Pepita Zorita (Lupe Vélez) when she is selling war bonds at the ballpark prior to a Sox game. Wacky and Pepita immediately fall in love, and not unexpectedly, Wacky can no longer throw the ball over the plate. So, as the Sox enter the Big Series, three of the wives conspire to keep Wacky and Pepita apart, including kidnapping Pepita and hiding her in a hotel room for several days, and later, once she escapes, tricking her into believing that she has an infectious disease. These story arcs are not very funny on paper, and they are even less funny when seen on the screen. Also, which one of the writers thought that having one of the wives hit Pepita over the head with a baseball bat (on two occasions) would be funny? Tastes in comedy change over time, and *Ladies' Day* seems dated from the perspective of more than seventy years after its release, but it is still hard to believe that anyone thought this stuff was funny back in 1943.

As to the baseball in *Ladies' Day*, there is not much of it, and what little is shown is badly filmed, consisting mainly of tight shots of the pitcher, batters swinging in front of projection screens, and long shots of the field, which are either stock footage or second-unit footage, with the viewer unable to see the stars of the movie. As to the play in the field, the batters display some of the worst swings ever shown in the movies, often lunging at balls (and hitting home runs when doing so). The pitcher often starts to throw his pitches before the catcher is fully down in his crouch.

Much like baseball movies from any era, the Sox games are narrated by a radio announcer who, in giving the play-by-play to his fictional radio audience is actually describing the events in each game for the movie audience. In most films, this play-by-play announcer contributes to the excitement of the game. In *Ladies' Day*, however, the announcer is one of the least exciting baseball announcers in the entire history of the game. At one point when a Sox player hits a long

Players, their wives, and the manager look on as Wacky Walters (Eddie Albert) talks on the phone to his wife, Pepita Zorita, in *Ladies' Day* (1943). The players in the back, from left to right, are Spike (Eddie Dew) and Marty (Jack Briggs). The manager on the far right, Dan Hannigan, is played by Cliff Clark. The three wives in the front, from left to right, are Kitty (Iris Adrian), Joan (Joan Barclay), and Hazel (Patsy Kelly). The others are unidentified.

ball, the announcer says without emotion, "That looks like a home run." When the ball goes foul, the announcer never says anything about it. Later, the wives listen to a game on the radio, and they hear the announcer say without emotion, "Here's the pitch. It's a home run and the ball game is all tied up." When Wacky wins the series for his team with a walk-off home run, the announcer can be barely bothered to say, "And the Sox win the 1941 Big Series, ladies and gentlemen, in one of the most exciting finishes in the history of the game." The announcer says that line as if he is reading his grocery list.

What happened to great home-run calls in baseball? Luckily, that same announcer was not around for the final 1951 National League playoff game between the Giants and the Dodgers, which ended with Bobby Thomson's walk-off home run, or fans would never have heard, in one of the most famous and exciting baseball calls of all time (by Russ Hodges on the radio), "The Giants win the pennant! The Giants win the pennant! The Giants win the pennant! The Giants win the pennant." If the *Ladies' Day* announcer were calling the game on that day, he would have made that momentous baseball event seem like the mundane.

Although *Ladies' Day* is far from awful, it is very hard to identify many positives for the film. The movie was designed as a star vehicle for Lupe Vélez, who plays Pepita in the movie. Vélez was a minor star of the day, perhaps best known for the seven-film Mexican Spitfire series that began in 1940, but the purported charms of Vélez are lost on a modern audience. There are a few good lines in the film, generally concerning a bank that has recently purchased the Sox and is loath to spend any money. The players' wives must now pay for their tickets when they want to attend Sox games, and Updyke, the bank's representative, played by Jerome Cowan in an unusual comedy role for him, complains about the laundry bill when the players dirty their uniforms, even suggesting that perhaps the players should no longer slide into bases when there is a close play.

Ladies' Day was produced at RKO, a major studio, but the film is minor, sometimes seeming more like a B film than an A production. The baseball scenes are ordinary. The film is also severely dated. *Ladies' Day* has little interest for baseball fans.

The Slugger's Wife (1985)

Neil Simon wrote many famous Broadway hits, including *The Odd Couple* (1965), *Sweet Charity* (1966), *The Sunshine Boys* (1972), and *Brighton Beach Memoirs* (1983). Many of his Broadways shows were then adapted into movies. Simon also wrote several original screenplays, including *The Slugger's Wife*. In fact, the film was promoted as "Neil Simon's *The Slugger's Wife*," which is how the title card for the movie reads on the screen. Neil Simon was so famous and successful in his writing career that his name alone was enough to bring large audiences to both theaters and the cinema. Unfortunately, if people came to see *The Slugger's Wife* based upon Neil Simon's reputation, they were sorely disappointed. To put it succinctly, *The Slugger's Wife* is one of the worst baseball movies ever made.

Darryl Palmer is a mediocre, self-centered Atlanta Braves ballplayer, who falls in love with a pretty young singer, Debby Huston. In order to get his first date with Debby, Palmer promises to hit two home runs in the Braves' next game, besting Babe Ruth's perhaps apocryphal story of promising to hit a home run in the World Series for young Johnny Sylvester. As Debby watches from the stands, Palmer accomplishes the task. From that point forward, Palmer's career takes off and he suddenly starts hitting home run after home run. Darryl and Debby marry, and with Debby in attendance at his games, Darryl looks like he could break the all-time season-home-run record, besting Roger Maris's mark of sixty-one home runs in 1961. Unfortunately for Darryl, Debby wants to pursue her singing career, and she decides to leave Darryl. At that point, Darryl's hitting falls off, putting the home-run record and the Braves' playoff hopes in disarray.

Darryl Palmer, as played by Michael O'Keefe, and Debby Palmer, as played by Rebecca De Mornay, are two of the least likable characters in the long history of romance films. Darryl is officious and overbearing, having little interest in Debby's hopes and dreams, only thinking of himself. Debby is also somewhat self-centered, abandoning Darryl at an important time in his career for her own self-interest. The film never convincingly explains why Debby married Darryl, and except for the fact that they repeatedly say they love each other, there is nothing in the film that convinces the audience that they really do. Since the audience has no interest in the characters, the audience never really cares whether or not the two will ever get together again.

For a Neil Simon comedy, it is surprising to find that there are no real laughs in the movie. Most of the "comedy" scenes are embarrassing for the audience, such as when the manager tells his other players to make sure that Darryl gets laid that night and they make an effort to do so, or when another young lady who resembles Debby impersonates Debby when Darryl is lying in a hospital bed, trying to convince Darryl that Debby still loves him.

Given how bad the rest of the film is, it would be nice if *The Slugger's Wife* were accurate in some of its baseball moments. In one important instance, at least, it is not. In the early scene in the movie where Darryl promises to hit those two home runs for Debby, the opposing pitcher is Mark Fidrych, also known as "The Bird." Fidrych plays for the Houston Astros in the film, a National League team, because Palmer plays for the Atlanta Braves, also a National

League team. Fidrych became a sensation in his rookie year with Detroit in 1976, where he led the major leagues in ERA among all pitchers and became Rookie of the Year in the American League. People flocked to his games that year because of his pitching skills and because of his antics on the mound, including repairing cleat marks on the mound, talking to himself, and talking to the ball.

Injuries shortened Fidrych's career, and he was out of baseball by the end of 1980. Fidrych played his entire career in Detroit, so why is he playing for the Houston Astros in the film? By 1985, the year that *The Slugger's Wife* was released, Fidrych was a forgotten figure in baseball. None of his famous mound behaviors are shown in the movie. Why include him in the film? This whole Fidrych incident in the movie displays a lack of feel of the filmmakers for the summer game, something that becomes more apparent as the film plods along.

In terms of the game action, most of the baseball scenes are shot with a camera on the first-base side of the field, showing Palmer either swinging and missing pitches or hitting a home run. There is little in between these two extremes. The rest of the action consists of Palmer standing in the batter's box and then trotting (more like walking) around the bases after hitting a home run.

In the baseball climax to the film, the Braves must beat the Astros in the last game of the season to get into the playoffs. Darryl is also one home run away from beating Roger Maris's home-run record. This should have been a great, tension-filled climax for a baseball movie. Instead, Darryl breaks the record early in the game, and because there has been no proper foundation laid in the movie as to the significance of that achievement or the difficulty of its accomplishment, and because Darryl is shown hitting a home run in just about every plate appearance in the film, Darryl's feat seems merely matter-of-fact.

The big game itself primarily involves random plays of no significance rather than plays used to set up the climax of the contest. In the bottom of the ninth inning, the Braves appear to be the victors when Moose Granger hits a long ball to center field, with two runners on base and two outs. The television play-by-play announcer describes the ball as "going, going," but it is then caught by the center fielder without much difficulty near the center-field wall. The cheat announcing would anger most viewers, but since no one is paying much attention to the film by that time, it is simply just another forgettable moment.

The Slugger's Wife does not work as a comedy, a romance, or a baseball film. That's three strikes and this film is out.

8

BASEBALL COMEDIES

√ *Major League* (1989)

If one ever wonders what would have happened if the Bad News Bears played professional baseball when they grew up, *Major League* provides the answer. The gang would have played for the Cleveland Indians, they still would have been prone to making horrific errors early in the season, their game would have improved throughout the season, a championship would be in sight near the end of the campaign, and their foul language would only have gotten worse. *Major League* is the adult version of *The Bad News Bears* (1976), and that is not a bad thing.

It seems that Rachel Phelps, a former Las Vegas showgirl, has inherited the Cleveland Indians from her deceased husband's estate. Mrs. Phelps does not like the city of Cleveland all that much, and she would like to move the team to Miami, which has lured her with a promise of a new stadium and personal memberships in all the right clubs. The only problem with Phelps's ambitions is the Indians' lease with the city, which cannot be broken unless fewer than 800,000 fans attend the Tribe's games in any one year. Phelps decides to artificially move the process along by forcing her general manager to fill the team with has-beens and never-weres, hopefully dampening attendance as the team goes on to lose game after game. Phelps's plan works at first, as the Indians play badly and attendance is low, but unfortunately for Phelps, the team eventually comes around, ending the season in a divisional tie, forcing a one-game playoff with the New York Yankees in front of a packed stadium.

That short plot summary of *Major League* highlights one of the prime criticisms of the film—its trite plot. Despite being an adult sports film, the basic structure of *Major League* is the same as many youth baseball films, such as *The Bad News Bears*, its progeny, and imitators. Every movie fan who starts to watch the film will know,

These are three of the stars from *Major League* (1989), clockwise from back, Corbin Bernsen as shortstop Roger Dorn, Tom Berenger as catcher Jake Taylor, and Charlie Sheen as pitcher Ricky "Wild Thing" Vaughn.

far in advance, that the Indians will get it together despite their obvious lack of talent and make a run for the championship by the end of the film. If a baseball fan is looking for an innovative story line, virtuoso direction, and a theme for the ages, *Major League* is not the movie to view.

If, however, a baseball fan is looking for an entertaining film with some good baseball action as an extra, then *Major League* is a good viewing choice. The film is marvelously funny. The Indians have an assortment of strange players, such as a convicted felon, a believer in voodoo, a shortstop who cannot field, a catcher with bad knees, and an outfielder named Willie Mays Hayes, who says he can hit like Mays (presumably Hall of Famer Willie Mays, who played most of his career with the Giants) and run like Hayes (presumably Bullet Bob Hayes, a football Hall of Famer after he was an Olympic sprinter who was once known as the fastest man alive). There are the usual assortments of strange batting rituals and swings, wild pitches high over the batters' heads, a player who tries to steal second but ends his slide about a foot short of second base, and high fly balls falling between three outfielders. There are also some not-before-seen incidents, such as the manager peeing on the contract of one of his players when the player raises a contractual issue; a runner picked off base when the first baseman tells him his shoes are untied; and a player, driving the bullpen cart, chasing a car on the street.

The comedy is held together by play-by-play announcer Bob Uecker, former major leaguer, beer spokesperson, and then the voice of the Milwaukee Brewers. He is full of sarcasm for the dim-witted play of the Indians, referring to the pitcher Rickey Vaughn as a juvenile delinquent in the off-season, calling pitches way outside as "just off the plate," and questioning how the batters can lay off such good pitches when Vaughn throws twelve straight pitches nowhere near home plate. Thanks to Bob Uecker, *Major League* is arguably the funniest baseball film ever made.

It is difficult to sustain a continuum of humor throughout the length of a feature film, and not surprisingly, the humor of *Major League* starts to tire in the second half, as the foul language, bathroom humor, and physical comedy start to wear thin. But just when it seems that *Major League* has gone on an uncorrectable downward spiral, the film reaches the one-game playoff between the Indians and the Yankees. Here, the comedy essentially ends and the game is treated for what it is — the most important game in the history of Cleveland Indians baseball in quite a while.

The Yankees are obviously the heavy favorites in the game. In a surprise move, manager Lou Brown starts the team's aging right-hander, Eddie Harris, rather than its young star, Ricky Vaughn, whose turn it is in the rotation. The game is a pitcher's duel, with the action mainly strikeouts, a catcher pickoff at first base, some slick infield work, and a circus catch above the outfield wall to rob a Yankees batter of a home run. In the top of the seventh inning, a two-run homer puts the Yankees in the lead, but in the bottom of the inning, the Indians respond with a two-out, two-run homer, tying the game. When the Yankees load the bases in the top of the ninth, the manager calls in Vaughn to pitch to a Yankees batter who has knocked him around all year. This time Vaughn succeeds, striking the batter out on three straight fastballs. In the bottom of the ninth, the Indians win on an exciting play, with Willie Mays Hayes scoring from second on a bunt toward third in a very close play at the plate.

In the scenes from the playoff game, the film excels because, much like both versions of *Angels in the Outfield* (1951, 1994), the viewer feels as if he is watching a complete, nine-inning ball game. By contrast, many baseball scenes in other films seem like a series of highlight footage that can be seen later that night on *SportsCenter*. In *Major League*, the filmmakers have taken time to provide the details of this important game, from good managerial moves to scoreless innings, from home runs to easy outs. There is also time taken between the pitches and the different batters to allow the suspense to rise, just as it does in a real game. When the Indians finally prevail, the movie audience is just as excited as the fans in attendance. While the game action could have done without the slow-motion footage of important plays or the side story of the feud between the shortstop and Ricky Vaughn, this baseball game is terrific, one of the best of the cinema.

As noted elsewhere in this book, it is always nice to see a baseball film about a city other than New York, Boston, Chicago, or any city in California. The local color and setting of a new city provides a special interest for the movie. In 1989, at the time *Major League* was made, the Indians played in Cleveland Stadium, usually known as Municipal Stadium, its part-time home from 1932 and its full-time home starting in 1947. Municipal Stadium was eventually demolished after the Indians moved to Jacobs Field in 1994. Thus, it is great to have the old ball yard captured on film in *Major League* so that it will never be forgotten. Or so it seems.

Unfortunately, all of the baseball scenes in *Major League* were actually filmed in Milwaukee at County Stadium, then the home of the Milwaukee Brewers. Milwaukee County Stadium has since been torn down. Thus, while there are nice establishing shots of the city of Cleveland in the film, particularly under the opening credits, and outside shots and second-unit footage of Cleveland Stadium, there is more of Milwaukee and County Stadium in the movie than Cleveland and Cleveland Stadium. Cleveland is probably the only city in the country in which a film about its professional baseball team ends up immortalizing a lost ballpark in another town.

Major League II (1994)

Major League (1989) was both a financial and critical success, leading to this sequel, although five years elapsed between the releases of the two films. Sequels to baseball movies have not been the norm with the only other examples being the trio of *Bad News Bears* films.

Despite the lapse of five years, *Major League II* picks up with the Cleveland Indians season right after the one shown in *Major League*. In the original, the Indians ended the movie by winning the division championship in a one-game playoff with the Yankees. The film never disclosed what happened to the team in the playoffs that year. *Major League II* provides the answer to that question. According to the film, the Indians lost to the White Sox in the American League Championship Series and never made it to the World Series, thus continuing the Indians' streak of non–World Series appearances since 1955.

The players who arrive for spring training in *Major League II* are almost the same as the ones who played for Cleveland in the prior successful year, but matters have changed significantly. Rick Vaughn, juvenile delinquent and "Wild Thing," is now clean-cut, dresses like a businessman, has a media agent, and is afraid to throw his fastball too often, because it could shorten his pitching career. Pedro Cerrano, the home-run hitter from the prior season, has given up voodoo for Buddhism, also causing him to be more carefree and less aggressive in the game. Willie Mays Hayes starred in a movie in the offseason, spraining his knee in the process, and he has become more interested in hitting home runs than getting on base as a leadoff hitter. Roger Dorn retired and then purchased the team. Jake Taylor eventually becomes a coach. It is therefore unsurprising that manager Lou Brown is not very optimistic about the upcoming season once he gets a good look at the crew on hand.

Brown is right about his team. The Indians perform poorly on the field, losing game after game early in the season. The Indians fall so far into the cellar that it will be impossible for them to get into the playoffs again this year, except that this is Hollywood, not reality. Not only is it Hollywood, David S. Ward, the director and primary writer of the original, performed similar functions in the sequel. Thus, the ending of *Major League II* is nearly identical to the one in *Major League* with, at the end of the sequel, the Indians one victory away from playing in the World Series.

In fact, *Major League II* appears to be more of a remake than a sequel, not just in the bad play of the Indians early in the season and the team somehow making it to the playoffs in the end but also in other significant matters. About halfway through the movie, Rachel Phelps purchases the team back from Dorn, and then once again she starts rooting for the team to lose. In this case, however, the whole plot point seems somewhat halfhearted. Why buy the team back if she still wants it to lose? That would only hurt her investment. Surely she made enough money from the original sale of the team to get whatever she desires. Phelps is neither an interesting nor funny character in the film. This story line only points to the paucity of good, new ideas for this sequel.

Just like the original, even though *Major League II* involves the Cleveland Indians, the film was not shot at a ballpark in Cleveland. The baseball scenes were shot at Camden Yards in Baltimore, Maryland, a field that was disguised to look like Cleveland Municipal Stadium. In 1994, the Indians had moved from Cleveland Municipal Stadium to Jacobs Field (now Progressive Field) and were playing their games that year in the new facility. Municipal Stadium was not torn down until 1996, after the Cleveland Browns fled the city for Baltimore. Thus, Municipal Stadium should have been available for filming in the summer of 1994, but for some reason it was not used in the movie. Once again, a film about Cleveland ends up immortalizing a ballpark in another town.

Major League II does not really have a plot. It is just a series of comedy vignettes, not tied together in any cogent manner. The best comedy moments in the film come not from the players but from Bob Uecker, reprising his role as the Indians play-by-play announcer, and Randy Quaid as an Indians fan who supports the team early on but once it starts to lose, becomes cynical about the team's chances. Uecker is hilarious, particularly when he bad-mouths the team, as, for example, when Willie Mays Hayes calls his home-run shot to left field on two successive occasions and flies out each time. Uecker comments that maybe Hayes was pointing his bat at the left fielder. Quaid's character becomes so down on the team that he never stops jeering, at one point yelling at Vaughn, parodying his theme song, "Vile thing. Mr. Choke thing. You make everything . . . embarrassing."

Despite some good humor sprinkled throughout the film, *Major League II* is simply boring, with not enough good comedy and no true plot. The film does improve at the end with its depiction of the seventh game of the American League Championship Series. The film takes the time to show much of the game, from the early innings through the ninth inning, which is always a plus for a baseball movie. The play in the field is good, although what baseball fan does not wish that the players would run out their home runs, at least until the ball goes over the fence? There is an epidemic of players in the film who watch what they hit, although in fairness to the film, that seems to happen often these days in the real major leagues.

The championship game is taut, hardly unexpected. Nor is the fact that Rick Vaughn is called from the bullpen to get the last out, against his season-long nemesis, Jack Parkman. Vaughn comes through, striking out Parkman. Wait—didn't the same thing happen at the end of *Major League*? Of course it did. In fact, since *Major League* is the far better film, and *Major League II* is really just a remake, it makes far more sense to re-watch the original than waste time on the remake.

Major League: Back to the Minors (1998)

Major League: Back to the Minors is the third movie in the *Major League* series, although it has little in common with the prior two films. One carryover is the character of Roger Dorn (Corbin Bernsen), who is now the owner of the Minnesota Twins, apparently acquiring the team after he sold his interest in the Cleveland Indians in the prior film. Dorn convinces a new character, minor-league pitcher Gus Cantrell, to retire as a pitcher and manage the Twins' Triple-A affiliate, the Buzz. The Buzz has a strange assortment of players, indeed, and in this regard, the movie has another link to the prior two films in the series. The players include a former ballet dancer, Lance

Pere, who uses ballet moves during games when running the bases; a medical school graduate, Doc Windgate, who throws the slowest fastball in professional baseball history; and twin middle infielders who run into each other trying to field batted balls and then get into fistfights on the field while the runners keep running.

Of course, that is not enough wacko players for any team in the *Major League* series, so some of the players from the prior films are back. They are Pedro Cerrano (Dennis Haysbert), the voodoo-loving home-run hitter; Taka Tanaka (Takaaki Ishibashi), a crazy Japanese ballplayer; and Rube Baker (Eric Bruskotter), the catcher who cannot throw the ball back to the pitcher or, for that matter, throw to any base properly. The return of these characters and the actors who previously portrayed the roles provides another link to the original films, but *Major League: Back to the Minors* would have been better if additional new wacky characters played for the Buzz, rather than the film employing retreads from the prior movies.

Major League: Back to the Minors has two story lines. One involves hitting prospect Downtown Anderson, who Cantrell believes needs more seasoning in the minors. The Twins manager, Leonard Huff, disagrees, and over the objections of Cantrell, Anderson is brought up to the major-league team. He immediately flames out. The other story arc is the rivalry between Cantrell and the obnoxious Huff, leading to two exhibition games between their teams. In the first game, when it looks like the Buzz will beat the Twins, Huff has the lights turned off at the Metrodome. The game is called for darkness with the game tied. The film ends with the second exhibition game, where there is much on the line. If the Buzz wins, Cantrell will become manager of the Twins. If the Twins win, Cantrell must give up an entire year's salary to Huff.

Surprisingly, the concept of a major-league team playing an exhibition game with its minor-league affiliate or any other minor-league team, although a rare occurrence these days (particularly in the middle of the season), is historically not that unusual an event. It used to be commonplace for a major-league team to play a minor-league affiliate once during the season. For example, according to baseball historian Brian C. Engelhardt, the Philadelphia Phillies played their minor-league affiliate, the Reading Phillies, almost once each year in Reading from 1967 through 1983 and then continued playing sporadically thereafter until 2000. Eventually, the long major-league schedule, concerns about player injuries, travel problems, and the fact that the major-league teams often rested their starters in the exhibition games led to a curtailment of the practice. Of course, playing two exhibition games during a single major-league season on the spur of the moment, as shown in *Major League: Back to the Minors*, never occurred.

By using the words and logo of the prior *Major League* films, the new film begs comparison with the prior films in the series, and in that regard, the new film comes up short. Although a very difficult negative to achieve, *Major League: Back to the Minors* has even less of a plot than its predecessors. Cantrell coaches a minor-league team, and his team plays in two exhibition games with a major-league team. That is about it. By repetitive use, the characters of Pedro Cerrano, Taka Tanaka, and Rube Baker have lost whatever charm they may otherwise have had. Bob Uecker is back, and surprisingly, he is not very funny. Most of his attempted humor comes, not by his play-by-play on the radio but by his comments under his breath after he gives his play-by-play. That undercuts the humor of Uecker, and, of course, the repetitiveness of his antics over three films also cuts his effectiveness.

Accordingly, *Major League: Back to the Minors* is not as funny as the prior films. The filmmakers may have believed that there were laughs in the antics of manager Leonard Huff, but the part is written as if Huff is a Disney villain, not a real person, and Ted McGinley overacts in the role to an outrageous degree. McGinley is more aggravating than funny.

Of course, the film has some positives. There is some reasonably good baseball action in the movie. Some of the humor in the film is funny, such as when one of Doc Windgate's pitches does not register on a radar gun, a coach tells Cantrell that the gun is from the Department of Transportation and does not measure speeds under 55 mph, or when a beanball incident is turned into a satire of Clint Eastwood's famous speech in *Dirty Harry* (1971) ("You've got to ask yourself one question: Do I feel lucky?"). Another plus is that the first exhibition game is shot on location in the Metrodome in Minneapolis, Minnesota, a domed stadium that was the home of the Minnesota Twins from 1982 to 2009. (Since *Major League: Back to the Minors* is not about the Cleveland Indians, the filmmakers apparently had no problem shooting on location in the actual stadium that was the venue of the fictional exhibition game in the film.)

If *Major League: Back to the Minors* were not part of the *Major League* series and evaluated solely on its own, it would probably not be so disappointing, just a light tale of players in the minor leagues working toward their goal of someday playing in the major leagues. But even there, the film falls flat. *Major League: Back to the Minors* never provides a feel for the atmosphere of the games down below, as *Bull Durham* (1988) and *Pastime* (1990) do. *Major League: Back to the Minors* is an okay film to watch, if there is nothing else to do on a rainy day, but a catch in the backyard is more interesting and much more memorable.

Fireman, Save My Child (1932)

For Pittsburgh Pirates fans, Joe L. Brown is an iconic figure. He was the general manager of the Pirates from 1956 through 1976, turning the Pirates from the worst team in baseball in the 1950s into world champions in both 1960 and 1971. Those were the years of Roberto Clemente, Willie Stargell, and manager Danny Murtaugh.

What many Pirates fans may not know is that Joe L. Brown has a connection to a trio of baseball movies made in the 1930s. Joe L. Brown received his love of baseball from his father, Joe E. Brown, a comedian and film actor. Most movie fans today probably remember Joe E. Brown, if they remember him at all, from his performance as Osgood Fielding III in *Some Like It Hot* (1959), where he falls in love with Jerry, played by Jack Lemmon, masquerading as a woman named Daphne. Brown has the last line in the film. When Jack Lemmon shows him that Daphne is really a guy, Brown replies, "Well, nobody's perfect." It is one of the most famous punch lines in all of film history and surely the most famous one Brown ever spoke in the cinema.

In his younger days, Joe E. Brown was an excellent baseball player, even receiving an offer to play for the New York Yankees organization. According to his autobiography, Brown turned that offer down because he was just getting started on Broadway, and he believed that he had a better chance of success in a career in entertainment than a career in baseball. He did, however, work out with the

Yankees for a few weeks, leading manager Miller Huggins to remark, "Well, he's not the first comedian I've seen in a Yankee uniform." Brown never forgot his baseball past, and in the 1930s, in the prime of his movie career, Brown starred in three light comedies set in the world of baseball.

The first was *Fireman, Save My Child*, released in 1932 by First National, an affiliate of Warner Bros. The story is about a fabulous baseball player, Smokey Joe Grant, who is more interested in fighting fires and working on an invention to suppress fires than playing the game of baseball. That is the reason why the film has such a strange title for a baseball movie. Actually, baseball film or not, the title is still strange, as Smokey Joe does not save any children in the movie.

The best parts of *Fireman, Save My Child* are the opening sequences in the small town of Rosedale on the day of the Valley Championship baseball game between the Rosedale Rosies and Orchid Center. These moments are true evocations of a bygone era, with a local game seemingly as important as a World Series, batters who do not wear batting helmets, and horse-drawn fire engines responding to a fire at a sauerkraut factory in town. The championship game does not have a rain delay. It has a fire delay, with the players, fans, and umpires content to let Smokey leave the game, put out a fire, and then return to the game to continue pitching where he left off. Smokey Joe's pitching motion, in which he wildly circles his arms above his head before throwing to the plate, is something to see. For some reason, Smokey Joe even pitches with this full windup when there are runners on base.

Smokey Joe is so successful that the St. Louis Cardinals offer him a position with the team. Smokey accepts the offer so that he can save enough money to marry his childhood sweetheart, Sally Toby. Smokey Joe is successful in the big leagues, but his life goes astray when June Farnum, a gold digger from the big city, bewitches him, even tricking him into becoming engaged. Matters work out in the end, as they always do. Smokey Joe's fire-extinguishing bomb appears to be a success, Smokey Joe pitches in the deciding game of the World Series and also scores the winning run, and at the film's conclusion, he finally marries Sally from Rosedale.

Once the story moves out of Rosedale, *Fireman, Save My Child* loses most of its charm. The melodramatic plot of June making a

This is a publicity photo for *Fireman, Save My Child* (1932), with star Joe E. Brown, who plays pitcher Smokey Joe Grant, posing before the fence of his boarding house in the film, flanked by two of the child actors in the movie. The child actor on the left is Dickie Moore; the one on the right is unknown.

fool of Smokey Joe is unconvincing, and the scene in which Sally, in a surprise visit to Smokey Joe, discovers his relationship with June can only be described as cringe-worthy. This story arc seems like padding, which is frequently the problem with light films about baseball. They often have such a weak primary story line that a serious subplot has to be inserted into the film just to keep the film going or to create a climax. This can also be seen in films as diverse as *Take Me Out to the Ball Game* (1949) and *Kill the Umpire* (1950). The problem is that the serious subplot often conflicts with the remainder of the film, both in tone and style, resulting in a detriment to the film. That is the case with *Fireman, Save My Child*.

Joe E. Brown, generally a very likable actor, grates on the audience's nerves once the setting of the film moves out of Rosedale with, on the one hand, his overblown hubris and, on the other hand, his incredible naiveté. Although director Lloyd Bacon brings the film alive with two early shots of Smokey Joe pitching in the major leagues, one from under the legs of the catcher and one through the mask of the catcher, the baseball scenes in the film are generally unconvincing. Smokey Joe begins to pitch in the middle of the final World Series game without warm-ups, and he scores the winning run after being caught in a rundown between third base and home plate. How many base runners in a major-league game get out of a pickle safely, much less move up a base in the process? Befitting the title of the film, the best moments in *Fireman, Save My Child* arise not from baseball but from fires, both the burning of the sauerkraut factory in Rosedale and the fire Smokey Joe starts in the offices of the Zenith Fire Extinguisher Company in St. Louis, Missouri.

Fireman, Save My Child rambles through several disconnected plot elements, from baseball players to fire extinguishers to good and bad women. There is no cohesiveness to the story lines. In fact, the story arc with the gold digger is never resolved; it is simply forgotten. While there were not that many baseball movies made in the 1930s, if a baseball fan is looking for a pleasant 1930s baseball movie, there are two better ones to view, both of which also star Joe E. Brown.

Elmer the Great (1933)

Elmer the Great is one Elmer Kane, a baseball player from the small town of Gentryville, Indiana. Elmer had been playing for Terre Haute, a minor-league team, but as the film commences the Chicago Cubs purchase his contract for $10,000, expecting Elmer to immediately play for the Cubs in the upcoming season. Elmer is in love with a local girl, Nellie Poole, and so he is reluctant to join the Cubs, but when Nellie pretends she does not love him, Elmer is off to the big leagues. The film ends with Elmer and the Cubs playing in the World Series.

Elmer the Great has its genesis in a short story by Ring Lardner, titled "Hurry, Kane," originally published in 1927. The story concerns a pitcher named Elmer Kane who wins the World Series for his team, but only after resolving his problems with women, some teammates who tease him, and some gamblers. The main carryover to the film is the story arc with the gamblers. The Lardner short story was adapted into a play also named *Elmer the Great*, written by Ring Lardner and produced by George M. Cohan. The play, which is the credited source material for the film, opened on Broadway on September 24, 1928, with Walter Huston playing Elmer Kane. Despite the fact that the play ran for only forty performances, it was the inspiration for two films, *Fast Company* (1929), with Jack Oakie as Elmer Kane, and *Elmer the Great*.

Even though *Elmer the Great* officially has its origins in a stage play, the similarities between *Elmer the Great* and *Fireman, Save My Child* (1932), the first film in the Joe E. Brown baseball trilogy, are patent. The protagonists of both films are country bumpkins who are enticed to play in the major leagues because they are great ballplayers. Both of the protagonists have a pretty love interest waiting for them back home, and in both films the girlfriend comes to town and finds her beau in the arms of a beautiful woman. Both ballplayers are incredibly egotistical about their baseball play but surprisingly naïve about life in the big city. In addition, at the end of both films, the hero scores the winning run in the deciding game of the World Series. *Elmer the Great* is not a remake of the prior film; it simply follows a formula that had previously proved successful.

Unfortunately, *Elmer the Great*, just like *Fireman, Save My Child*, has almost no plot. It is really just a series of vignettes, initially about small-town life and later about life on a baseball team. The story lines, such as they exist, are totally unconvincing. No one can be as dumb as Elmer, even someone from Gentryville, Indiana. Elmer's lack of street smarts and his constant changing of his mind in the film are particularly grating on the viewer.

In addition to its plot problems, *Elmer the Great* is disappointing because of little matters that are annoying to baseball fans. Elmer is a prodigious home-run hitter and that is fine. Yet there is a slide in the film that states that Elmer has hit sixty-seven home runs that season, and the season is not yet over. Most baseball fans know now, and those watching in 1933 knew then, that Babe Ruth set the season home-run record of sixty home runs in 1927. (That record, of course, was subsequently broken by Roger Maris in 1961 and then again later in baseball's steroid era.) Before 1927, the only batter to hit more than fifty home runs in a season was also Babe Ruth, hitting fifty-four in 1920 and fifty-nine in 1921. Between 1928 and 1932, the years before the film was made, only Babe Ruth in 1928 (54), Hack Wilson in 1930 (56), and Jimmie Foxx in 1932 (58) hit over fifty home runs. To suggest that Elmer hit over sixty-seven home runs in one season is just too much. It also demonstrates that the filmmakers were out of touch with what was going on in baseball at the time.

The World Series finale in the film is played at the home of the Chicago Cubs, Wrigley Field, one of the most storied ballparks in all of Major League Baseball, still being used today, more than one hundred years after its opening in 1914. However, other than an establishing shot of the outside of Wrigley Field and some second-unit footage of the inside, it is clear that the film was not shot inside Wrigley Field. Having identified Elmer as playing on the Cubs and having identified the site of the final game as Wrigley Field in Chicago, it was incumbent on the filmmakers to shoot some scenes on location in the famous edifice, B movie or not, just because Wrigley Field is such an iconic structure in American sports. This failure in the production adds to the disappointment of the film.

To be fair to the filmmakers, the baseball scenes were shot at a Wrigley Field. Unfortunately, it was Wrigley Field in Los Angeles, a real field that was used by the Los Angeles Angels of the Pacific Coast League from 1925 to 1957, also used from time to time by the Hollywood Stars of the Pacific Coast League, and which eventually became the home of a major-league team, the Los Angeles Angels, when it became an expansion team in the American League in 1961, but only for the team's inaugural season.

Elmer the Great is redeemed somewhat by the World Series game that concludes the film. The latter stages of the game resemble a cartoon more than a real baseball game, with many surreal elements. In these scenes, the film becomes less grating and more ingratiating. The cartoon aspects start with the field announcer who speaks through an incredibly large megaphone. His announcements are shot through the open end of the megaphone, with only the announcer's large mouth, opening and closing, being seen. It is a weird beginning to the game. In the seventh inning, when Elmer comes to bat for the first time, he is hit in the head with a pitch, resulting in him dizzily walking to first base on a weaving course, instead of in a straight line.

At that point, a terrific rain begins, turning the field into a morass of mud. A ball is hit to Elmer at second base and lands in a large puddle at his feet. Elmer cannot find the ball in the mud, resulting in the other team scoring three runs. The rains continue, and when Elmer comes to bat in the bottom of the ninth inning, with the bases loaded and his team behind by three runs, visibility is so low that the pitcher pretends, on two occasions, to pitch the ball to Elmer, the catcher pretends to catch the ball and the umpire actually calls a strike. Elmer finally gets matters straightened out, and on the next pitch, he hits an inside-the-park, grand-slam home run, winning the game for his team. Because of the mud, Elmer is able to start his slide into home plate from quite a distance away, another cartoonish aspect of the game.

The concluding baseball game of *Elmer the Great* is stylish in the extreme, and the cartoonish and surreal aspects of the game make the film worth a viewing, just because the game is so unusual. In addition to the fun of watching the game, there are two interesting aspects of that ninth inning for baseball fans. In the long history of Major League Baseball, there has only been one walk-off, inside-the-park, grand-slam home run. On July 25, 1956, Roberto Clemente hit just such a home run in the bottom of the ninth inning in a game at Forbes Field in Pittsburgh, and the Pirates beat, coincidentally, the Chicago Cubs, 9–8. Also, the owner of the Cubs permits Elmer to bat in the ninth inning, despite his worries that Elmer may be throwing the game, when Elmer explains that he bet all of the money he received from the gamblers on the Cubs to win. The fact that Elmer admits to betting on baseball may seem somewhat unusual to modern-day baseball fans who are familiar with the saga of Pete Rose.

Alibi Ike (1935)

Joe E. Brown is back playing for the Chicago Cubs in this final film in the Joe E. Brown baseball trilogy of the 1930s. Based upon a 1915 short story of the same name by Ring Lardner, Brown plays Frank X. Farrell, a rookie pitcher who is the main hope for success of the Chicago Cubs in the upcoming season. As a result of Farrell's penchant for providing excuses for everything that goes wrong and his unwillingness to tell the truth when his teammates press him for answers about his personal life, Farrell's teammates begin to call Farrell "Alibi Ike." Farrell falls in love with Dolly Stevens, the manager's sister-in-law, and the two become engaged, but Farrell's mendacious comments result in Dolly running away. At the same time, some tough gamblers threaten Farrell with personal injury if he does not throw the games in which he pitches. In the end, of course, all turns out well, as Farrell defies the gamblers, wins an important game, and gets the girl.

Alibi Ike is the best of the three Joe E. Brown baseball movies, even though, like the other films, *Alibi Ike* does not have much of a plot. What makes *Alibi Ike* better than the prior two films in the series is its genuine humor and the likability of the performers.

Alibi Ike contains Joe E. Brown's best performance in the series. While he still plays an overly conceited baseball player, there is none of that country-bumpkin naiveté that did not work well in the other films. Also, Farrell gets a well-deserved comeuppance early in the film, when he deliberately walks the bases full, demands that his fielders leave the field of play because he is going to strike out the next three batters, but then gives up a grand-slam home run. This makes Farrell more likable throughout the remainder of the film, even though he has an alibi for that mistake. According to Farrell, the manager shook Farrell's hand prior to Farrell throwing the home-run ball, injuring Farrell's hand.

Another reason Joe E. Brown gives a good performance is that he is often playing off of a great second banana, William Frawley. Frawley plays Cap, the manager of the Chicago Cubs. Frawley was a regular character actor in films in the 1930s and 1940s, but he is best known today for his role as Fred Mertz in the television series *I Love Lucy*. Frawley is excellent in *Alibi Ike*, alternately gruff, exasperated, and sarcastic, similar to his Fred Mertz character. In the scenes with Frawley and Brown, Frawley always makes Brown look good. It is easy to see why Frawley was never out of work in the first two decades of the sound cinema.

As Frank X. Farrell, Joe E. Brown brings back the same pitching motion that he employed as Smokey Joe Grant in *Fireman, Save My Child* (1932). Brown may have learned that complex pitching motion while playing baseball in his younger days, but when Brown's feet are shown in the film when he is pitching, his back foot is often behind the rubber, rather than in front of the rubber and touching it. Strange windup or not, it is hard for Farrell to achieve much velocity in his pitches when his feet are in the wrong place. And, in fact, Farrell's pitches to the plate in *Alibi Ike* seem awfully slow.

Despite the title, *Alibi Ike* is not so much about alibis but rather about Farrell being afraid to admit anything about his personal life, such as being in love with Dolly, and then making up tall tales just to avoid any admissions. Many of Farrell's ridiculous evasions in the film come directly from Ring Lardner's short story, such as the time that he has tickets to take Dolly to a show but tells his teammates that a friend of his is going with him, or getting letters from Dolly and telling his teammates they are from a college friend. As his team-mates question Farrell closely over his obvious prevarications, his explanations for each situation become wilder and wilder.

As was usually the case when a baseball film has almost no plot, a melodramatic story arc is inserted into *Alibi Ike* just to create a climax. Here, it is gamblers threatening Farrell with physical harm in order to convince him to deliberately lose some ball games. Gambling seems to be a common theme of 1930s baseball movies. Either gambling on baseball by nefarious professional gamblers did exist to a large degree in the 1930s or filmmakers just had no new ideas to use in their films. One suspects that the latter is the correct answer. In *Alibi Ike*, however, the insertion of this new story line into the film does not seem intrusive, probably because it is very brief, but more importantly, because it is not used for melodramatic purposes. Rather, the story arc is used as a platform for some broad humor.

That broad humor includes a car chase, with Farrell escaping from the gamblers in an ambulance with the siren screaming; Farrell unknowingly driving the ambulance up a ramp onto a flatbed truck carrying cars, resulting in Farrell honking his horn at the cars on the truck in front, cajoling them to get out of the way; Farrell taking over the large truck and crashing it through the outside wall of the stadium; Farrell ready to pitch in the big game in his pajamas but instead taking someone else's uniform and pitching in an outfit that seems about ten sizes too large; Farrell losing a batted ball in the oversize uniform and then tagging a runner out at home plate with a headfirst leap; and Farrell scoring the winning run by leaping over the catcher after running through a stop sign at third base. It is all pretty silly stuff, but there are still some good laughs in these scenes.

In the big game at the end of the film, it is time for a cliché, as Brown scores the winning run on an inside-the-park home run, a popular finish for baseball movies of the 1930s. However, there is something unique about the big game. It is played at night, under the lights. The reason for this is readily apparent—budgetary issues. Wrigley Field in Los Angeles, the location of the baseball scenes in *Alibi Ike*, had lights installed in 1931, so it was not very costly for the filmmakers to shoot a night ball game there. Using the darkness to their advantage, the filmmakers shot most of the game's events with one camera, from behind home plate, with the infield brightly lit and the rest of the film cloaked in darkness. Sometimes it seems as if there are no outfielders present during the game, even on Brown's inside-the-park home run.

Although the game was shot at night for budgetary reasons, the scene is actually ahead of its time. *Alibi Ike* was first released on June 15, 1935. The first night game ever played in the major leagues occurred about three weeks before, on May 24, 1935, when the Cincinnati Reds beat the Philadelphia Phillies, 2–1, under the recently installed lights in Crosley Field in Cincinnati. The makers of *Alibi Ike* could hardly have been aware of that night game when the film was in production. The filmmakers probably took their cue from Minor League Baseball. The first-ever night games in professional baseball took place in the minor leagues in 1930, and thereafter, there were a number of night games in the minor leagues prior to 1935.

Farrell pitches for the Chicago Cubs, and the final game in the film is a home game. While there is no mention of Wrigley Field in the film, that must be where the final game is played. The filmmakers could not have known it in 1935, but Wrigley Field was the least likely ballpark to use as the setting for a night baseball game. Wrigley Field was the last of the old ball yards to install lights. The first official night game in Wrigley Field was not played until August 9, 1988, when the Cubs beat the Mets, 6–4. Therefore, *Alibi Ike* was fifty-three years ahead of its time.

Hot Curves (1930)

The template of many of the baseball movies from the 1930s includes a young and gregarious baseball star who is in love with a girl-next-door type, the star waylaid by a gold digger who breaks up the romance, the star finally seeing the errors of his way, and the star then winning the World Series for his team, with a walk-off, inside-the-park home run. This story line can be seen in *They*

Learned About Women (1930), *Fireman, Save My Child* (1932), and *Hot Curves*. If the other baseball films from the 1930s do not use this exact plot, they still employ the walk-off, inside-the-park home run to win the final game.

The plot of *Hot Curves* is no better and no worse than those other 1930s films, but, in any event, the plots of all of those films seem horribly out-of-date. Here, Jim Dolan, the star pitcher of the Pittsburgh team (no nicknames are given for the major-league teams in the film), falls in love with Elaine, the manager's daughter, but he strays when Maizie, an aggressive and dangerous female, gets her claws into him. Near the end of the movie, Jim finally realizes what he has done (particularly after Maizie steals his watch, ring, and some money). Jim returns to Elaine, and he then pitches for Pittsburgh in the seventh game of the World Series, becoming the hero by hitting a two-run home run in the bottom of the ninth inning, winning the game for his team.

While there are some scenes of baseball tryouts early in the film, much of *Hot Curves* strays far from its baseball setting. In fact, after the opening, the next significant game footage in the film occurs at the climax, during the last game of the World Series. Also, the baseball action is not that convincing. For example, when Dolan scores the winning run in the World Series, he executes the worst headfirst slide into home plate ever seen on a field or in a movie theater. Dolan does a slow flop on the pitcher's side of the plate, yet somehow scores, perhaps because the catcher tries to take the throw from behind home plate instead of in front of the plate and on its third base side. Put simply, there is not a lot of baseball authenticity in *Hot Curves*. The movie would have been much better if more attention were paid to its baseball elements, instead of just its romantic and comedy elements.

In fact, most of the joy in the film comes from Jewish comedian Benny Rubin, who plays Benny Goldberg, the new catching sensation for the Pittsburgh team. Benny Rubin speaks with a thick Yiddish accent, employs impossible sentence constructions, and overacts just a little, in the comedic manner of the vaudeville stage where Rubin obtained his start in show business. Rubin is endearing in the role, and just about all of the laughs in *Hot Curves* come from Rubin. Rubin had a long film career but usually in small parts (including a supporting role in another baseball film, *They Learned About Women* [1930]). He is best known today for his appearances on Jack Benny's radio and television programs.

The manager of the Pittsburgh team is named John McGrew, an obvious reference to John McGraw, the manager of the New York Giants from 1902 to 1932. Some have seen a similarity in Pittsburgh having a Jewish ballplayer on the team in *Hot Curves* to John McGraw's interest in finding a Jewish player for the Giants in the 1920s in order to help draw Jewish fans in New York to the Polo Grounds. The Giants were in a fierce competition with the New York Yankees for baseball fans at the time. One Jewish player McGraw brought to the New York Giants, near the end of the 1923 season, was Mose Solomon, nicknamed the Rabbi of Swat as a result of his home-run-hitting abilities in the minor leagues, but whose lack of fielding skills (or a dispute with McGraw) resulted in him playing in only two games in the major leagues. Another was Andy Cohen, who played second base for the Giants for several years starting in the middle of the 1926 season. Perhaps Cohen

John McGraw is here pictured at the Polo Grounds c. 1912. The legendary manager of the New York Giants searched for a Jewish ballplayer for his team in the 1920s, perhaps the inspiration for *Hot Curves* (1930). *(Library of Congress, LC-DIG-ggbain-11245)*

was the true inspiration for Benny Goldberg in the film, as Cohen performed in vaudeville during the off-season.

Early in *Airplane!* (1980), a passenger asks the stewardess for something light to read. From the magazines she is carrying, the stewardess pulls out a small brochure and says, "How about this leaflet—*Famous Jewish Sports Legends?*" While this variation on an old joke may be relevant to other sports, it does not truly apply to baseball because there have been lots of Jewish major leaguers over the years, many of whom have attained stardom. The two most famous examples are Sandy Koufax, a Hall of Fame pitcher and three-time Cy Young Award winner for the Dodgers in the 1950s and 1960s, who pitched a perfect game in 1965, and Hank Greenberg, the Hall of Fame slugger for the Detroit Tigers in the 1930s and 1940s, who hit fifty-eight home runs in 1938. The writers of *Hot Curves* could not have known it at the time, but by providing the Pittsburgh team with a great Jewish ballplayer, Benny Goldberg, they were being prescient. For the 1947 season, the Pirates bought the contract of Hank Greenberg from the Detroit Tigers, and for one season Pittsburgh did have a great Jewish ballplayer on its team, even if it was at the end of Greenberg's illustrious playing career.

Whistling in Brooklyn (1943)

In the 1940s, Red Skelton made three mystery-comedies at MGM that are sometimes known as the "Whistling" series, because of the titles of the films in the trilogy. In all of them, Skelton portrays actor Wally Benton, the star of a popular detective series on the radio, whose character, the Fox, is a detective who always solves the crime.

The first film in the series, *Whistling in the Dark* (1941), is one of the best comedy-mysteries ever made. However, each of its two sequels is worse than the picture that preceded it, with *Whistling in Brooklyn*, the last film in the series, being clearly the least of the three films. For baseball fans, however, it is *Whistling in Brooklyn* that has the most interest among the three "Whistling" movies.

Near the end of the film, the police chase Benton to Ebbets Field, believing he is a serial killer known as Constant Reader. In order to escape, Benton disguises himself as the bearded pitcher for the Battling Beavers, and as a result is forced into pitching one inning of exhibition baseball against the real Brooklyn Dodgers, while at the same time, trying to prevent Inspector Holcomb, a police inspector from New York, from becoming the next murder victim of the real Constant Reader. Reader intends to stab Holcomb while he is seated next to him at the exhibition game, thereby framing Benton for the crime.

During the game, Benton pitches several balls with warning messages into the field box where Holcomb is sitting, once accidentally picking a runner off first base when the first baseman intercepts a ball. He has trouble seeing the signals from the catcher and has to walk almost on top of home plate to see them; he catches a ball in his long, thick beard for the third out in an inning of scoreless pitching; and when he comes to bat, takes several very close pitches, one breaking a button on his shirt, which comes open, and another splitting the belt on his pants, which comes loose. (Actually, Benton should have been awarded first base on each of those pitches, because when a pitched ball touches the batter's clothing, it is the same as if the ball touches the batter's body, thereby becoming a hit-by-pitch.)

Red Skelton was an excellent comedian in his early years at MGM, and the scenes with Benton on the field in *Whistling in Brooklyn* generate some laughs. However, it is the location shooting and the real players who appear in the film that engender the most interest. Wally Benton is not much of a pitcher, and he hits the first three Brooklyn Dodgers he faces. All three batters are played by real Brooklyn Dodgers, who despite appearing in this film were subsequently elected to the Baseball Hall of Fame. The batters are Billy Herman, who was then the second baseman for the Dodgers but who spent most of his career with the Chicago Cubs; Arky Vaughan, who was then the third baseman for the Dodgers but who spent most of his career with the Pittsburgh Pirates as a shortstop; and Ducky Medwick, who was then the left fielder for the Dodgers.

Another Brooklyn Dodger in the film who is somewhat famous is Mickey Owen, who plays the Dodgers catcher when Benton is batting. Throughout his career, Owen was a good hitting and fielding catcher, but unfortunately for him, he is primarily remembered today for dropping a third strike in the fourth game of the 1941 World Series between the Dodgers and the Yankees (a strikeout that would have sealed the win for the Dodgers that day), allowing the Yankees to win that game and capture the world championship the following day.

The most famous baseball personality in the film, however, is Leo Durocher, who was then the manager of the Dodgers and who would eventually become another Hall of Famer. During his brief scene in the film, Durocher gets into a tiff with both Benton and an umpire, not unexpected from a man who became famous for arguing with umpires and for one of his sayings which endures to this day— "Nice guys finish last."

Although *Whistling in Brooklyn* is a disappointing film, it endures as a memorial to a piece of Americana. Some of the movie was shot on location in Brooklyn, and there are therefore some historic shots of 1940s Brooklyn that have been preserved. These include shots of Ebbets Field, home of the Dodgers from 1913 to 1957, until the Dodgers moved to Los Angeles. The first shot of the edifice is a famous view of the ballpark from the outside of the home plate area, with Ebbets Field lettered along the top of the structure, windows in the façade and a striped awning over the entranceways. While there is some process screen footage employed during the actual baseball game, Red Skelton is usually really out there pitching from the mound and running the bases at the real Ebbets Field.

One of the ways to confirm that fact is that there are several shots in the background of the famous sign at the bottom of the Ebbets Field scoreboard in right-center field, which reads, "Hit Sign, Win Suit. Abe Stark 1514 Pitkin Ave. Brooklyn's Leading Clothier." The sign was first put in the location shown in the film in the early 1930s and remained there until the field was demolished in 1960. Any player who hit the sign on the fly would earn a free suit from Abe's store. Because the sign was only three feet tall and Brooklyn had such good fielding outfielders, few players were able to cash in on Abe Stark's promise. Many people today believe that such a sign can only be a baseball legend, but it really existed for a time in Brooklyn, thereby adding to the character and mystique of Ebbets Field.

The Naked Gun (1988)

Many of the great screen comedians have appeared in baseball sequences, whether in feature-length movies or shorts, including Buster Keaton, Harold Lloyd, Charley Chase, Shemp Howard, and Red Skelton, but by far, the funniest baseball sequence ever filmed stars a man who came late to the world of comedy, Leslie Nielson. Neilson was primarily a dramatic actor in film and television until he played the role of the doctor in *Airplane!* (1980). ("I *am* serious and don't call me Shirley.") Nielson stood out among the other dramatic actors in the film, Robert Stack, Lloyd Bridges, and Peter Graves, leading to Nielson starring in *Police Squad!*, a 1982 television series written and shot in the style of *Airplane!* Nielson played Detective Frank Drebin in the series, and although the show is now considered a cult classic, only six episodes were produced.

That seemed to be the end of *Police Squad!* until the makers of *Police Squad!* and *Airplane!* decided to revive the character of Lieutenant Frank Drebin for *The Naked Gun: From the Files of Police Squad!* in 1988. In the film, Drebin is investigating the mysterious shooting of a fellow officer, Nordberg, while the police force is trying to prevent an assassination attempt on Queen Elizabeth, who is visiting Los Angeles. Durbin is suspicious of Vincent Ludwig, a millionaire who seems to make most of his money in the drug trade and, apparently, in killings for hire.

Late in the film, Drebin gets a tip that Ludwig is going to have an unnamed, brainwashed baseball player assassinate the Queen during the seventh-inning stretch of a ball game between the California Angels and the Seattle Mariners at Anaheim Stadium, called in the film by its nickname, The Big A. The big game is announced on television by famed broadcaster Curt Gowdy, along with his color announcers, Jim Palmer, the Hall of Fame pitching star of the Baltimore Orioles, All-Star catcher Tim McCarver, and Dick Vitale, Mel Allen, Dick Enberg, and Dr. Joyce Brothers. Drebin is determined to get down on the field and search each of the players for a weapon. He accomplishes this by knocking out the home-plate umpire and taking his place on the field.

As everyone knows, there is a lot of spitting in baseball, but in this game, some even comes from the players' wives sitting in their special seats. Signals to the base runners come from the dugout via signal flags and a semaphore. Queen Elizabeth has to pass a hot dog down her row and even participates in a wave. At one point, the umpires get a base runner into a rundown! All Mel Allen can do is employ one of his catchphrases, "How about that?"

Drebin is an unusual home-plate umpire. When he receives some positive fan reaction to a strike call he makes, he starts making more and more outrageous gestures during his strike calls, including a little bit of a moonwalk at one point. At first, Drebin cleans home plate with the traditional brush, but later he uses a hand vacuum and then a full-size vacuum cleaner.

While all of this is going on, Drebin is searching the players, trying to find a potential murder weapon. At one point, he searches the pitcher, and although he finds sandpaper, an electric sander, and a full container of Vaseline, Drebin does not care because there is no hidden weapon. Drebin fails to search the right fielder, however, and when the seventh-inning stretch arrives, it turns out that the killer is none other than Reggie Jackson, the Hall of Fame slugger and right fielder who once played for the California Angels in the mid-1980s. What a neat twist!

The baseball scene in *The Naked Gun!* is only a small portion of the film's running time, but it is hilarious. Who would have thought there were any laughs in the singing of the National Anthem or in an umpire calling balls and strikes or dusting off home plate? It turns out that there are lots. The humor in the baseball scene in *The Naked Gun!* flows from the game itself and its many idiosyncrasies, making the film very special for every baseball fan with a good sense of humor about the game.

Kill the Umpire (1950)

William Bendix, who commenced his cinematic baseball career portraying the Sultan of Swat in *The Babe Ruth Story* (1948), continues his cinematic involvement in baseball by moving behind the plate to play Bill "Two Call" Johnson, a minor-league umpire, in the 1950 film *Kill the Umpire*. The phrase "Kill the umpire" has multiple meanings within the context of the film. The obvious reference is to a common baseball expression that goes back to the early days of the game. While it is unknown when the phrase first became popular among baseball fans, it was clearly in use by 1888, when the famous baseball poem "Casey at the Bat" by Ernest Lawrence Thayer was published. After Casey takes his first called strike in the poem, the verse reads:

"Kill him! Kill the umpire!" shouted some one on the stand;
And it's likely they'd have killed him had not Casey raised his hand.

"Kill the umpire" is also the favorite line of the film's protagonist, Bill Johnson, a baseball fanatic who cannot seem to hold a job because he is always out at the ballpark. Even though Johnson is a baseball fanatic, he is the last person with whom anyone who ever want to attend a game. At the beginning of the film, Johnson is loud and officious. He always disagrees with the umpire's calls, whether right or wrong, resulting in his constantly bellowing his catchphrase, "Kill the umpire." In fact, the first time Johnson hollers the phrase, he is walking into the ballpark and not even looking at the game when he hears the umpire's strike call. On other occasions when he shouts his favorite three words, the umpire's call is clearly correct. Johnson would seem to be the last person anyone would consider to be umpire material.

Nevertheless, after Johnson loses another job because of his fanaticism about baseball, Johnson's father-in-law, a retired major-league umpire, suggests that Johnson become a professional umpire. After much reluctance and varied attempts at being kicked out of umpire school, Johnson graduates and obtains an umpire's job in the Texas League. There, he refuses a gambler's bribe and makes a controversial call at home plate, resulting in a mob of crazy Texans trying to get Johnson before he can umpire the next game. The gamblers actually take several shots at Johnson, trying to kill him for reasons unknown. At that point, the title of the film takes on its literal meaning, as several people really are trying to murder the umpire.

Kill the Umpire, with its relatively low budget and family scenes, sometimes looks more like a television situation comedy than a feature film. One can almost imagine the description of the show in the fall preview of *TV Guide*: "Comedy hijinks as a man who hates umpires becomes an umpire himself."

The screenwriter for *Kill the Umpire* is Frank Tashlin, who

Before he becomes an umpire in *Kill the Umpire* (1950), "Two Call" Johnson (William Bendix) is always happy to yell at umpires.

started his cinema career working in animation, including a stint at Warner Bros. where he worked on the Looney Tunes and Merrie Melodies series. Tashlin then became a director, reaching his greatest success in the 1950s, directing several Martin and Lewis and then Jerry Lewis solo films. *Kill the Umpire* presages the cartoonish and broad humor of Tashlin's later work. As one of many examples of the visual humor of a cartoon, while in umpire school, Johnson blows so much air into his chest protector that it becomes like a balloon, so that when Johnson is stuck to the floor in his spiked shoes, he bounces back and forth off the floor and the wall. As to broad humor, the climatic car chase, some of which is shown in fast motion, includes a sequence with Johnson unwittingly skiing along paved roads on skis made from the wooden fence of a farm, creating slapstick humor in the extreme.

Kill the Umpire is not much of a baseball film; there are very few scenes of actual baseball being played. There are also several missed baseball opportunities, particularly at the umpire school. If *Kill the Umpire* is accurate, umpire school consists mainly of calisthenics, learning how to shout "Safe" and "Out," and studying proper hand signals. The scenes at the school were an opportunity for some realistic moments in the otherwise outrageous story line of the film. It would have been nice to have learned about proper umpire positioning in calling the bases, what exactly a balk is, and the intricacies of the infield fly rule. Instead, the school scenes are filled with a quick montage of school activities and more buffoonery.

Kill the Umpire has its interest, particularly for someone who likes broad slapstick humor. William Bendix is likable enough in the starring role. For baseball fans, however, the film will seem fanciful and unconvincing, with not enough emphasis on the sport itself. It is therefore difficult to recommend *Kill the Umpire* to baseball fans, even those who are as ardent about the game as Bill "Two Call" Johnson.

Rhubarb (1951)

Rhubarb, based on a novel of the same name by H. Allen Smith, is a fantasy-comedy film about a cat named Rhubarb who inherits an unsuccessful major-league baseball team known as the Brooklyn Loons (although the team's name morphs into the Brooklyn Rhubarbs at some point during the story), along with $30 million, from Thaddeus J. Banner, an eccentric millionaire who loved the cat's spirit and did not care much for his other potential heir, unpleasant daughter Myra. Because it is difficult to imagine a cat owning a major-league ball club (even in Hollywood), Banner's will appoints Banner's press agent, Eric Yeager, as Rhubarb's guardian. At first, the Loons players are reluctant to play for a cat, but once they realize that Rhubarb brings good luck to the team, they become enthusiastic about the feline, usually petting the animal before they step to the plate. With the addition of Rhubarb, the Loons start to play better, rising from the cellar of the league and making it to the World Series. If only Eric can keep Rhubarb out of trouble and have him attend each of the Loons games, a World Series victory for Brooklyn appears imminent.

As can be seen from that short plot summary, Rhubarb is the owner of the team in name only. Unlike that famous mule named Francis, Rhubarb does not talk, so Rhubarb cannot run the team in any meaningful manner. Rhubarb does not have mental or supernatural powers to assist the team. The real owner of the team after Banner dies is Eric Yeager. Rhubarb is simply an animal that comes to each game, sits in particularly good seats, and provides the team with good luck. Contrary to just about every blurb about the film, *Rhubarb* is not really the story of a cat that inherits a major-league baseball team. It is really just the story of a major-league baseball team that has a feline mascot.

While the concept of *Rhubarb* must have seemed funny to somebody, every concept needs a plot, and in this case, a single compelling story line must have been hard to devise. Therefore the screenwriters chose to devise several different story arcs to fill the running time of the feature-length film, including T. J. Banner's request that Eric capture Rhubarb and bring him home, a very difficult task indeed; convincing the ballplayers to play for a team owned by a cat; Myra suing to wrest the team from the cat, resulting in a court trial; and gamblers kidnapping Rhubarb in the hope that Brooklyn's game will fall apart without the presence of Rhubarb.

While these several story lines are uninvolving, there are still some good laughs in the film. It is fun watching Rhubarb steal golf balls right in front of some pompous golfers and then scare one of the golfer's dog; Eric attempting to trap Rhubarb but unable to find any net strong enough to hold him; the worldwide newspaper headlines about a cat inheriting so much money; and the overreaction of the Brooklyn fans to the cat in their midst. The problem with *Rhubarb* is that there are simply not enough good laughs in the film, and without engaging story arcs or more laughs, *Rhubarb* is a bore.

Another attempt at humor is the satirical material in the film, primarily about television, satirizing the intrusive commercials (including one that preempts the showing of part of the game), and the poor television reception of the day. Unfortunately, these vignettes are not particularly funny to a modern viewer. They are only interesting as curios.

In addition to *Rhubarb*'s premise being lacking, the production itself has several problems. The movie was filmed in California, not New York, and as a result, even though the bulk of the film supposedly takes place in Brooklyn, there is no real feel of Brooklyn in the film. The human performances are nothing special except for Gene Lockhart in the role of the eccentric millionaire, T. J. Banner. Lockhart is engaging in whatever Banner does, whether reveling in the high spirit of the cat, fighting with Myra, showing his tenderness and love for Rhubarb, or stating his last wishes on his death bed. Unfortunately, Lockhart's character exits the film early, and *Rhubarb* is not as much fun once Lockhart is gone.

The other good performance is by Orangey the Cat as Rhubarb. Orangey, a male marmalade tabby cat, plays Rhubarb against type, not as a cute, loving cat, but as a vicious one who bares his teeth, scratches people, scares dogs, and is difficult to catch. In 1952, Orangey received a PATSY Award for his performance in this film. A PATSY is the animal kingdom's version of the Oscar. In 1962, Orangey became a two-time winner, receiving the award again for his performance in *Breakfast at Tiffany's* (1961). Orangey appeared in other films and television shows, but many people remember the cat best for its role as a housecat that attacks its owner, Scott Carey, the title character in *The Incredible Shrinking Man* (1957), after Carey becomes small.

The baseball footage in *Rhubarb* is disappointing, consisting primarily of stock footage of games shot from a long distance, a few shots of batters swinging at balls, and footage facing into the stands or into the dugout with some crowd noise in the background, confirming that those scenes were not shot anywhere near a ball field. Just as with *It Happens Every Spring* (1949), none of the real names of any Major League Baseball teams or their ballparks is used in the film. Perhaps in this case, Major League Baseball did not want to be associated with such a silly film (or perhaps this is a characteristic of baseball movies starring Ray Milland, who plays Eric Yeager in this film).

There is one interesting and funny bit of baseball in the movie. With two runners on base for Brooklyn, the batter hits a slow, looping ball down the third base line. Rhubarb jumps onto the field to steal the ball while the St. Louis mascot, a dog, runs onto the field to chase Rhubarb. Two infielders, the dog, and the cat collide on the third base line, and with some errant throws, all three base runners score. There is a clever shot above and to the left of home plate as first the dog, then the cat, and then a base runner cross home plate. An argument ensues as to whether Brooklyn had two many men on the field during the play (does Rhubarb count as a player?) before the umpire rules that the ball had rolled foul.

Fantasy baseball films can work if the film remains consistent within its fantasy elements. It is obviously ridiculous for a cat to inherit $30 million, but as a premise to a film, that idea can work. Rhubarb is just a regular cat, but the baseball players and fans have such a strong, superstitious attraction to the animal that the Loons start to play better. That is not an unbelievable premise either. What baseball players (and their fans) are not superstitious to some degree, such as Joe DiMaggio always touching second base on his way in from center field or Roger Clemens always touching the head of the Babe Ruth statue in Monument Park before he pitched in Yankee Stadium? Rhubarb can be viewed as a good-luck charm for the Loons, not that hard to believe, particularly in a baseball setting.

Unfortunately, as the film progresses, the fantasy becomes more outrageous. Eric causes a rainout of a World Series game by dropping dry ice onto the field from a propeller plane. Really? Rhubarb escapes from gangsters on his own, makes his way to the ballpark without any guide, scales the outfield wall without assistance, and then goes back to his usual seat in the stands, not for the game but to see the female cat that usually has the seat behind Rhubarb's. Really? When a fantasy film turns into a cartoon, much of the impact is lost.

There are no important child characters in the film, which is surprising because the film has a child-oriented story line and might have worked better if written with a youth audience in mind. Instead, the film is directed toward an adult audience, although unlike the novel, the film is less satire and more screwball comedy. Frankly, *Rhubarb*, with its sporadic comedy, uneven story arcs, inconsistent fantasy elements, and only one good baseball scene, is quite dreadful. A better baseball fantasy-comedy of the same year, *Angels in the Outfield* (1951), is by far the more enjoyable film. In fact, Paul Douglas, the star of *Angels in the Outfield*, makes a cameo appearance at the end of *Rhubarb*, and while it is nice to see Douglas in another baseball movie, even he does not have enough screen presence to make *Rhubarb* into a fun film.

The Bingo Long Traveling All-Stars & Motor Kings (1976)

The Bingo Long Traveling All-Stars & Motor Kings, based on a book of the same long name by William Brashler, has a number of unique characteristics. First of all, it has, by far, the longest title of any film about baseball and is probably right up there with the longest film titles of all time. Second, it has an almost all-black cast, groundbreaking for any baseball film, even today, although perhaps not that unusual for a movie released in the mid-1970s. Also, while *Bingo Long* is not really about the Negro Leagues, it is about Negro League players, making *Bingo Long* a rare baseball film to address any aspect of the Negro Leagues.

Bingo Long, a pitcher for the Ebony Aces, has become tired of being mistreated by the team's owner, Sallie Potter. Bingo decides to steal some of the best black players from around the Negro Leagues and form the All-Stars, his own barnstorming team. At first the All-Stars are a success, but when Sallie puts pressure on the All-Stars and its opponents, the team starts to flounder. Sallie then proposes a challenge—one game between the All-Stars and the stars of the Negro League teams. If the All-Stars win, they become a new franchise in the Negro Leagues. If they lose, the All-Stars must disband and the players must rejoin their prior teams. Bingo accepts the bet. Sallie leaves nothing to chance, kidnapping Leon Carter, the star catcher and slugger of the All-Stars, trying to keep him out of the big game. Carter escapes and manages to make it to the big game by the final inning, hitting a walk-off home run for the win.

The Bingo Long Traveling All-Stars & Motor Kings has its entertaining moments. The acting is wonderful, with the two stars, Billy Dee Williams as Bingo Long and James Earl Jones as Leon Carter, particular standouts. There is special interest in seeing a younger, slimmer James Earl Jones playing an athlete, although, of course, he did play a boxer in a slightly earlier film, *The Great White Hope* (1970). The other big name in the cast is Richard Pryor, playing right fielder Charlie Snow, who is trying to make it into the big leagues posing as a Cuban (there were Cubans in the major leagues at least as late as 1911 and probably for some time thereafter) and later as an American Indian. Pryor, as always, is funny.

The promotional aspects of the All-Stars are also entertaining. When they arrive in a new town, the All-Stars cake-walk down Main Street, singing and clowning around, in order to rouse interest in their games. Bingo Long has an "Invite Pitch," which he throws at the beginning of a game to the first batter, with no other players on the field. Long sometimes dresses in a gorilla suit while he is pitch-

From left to right, Louis Keystone (Sam "Birmingham" Brison), Willie Lee Shively (Rico Dawson), and Leon Carter (James Earl Jones) celebrate a victory in the locker room in *The Bingo Long Traveling All-Stars & Motor Kings* (1976).

ing, the team sometimes has a midget catcher and a one-arm player, and before each game, the All-Stars entertain the fans with their comedy routines. Any similarities to the Harlem Globetrotters are probably intentional. (Actually, the All-Stars are based more on a black barnstorming baseball team, the Indianapolis Clowns, who also performed comedy routines before their games. The Indianapolis Clowns usually played in the Negro American League.)

Many of the characters in the film are caricatures. Sallie Potter, the owner of the Ebony Aces, who tries to destroy the All-Stars by nefarious means, is pompous and evil. Bertha DeWitt, the only female owner in the league, is incredibly obese and addicted to sex. A player, Rainbow, gets hit in the head with a pitch and can no longer talk. Joe Calloway, a farm boy that the All-Stars take from another team, becomes a great player. It is all quite silly, but if the viewer can get into the swing of things, the film can be quite amusing.

For all of that, *Bingo Long* is a disappointing film. There are simply too many comedy elements in the film, and most of the comedy is too broadly played. Much of the humor is caused by the fact that once the All-Stars decide to play against white teams, and usually beat them, they realize that they have no choice but to act like fools in front of the white fans, or they will get no more games or be run out of town. The black players have to shame themselves in order to make a living. Viewers can laugh about the antics in the film, but they mask the racism of the white fans and the inability of the black players to play in the white major leagues. There was a good opportunity for *Bingo Long* to address some serious issues, but that opportunity is squandered in the name of light entertainment.

While *Bingo Long* is not about the Negro Leagues, it does show some aspects of their baseball. The character of Bingo Long, the leader and pitcher of the All-Stars, is inspired by one of the greatest baseball pitchers of all time, Satchel Paige. Paige actually made it to the white major leagues as a forty-two-year-old rookie playing for the Cleveland Indians in 1948. Bingo Long's invite pitch is probably inspired by one of Satchel Paige's routines. Sometimes when Paige was pitching on his barnstorming tours, he would have the fielders behind him sit down. Paige would then strike out the side.

Some sources state that the character of Leon Carter is based on Josh Gibson, a catcher primarily for the Homestead Grays and the Pittsburgh Crawfords in the Negro Leagues. Gibson was a fabulous hitter with a high lifetime batting average. He was also known as a slugger, purportedly hitting almost 800 home runs in his professional career. In *Bingo Long*, Leon Carter is a catcher and a slugger, but there do not seem to be any other tie-ins to Josh Gibson.

Near the end of the film, Charlie Snow, the character played by Richard Pryor, comes up with a new idea to sneak into the white major leagues. He decides to masquerade as an American Indian by the name of Chief Tokohama, thereby avoiding the major leagues' unwritten ban against African American ballplayers. This is a clever reference to a black baseball player named Charlie Grant, who played second base in the Negro Leagues. In 1901, during spring training, John McGraw, then the manager of the Baltimore Orioles, saw Grant, who was working as a bellhop at a hotel, playing ball with some of his co-workers. Grant was light-skinned and had wavy hair. Recognizing Grant's potential, McGraw decided to disguise Grant as a Cherokee Indian, give him a new name, Charlie Tokohama (based on the name of a creek McGraw spotted on a map), and try to get him into the big leagues. The secret did not last long, however, and Grant never played in a regular-season baseball game.

At the end of the movie, Joe Calloway is signed by a team from the white major leagues. While the players are excited for Joe, Leon

Carter recognizes the significance of the event for the All-Stars. Leon understands that once the white major leagues decide to accept black players on a regular basis, the Negro Leagues are doomed. Joe Calloway's good fortune is a true catch-22 for black players. Finally, there is a touch of realism in the film because, in fact, the Negro Leagues were essentially out of business after the 1951 season, just a few years after the action in *Bingo Long* apparently takes place.

The Scout (1994)

Following his last screw-up with a failed pitching prospect, Al Percolo, a scout for the New York Yankees, is banished to Mexico to look for players in the backwaters of that country. After a long period of terrible bus rides, bad food, and awful baseball, Percolo comes upon a true phenom, Steve Nebraska, who can consistently throw a ball for strikes at over one hundred miles per hour and hit record-distance home runs at seemingly every at bat. Percolo brings Nebraska back to the states, where he is signed by the Yankees for $55 million dollars.

Percolo's agreement with the Yankees is that Nebraska does not have to pitch in his first year with the team, unless the Yankees make the World Series, a highly unlikely event at the time the deal was made. To no viewer's surprise, the Yankees do make the World Series that year, and Nebraska, after initially running away from the game, agrees to pitch the first game of the Fall Classic. He strikes out twenty-seven straight batters and hits a home run, winning the game for the home team.

The Scout is part comedy, part fantasy. Most viewers will probably be willing to suspend their disbelief and accept a pitcher who can throw a pitch at 112 mph; throws so fast that when the catcher receives the ball, he is knocked back several feet; only throws strikes; and does not need warm-ups before he pitches. What may be harder to believe is that such a good pitcher is also a good hitter. Where does that idea come from?

The film is generally funny, with the best comedy moments always involving Albert Brooks as Al Percolo. In order to convince religious parents to allow their son to quit college and turn pro, Percolo wears a large cross to the family's dinner, mentions that there is a large picture of Christ in the Yankees locker room similar to the one

This is a publicity photo for *The Scout* (1994). On the left is pitcher Steve Nebraska (Brendan Fraser) and on the right is baseball scout Al Percolo (Albert Brooks).

in the family's house ("terrific likeness, isn't it?"), and provides the dubious facts that Mickey Mantle's sister, also named Mickey but spelled "Micki," is a nun, and that Lou Gehrig contracted his fatal disease in college. On Al's banishment to Mexico, he watches games with animals in the outfield and one in which a pitcher leaves the mound to take a telephone call, not to mention the strange food that the fans eat in the stands.

Some of the baseball-oriented jokes are the best. When Al needs to find a psychiatrist for Steve Nebraska in New York, he consults the telephone directory and going in alphabetical order, discovers a psychiatrist named "Aaron, H." Percolo sees that as a good omen. When Bret Saberhagen (All-Star and Cy Young Award–winning pitcher, playing for many teams) comes in to pitch against Nebraska at his tryouts and asks Percolo for his money in advance, Percolo sarcastically says under his breath, "Nine million dollars; he needs my money!" When Nebraska keeps overeating, Percolo says that he has two words for Nebraska: "Fernando Valenzuela. Started out a pitcher, wound up a truck."

The Scout is the only baseball film that is based more on *King Kong* (1933) than the game of baseball. Percolo is a big fan of the movie and can quote the dialogue word for word. In his scouting trips, he tells people that he is looking for the next King Kong, and when he first spots Steve Nebraska, he believes he has found him. Nebraska is substantially larger and stronger than the other ballplayers. There is never any explanation of where he came from. Nebraska is a god in his little baseball world in Mexico, far off the beaten path. Percolo decides to bring Nebraska to New York, primarily for Percolo's fame and fortune. At an early press conference, flashbulbs disturb Nebraska, just as they disturbed King Kong many years ago. The apparent conclusion of the film has Nebraska on the roof of Yankee Stadium, a parallel to the Empire State Building of the older film.

The problem with the *King Kong* analogy is that *The Scout* never takes the analogy to its natural end. King Kong did not survive the conclusion of his film. He died from those airplane attacks up on the Empire State Building. Similarly, Nebraska, while he does not have to die at the end of *The Scout*, should have come to a sad end, either because he was too nervous to play in the World Series or because he did not pitch well in the game. If it was beauty that killed King Kong, then Nebraska's time in New York or his sessions with the psychiatrist should have put enough of a dent in his mental attitude that his career would have come to an end. Instead and despite the *King Kong* thread running throughout the movie, the filmmakers went for a happy and sappy ending. If the filmmakers were unwilling to take the *King Kong* analogy to its natural conclusion, why make the analogy at all?

Not only is the ending of *The Scout* happy and sappy, it also strains the credulity of the viewer. After some self-doubts, Nebraska throws the most perfect game of all time—twenty-seven batters up and twenty-seven batters striking out, on only eighty-one pitches. That is a statistic that no baseball fan can believe, no matter how much they want to suspend disbelief. In fact, the only times such pitching miracles occurred were in the film *It Happens Every Spring* (1949) and in the novel *The Curious Case of Sidd Finch* by George Plimpton. In fact, the hard-throwing Sidd Finch, who never needs warm-ups before he pitches, can be seen as the inspiration for the Steve Nebraska of *The Scout*.

It is nice to see some of the major leaguers and former major leaguers who appear in the film, including Tim McCarver (All-Star

This is a photograph of the original Yankee Stadium in New York City, around the time when pitcher Steve Nebraska first pitches there in *The Scout* (1994). *(Photographs in the Carol M. Highsmith Archive, Library of Congress, Prints and Photographs Division, LC-DIG-highsm-14721)*

catcher, playing for many teams, later a broadcaster), Keith Hernandez (All-Star first baseman, primarily for the Mets and the Cardinals, later a broadcaster), Ozzie Smith (All-Star shortstop, primarily with the Cardinals), and Bob Tewksbury (All-Star pitcher, playing for many teams). Those are mere cameo roles, but George Steinbrenner, then the owner of the Yankees, has a slightly longer part in the film, playing himself. The characterization of the Yankees owner in the film is a subtle jibe at Steinbrenner's large personality and pomposity. Steinbrenner's willingness to play himself in the part makes him both amusing and endearing, and there are few times in the world of baseball that the adjective "endearing" has been properly applied to George Steinbrenner.

However, having blown the *King Kong* analogy and gone for what they must have believed was a happy ending to the film, the filmmakers made a significant error, because a movie about the Yankees buying another World Series is hardly a happy ending for non-Yankees fans. Laughs and all, *The Scout* is a disappointing film.

Mr. 3000 (2004)

Through the end of the 2016 season, there were only thirty players in Major League Baseball's exclusive 3,000-hit club. The all-time leader in career hits is Pete Rose with 4,256. The next in line is Ty Cobb with either 4,191 or 4,189, depending on the reference source. The last player to reach this milestone was Ichiro Suzuki, who accomplished the task on August 7, 2016, while playing for the Miami Marlins. Since only thirty players have reached that milestone in the long history of Major League Baseball, 3,000 hits in a career is clearly an incredible accomplishment.

Mr. 3000 concerns another member of that club, or so it seemed at one time. Mr. 3000 is the sobriquet for Stan Ross, a fictional player for the Milwaukee Brewers. During the 1995 season, Ross reached the 3,000-hit plateau and immediately quit baseball, even though the Brewers were in the middle of a pennant race. Ross quit at that time because he believed that reaching the 3,000-hit club would result in his automatic election into the Baseball Hall of Fame. In that regard, Ross was generally correct. Every major-league ballplayer who has 3,000 career hits, and is otherwise eligible for the Hall of Fame, and does not have other special reasons for disqualification, has been inducted into the Hall of Fame. The other players who have 3,000 hits, are eligible, but have not made the Hall of Fame are Pete Rose, banned from baseball for gambling, and Rafael Palmeiro, who tested positive for the use of anabolic steroids.

After leaving baseball, Ross hit it big, opening numerous successful businesses, capitalizing on his self-given nickname, Mr. 3000. Unfortunately, seven years after he left baseball, Ross's most important goal, induction into the Hall of Fame, had not been met. During his playing days, Ross upset so many sportswriters, fans, teammates, and others with his arrogant behavior that he never received enough votes for the Hall. Then, to make matters worse, the unthinkable happens, at least for Ross. The Hall of Fame determines that a mistake was made in calculating Ross's career hits, counting three hits twice in a game suspended by rain. Thus, Mr. 3000 only has 2,997 career hits.

This situation is not unprecedented in baseball. In 1910, Ty Cobb of the Detroit Tigers won the American League batting title by approximately one percentage point over Nap Lajoie of the Cleveland Indians. However, years later it was discovered that through a clerical error, one game of Ty Cobb's was counted twice that season, and if that had not happened, Lajoie would have won the title. Although this is a matter of some controversy even to the present day, Cobb is still considered by Major League Baseball to be the 1910 batting champion, even though Lajoie had the higher batting average that year.

Ross decides to return to baseball at the age of forty-seven, get three more hits, and hopefully succeed in his quest for admission to the Hall of Fame. At first, things are difficult for Ross as three hits seem hard to come by at Ross's age. However, Ross does get an in-field single in one game, a homer in another, and on the last day of the season, he is hopeful of finally reaching his goal.

Mr. 3000 is hardly a classic baseball film, but it is still quite enjoyable. Bernie Mac as Stan Ross is engaging in the title role, likable even when he is playing Ross as a pompous ass. Mac has the size and the skills to portray a great baseball player, which contributes to the overall effectiveness of the baseball scenes. It is surprising that Mac did not go on to other good film roles in his career. Among other recognizable actors in the film is Paul Sorvino, playing the Brewers manager. It is an unusual part for Sorvino. He has no lines at the beginning of the story, and when Ross comes back from retirement, Sorvino does little more than sit at the end of the bench and scowl. His first lines are at the end of the film, when he gets into an argument with the umpire.

Mr. 3000 is only a light comedy, but there are a few good laughs in the film. When Ross forcibly takes his original 3,000-hit ball from a young boy in the stands, his father shouts, "Why don't you take his cotton candy while you're at it?" Coming out on the field on the day his number is retired by the Brewers, Ross appears to be appreciating the fans, but he is really appreciating his handsome image on the Jumbotron. When Ross returns to the Brewers locker room for the first time, he finds that his teammates have left a walker in front of his locker. Later, Ross helps to teach a foreign-born player to swear in English.

Some of the strengths of *Mr. 3000* are in the little things. The film is a virtual time capsule of the pop culture of the early 2000s, with clips about the fictional Ross from *The Tonight Show with Jay Leno*,

ESPN's *SportsCenter* and *Pardon the Interruption*, and Fox's *The Best Damn Sports Show, Period*. Even Larry King from CNN gets into the action. At the end of the film, Ross appears in a commercial for Viagra, which is fitting given Ross's age. There is even a moment of older pop culture, with a clip from a Bugs Bunny cartoon.

The game action was filmed at Miller Park in Milwaukee, Wisconsin. The park, which is named after one of the beers that made Milwaukee famous, looks spectacular in the film. It is a perfect setting for the games, with the producers somehow convincing lots of fans to attend the cinematic contests. The baseball action on the field seems legitimate. Viewers even get to see the end of a race between the four Milwaukee sausages, providing some local color to the action. Indeed, some of the funniest moments in the film are the insults from one of the sausages to Stan Ross. It is hard not to laugh when a man dressed in a tall sausage outfit is making smart remarks at a ballplayer.

Baseball films tend to be centered on the baseball stadiums of New York, Chicago, Boston, or Los Angeles, and so when films are shot in other ballparks, such as *Angels in the Outfield* (1951), shot at Forbes Field in Pittsburgh, or *Little Big League* (1994), shot at the Metrodome in Minneapolis, it is a nice change of pace for baseball fans. How many other baseball movies will be filmed at Miller Park in Milwaukee?

The film does seem insensitive in one respect. The only real player to end his career with exactly 3,000 hits is Roberto Clemente of the Pittsburgh Pirates. He accomplished that goal at the end of the Pirates' 1972 season. The only reason Clemente's total career hits concluded with number 3,000 was that he died in a plane crash after the 1972 season. So, did Stan Ross, who quit the game when he could still play, really have to wear number 21 on his back, just as Clemente did?

Mr. 3000 has some of the usual clichés of baseball films. Not unexpectedly, the arrogant Stan Ross does mellow and finally becomes a team player and team leader on his return to the Brewers. As a result, his new teammates and even his old manager finally come around and support him. Ross's last chance to reach 3,000 hits occurs in his last career at bat in the last inning of the last game of the season. As they say, it all goes down to the wire.

However, *Mr. 3000* is not all clichés. After becoming a team leader, Ross lets his team down again, by going on *The Tonight Show* and missing a team practice that he called. On *The Tonight Show*, Ross insults his teammates once again, just to get a laugh. And the ending of the film is quite a surprise. So, for some laughs, some good baseball, and a few surprises along the way, *Mr. 3000* is worth a view.

9

BASEBALL MUSICALS

They Learned About Women (1930)

Given the title of the film, it is not surprising that *They Learned About Women* is more about romance than baseball. The story involves two players from the Blue Sox baseball team, Jerry Burke, the catcher, and Jack Glennon, a pitcher. Burke and Glennon are also vaudeville performers in the off-season, although they have a tendency to break into song even during the regular season. Jack is in love with Mary, the club secretary, but when a gold digger named Daisy Gebhart gets her hooks into Jack, he drops Mary and marries Daisy. Daisy also talks Jack into quitting baseball. In the end, Daisy drops Jack for a different entertainer. Jack then returns to the Blue Sox and Mary, and in the climax of the film, Jack pitches for the Blue Sox in the final game of the World Series.

They Learned About Women stars Gus Van and Joe Schenck, who had an act in vaudeville and on Broadway known as Van & Schenck, in which the two sang songs, performed comedy routines, including comedy dialect songs, and performed minstrel acts. Schenck also played the piano. Examples of these types of performances by Van & Schenck are included in *They Learned About Women*. The two also worked in radio and released several records. Schenck died on June 28, 1930, at the age of thirty-nine, about six months after *They Learned About Women* was released.

Surprisingly, it is not so far-fetched to find Major League Baseball players who also performed in vaudeville during the off-season. It was not all that long ago that many ballplayers did not make enough money from the sport for a whole year of living, and they had to obtain additional income during the winter months. In the 1920s, some of those players turned to vaudeville for extra cash. For example, Waite Hoyt, the pitcher with the most wins for the New York Yankees in the 1920s and a future Hall of Famer, performed in vaudeville during the off-season, as did the comedy team of Cohen & Hogan, which was comprised of James Francis "Shanty" Hogan, a major-league catcher from 1925 to 1937, primarily with the Boston Braves and the New York Giants, and his Giants teammate and second baseman, Andy Cohen. According to Ken Burns's *Baseball*, famous ballplayers such as Cap Anson, Rube Waddell, and Christy Mathewson and manager John McGraw performed on the circuit.

Van & Schenck were obviously very popular in their day, but whatever charm they may have had is lost on a modern-day audience. Although their singing is adequate in *They Learned About Women*, the two are not very funny, with, at one point, the film coming to a screeching halt in a very long segment in which the two perform their vaudeville act onstage. The film actually gets worse after that, when Benny Rubin and Tom Dugan, playing two of the other Blue Sox players, perform a "comedy" routine in front of an agent in the hopes of also being signed for a gig in vaudeville. Rubin and Dugan are even less funny than Van & Schenck, and it is easy to joke that Van & Schenck (and Rubin and Dugan) killed vaudeville, but what is clear is that *They Learned About Women* did nothing positive to promote movie musicals at MGM in the early 1930s, with very few being made at the studio after *They Learned About Women* was released.

The climax of the film depicts the World Series between those famous and bitter rivals, the Blue Sox and the Bisons, whoever they are. The Blue Sox win the seventh game of the series, 8–7, when Jerry Burke hits a walk-off, inside-the-park homer, with Jack Glennon, who had been hit on the head with a pitch, on base at the time. Of course, the terms "walk-off home run" and "walk-off hit," which describe the game-winning RBI for the home team in the bottom of the ninth inning or in extra innings, were not in use in 1930. The terms came into vogue in the 1990s. The terms arise from the fact that when there is a walk-off hit, all the losing team can do is walk off the field.

They Learned About Women provides the term with an additional meaning. As Jerry Burke rounds the bases in the film for his walk-off home run, he is running as slowly as can ever be imagined. How he even makes it to third base without being thrown out is amazing. Then Burke actually has to stop between third and home to allow Glennon, who has fallen, to get up and make it to the plate. Mercifully, the film does not show what is happening with the ball in the outfield while Burke is "running" the bases. This must be the slowest inside-the-park home run ever hit. So, for once in real life or fiction, an inside-the-park home run can be accurately described as a "walk-off home run," because the batter appears to be walking around the bases.

They Learned About Women is not the first sound film about baseball, but it is the earliest one extant today. Many of its techniques were employed in subsequent films, such as its mixing of archive footage (showing large crowds in large stadiums) with shots of the actors playing ball on only a portion of the field, a radio announcer narrating the events of the game, and the game ending with an inside-the-park home run. However, the archive footage in this film is so bad that in one scene, the radio announcer comments on a circus catch that cannot be seen in the archive footage, although a man in a hat partially blocking the camera is clearly visible. While Joe Schenck employs a reasonable pitching motion on the mound, his pitches to the plate seem awfully slow. The technology was not there in 1930 for the use of a radar gun to measure the velocity of the pitches, but if Schenck's pitches are over 50 mph on the gun, it would be surprising. Whether his pitches are down the middle or high, the batters still swing at them, missing them by a mile. Apparently none of the actors ever heard the advice to "swing level."

The 1930s was not the best decade for baseball in the cinema, with *They Learned About Women* setting the tone for the next several years of films. It was not until 1942 and *The Pride of the Yankees* that baseball films became part of the mainstream of Hollywood filmmaking, when a great baseball film could also finally be a great film.

Take Me Out to the Ball Game (1949)

Take Me Out to the Ball Game is part of a series of color musicals produced by MGM after World War II and continuing into the 1950s, often starring the aging Fred Astaire or the younger and more athletic Gene Kelly. In this film, Kelly is the star along with Esther Williams, who performed in many of the MGM musicals of this time period, and Frank Sinatra, who performed in a few.

The story involves a professional baseball team known as the

Wolves and, in particular, the team's shortstop, Eddie O'Brien, and its second baseman, Dennis Ryan, who perform song-and-dance routines in vaudeville in the off-season. They are also part of a famed double-play combination, along with first baseman Nat Goldberg, thus the song "O'Brien to Ryan to Goldberg." As O'Brien and Ryan join the team for spring training after its championship season of the year before, things are changing for the Wolves. The team's owner recently died, and his young and distant female relative, K.C. Higgins, has inherited the team.

At first, the Wolves players are unhappy with a female owner, but once she demonstrates her knowledge of baseball, they warm up to her. The film then turns into a love story, as K.C. and Eddie O'Brien start to have feelings for each other, but circumstances prevent them from getting together, and baseball fan Shirley Delwyn falls in love with a reluctant Dennis Ryan. As the baseball season draws to a close, the Wolves appear to be well on their way to another world championship, when gamblers attempt, by illicit means, to force Eddie out of the Wolves' lineup. Things work out in the end, with the Wolves winning the championship and all of the lovers coming together.

The title of the film is based on what is the most popular sports song of all time, "Take Me Out to the Ball Game." In fact, it has been said that "Take Me Out to the Ball Game" is the third-most performed song in America, behind only "The Star Spangled Banner" and "Happy Birthday." The song was written in 1908 by Jack Norworth, the lyricist for many popular songs, including "Shine On, Harvest Moon," and set to music by Albert Von Tilzer, a prolific song composer whose works include "I'll Be With You in Apple Blossom Time." As the story goes, neither of the collaborators had seen a baseball game at the time the song was written.

"Take Me Out to the Ball Game" is traditionally played during the seventh-inning stretch of Major League Baseball games, with the fans singing along. That was not, however, always the case. Despite the fact that the song was written in 1908, it was not until the 1930s that the song was first performed at a baseball game, and many years thereafter before it was regularly performed during the seventh-inning stretch of Major League Baseball games. Also, the entire song is not performed at the games; the fans only sing the chorus of the song. "Take Me Out to the Ball Game" has two other verses that are almost forgotten. In the first verse of the revised 1927 version, a boy asks his girlfriend, Nelly Kelly, out on a date to Coney Island, but she prefers that he take her out to the ball game. The second verse is about Nelly's interest in the game. Unlike the well-known chorus, the other two verses of "Take Me Out to the Ball Game" are seldom sung or heard, unless one watches *Take Me Out to the Ball Game*. Baseball fans can hear the first verse sung by Frank Sinatra and Gene Kelly in the opening song-and-dance routine of the film.

In *Take Me Out to the Ball Game* (1949), manager Michael Gihuly (Richard Lane) and the new owner of the Wolves, K. C. Higgins (Esther Williams), watch as the vaudeville team (and double-play combination) of O'Brien, Ryan, and Goldberg perform before a game.

Take Me Out to the Ball Game is a disappointing movie, both as a baseball film and a musical. Of course, no one expects a baseball musical to present a realistic evocation of the summer game. All musicals are, to a degree, unrealistic. But *Take Me Out to the Ball Game* takes the matter to the extreme, with a world-championship baseball team that seemingly belongs to no city and calls itself the Wolves (not exactly a baseball name), a shortstop and second baseman who perform in vaudeville in the offseason, and a double-play combination that performs a comedy act for the fans before the games. The baseball skills of the actors are, to be kind, awkward. The story arc of a gambler improperly trying to influence the results of the games is totally unconvincing, especially because *Take Me Out to the Ball Game* is a family film, and the filmmakers were apparently reluctant to show what real-life gamblers would probably do to a real-life baseball player who screwed up their betting operation, at least before the 1919 Black Sox scandal. In addition, that kind of realism would make the musical numbers totally inappropriate.

When one thinks of the great MGM musicals of the post–World War II era, titles that come to mind are *On the Town* (1949), *An American in Paris* (1951), *Singin' in the Rain* (1952), *The Band Wagon* (1953), *Seven Brides for Seven Brothers* (1954), and a few others. *Take Me Out to the Ball Game* is never on the list. The problem with the film is that all of the songs, except for the title song, are easily forgettable. Also, and unexpectedly for a Gene Kelly film of the time period, there are no striking dance routines. Most viewers probably expect, at the least, a stunning dance sequence to conclude the film, such as the "Broadway Ballet" in *Singin' in the Rain* or the "American in Paris Ballet" in *An American in Paris*, but *Take Me Out to the Ball Game* ends with only a mild and unmemorable song and dance performed on a stage by the four principals, as they get out of character and mention contemporary musical names such as Fred Astaire and Judy Garland. That supposedly clever scene hardly befits a baseball movie set just after the turn of the century.

In fact, the only memorable musical moments in the film are those performed outdoors in the ballpark. The first is the singing of the song "Yes, Indeedy" by Sinatra and Kelly, and the dance routine performed on the roof of the dugout, on the steps of the grandstand, and on the dirt of the field. Later, "It's Fate, Baby, It's Fate" sung by Betty Garrett, while not exactly a dance routine, being more like a brisk walk or a chase, is performed by Garrett and Sinatra in the stands of the baseball stadium. While there were dance routines that appeared to be performed outdoors in films before *Take Me Out to the Ball Game*, most, if not all of those, were actually shot on a Hollywood soundstage or on the city street of a studio back lot. It is therefore refreshing to see dance routines performed in a real stadium, in the real outdoors.

However, those two sequences, as notable as they may be, are not enough to save *Take Me Out to the Ball Game*. Baseball and music are a mismatch in this film. The only thing they have in common is that for the movie fan, not only are there substantially better baseball movies available for viewing, there are also substantially better MGM musicals to see.

Damn Yankees (1958)

If the Pittsburgh Pirates of the 1950s needed angels in their outfield to turn the team's fortunes around, *Damn Yankees* suggests that the Washington Senators of that same decade needed help from the devil himself to win the American League pennant. In this case, after the Senators lose another ball game to the New York Yankees, Joe Boyd, an ardent fan of the Senators, offers to sell his soul for one long-ball hitter for his team, and the devil, employing the name of Mr. Applegate, is happy to oblige. Applegate turns Joe Boyd into a young ballplayer, Joe Hardy, who is so exceptional that he leads the Senators to a chance at the pennant on the last day of the season. But, in the process, will Joe be permanently separated from his wife, Meg, and will Joe permanently lose his soul to the devil?

Damn Yankees is based on the very successful Broadway musical of the same name that opened on Broadway on May 5, 1955, and ran for 1,019 performances. It won seven Tony Awards, including Best Musical, Best Performance by a Leading Actor in a Musical (Ray Walston, as Mr. Applegate), and Best Performance by a Leading Actress in a Musical (Gwen Verdon, as Lola). The musical was based on a 1954 book by Douglass Wallop, titled *The Year the Yankees Lost the Pennant.*

Damn Yankees is a fun movie, surely the best movie musical about baseball, and also one of the best of the fantasy movies about the game. One of its positives is that even though it is a story about the devil, its underlying premise has a solid foundation in the real world of baseball. The Washington Senators, founded in 1901, was one of the original teams in the American League. While the franchise had successes prior to 1934, including the years with one of the most famous pitchers of all time, Walter Johnson, the team was often less than mediocre in the next two decades, with six last-place finishes in the 1940s and 1950s. At the same time, the Yankees were one of the most successful franchises in baseball history. No wonder Joe Boyd refers to the Yankees as "those damn Yankees."

Another important positive of the film is its sensitive handling of the relationship between Joe and Meg. When Joe departs in the middle of the night, he leaves a note for Meg in the form of the beautiful song "Goodbye Old Girl." Even as a successful ballplayer, young Joe Hardy misses Meg and decides to room with her so that he can be near her. At the end of the film, Joe and Meg defeat the devil by demonstrating their love in the reprise of the song "There's Something About an Empty Chair."

Just about every actor and actress who appears in the movie is reprising his or her role from the original Broadway production. They give uniformly excellent performances. In particular, Ray Walston is outstanding as Mr. Applegate, alternately clever, deceptive, charming, funny, and, of course, devilish. Walston is also lucky to have some of the best lines in the film. When Applegate produces a light for his cigarette out of thin air and Joe asks him how he does it, he says, "I'm handy with fire." When Applegate makes his deal with Joe and they just shake hands on it, he says, "What did you expect to do? Sign your name in blood or some other phony stunt like that?" When Lola, the devil's temptress, starts to disagree with him, he tells her, "You get too fresh with me or I'll put you back on your broom." Those lines may not seem so funny on paper, but when they are delivered in the film by the irresistible Ray Walston, it is hard not to chuckle. Also, Gwen Verdon as Lola is credibly seductive early in the film as she attempts to vamp Joe Hardy, and then sympathetic later when she begins to show true human emotions.

Tab Hunter, as Joe Hardy, is new to the film, not having appeared in the Broadway version. He is an unusual choice for the film, as he is not known as a singer or a dancer. Hunter does nothing in the film to change that reputation, and even as an actor, he is somewhat bland in his role.

There are several memorable songs in the film: "(You Gotta Have) Heart," sung by the manager and his ballplayers; "Whatever Lola Wants," sung and danced by Gwen Verdon; and the less well-known "A Little Brains, a Little Talent," sung and danced by Gwen Verdon. A cynic might argue that if the Washington Senators spent less time on their singing and dancing and more on their ball playing, they might not need the help of the devil for attaining success, but since this is a movie musical, it is better to suspend disbelief than to be cynical.

When a Broadway play is adapted to the cinema, it is almost always opened up, with scenes occurring in multiple locations and often outdoors, instead of being limited to the few sets that a play usually employs. Sometimes that approach hurts the film because the story

Lola, the devil's temptress (Gwen Verdon), and Joe Hardy, the new ballplayer for the Washington Senators (Tab Hunter), share a moment out of the ballpark in *Damn Yankees* (1958).

line does not require these multiple changes of scenes, which then makes these extra scenes seem artificial. In a movie about baseball, however, the required baseball scenes are a natural way to open up the film. In *Damn Yankees*, however, while there are some realistic scenes outside on the ball fields, particularly early on when Joe Hardy receives his tryout with the Senators, most of the baseball scenes in the film are disappointing. Apparently the real baseball action was shot by a second unit at several games between the Yankees and the Senators, but since they are shot from a long distance away, they are uninvolving for the film audience. In fact, it is almost impossible to spot Tab Hunter in any of the action, probably deliberate on the part of the filmmakers but detrimental to the verisimilitude of the story.

Just when all seems lost in terms of real baseball footage, the last baseball scene is a knockout. With the Senators winning, 1–0, in the ninth inning, with two men out, and the opposition with one last chance, a fly ball is hit to Joe in left field. As Joe goes back to catch it, Applegate turns Joe Hardy back into Joe Boyd. The older Boyd falls down, gets back up, and then stumbles again. While sitting on the ground, he puts his glove up and catches the ball. The Senators win the pennant!

Damn Yankees ends on a happy note, as all musicals of the era do, with Meg and Joe happily reconciled and the Senators winning the pennant. Also, there is still a chance that the Senators can win the World Series, even without Joe, so long as they play with heart.

Alas and alack, in real life it appears that Mr. Applegate got his way. Just two years after the film was released, the Washington Senators abandoned Washington and moved to Minnesota, becoming the Twins. In 1961, Washington received a new expansion team, also named the Washington Senators, but that team never came close to winning the pennant. After the 1971 season, the new Senators moved to Texas and became the Texas Rangers. Washington did not have a professional baseball team again until 2005, when the Montreal Expos moved there and changed their name to the Washington Nationals. As of this writing, the Nationals have yet to win a pennant.

10

BASEBALL IN DIVERSE CULTURES

√ *Mr. Baseball* (1992)

Mr. Baseball is Jack Elliot, a Yankees ballplayer who just four years ago was the Most Valuable Player in the World Series and who is now struggling at the game. When a hotshot rookie first baseman arrives with the team in spring training, Jack is traded to the only team that will now take him, the Chunichi Dragons of a Japanese professional baseball league. At first, Elliot is unhappy with the situation, is arrogant to his manager and other Japanese people, and does not hit very well, but by the end of the film, Elliot turns things around, leading his team to a championship season.

Mr. Baseball is built upon movie clichés. Is there any movie viewer in all the world who does not know, well in advance of the ending of the film, that Jack will finally see the light, change his attitude, and become a team player, leading his team to victory in the final game? Is there any movie viewer in all the world that does not know, well in advance of the ending of the film, that Jack will fall in love with the manager's daughter, Hiroko, even though they seem to dislike each other when they first meet, and even after they start to date, have serious clashes over important issues?

Now, the fact that the plot of *Mr. Baseball* is based upon movie clichés does not, in and of itself, make *Mr. Baseball* a bad film. After all, movie plots become movie clichés only because the formula has been shown to be successful over time. Most everyone likes a story in which good triumphs over bad, a romance is successful, and there is a happy ending for all involved (no matter how contrived the ending turns out to be). The formula has been used with great success in several sports films over many years, providing substantial enjoyment for movie and sports fans.

Also, *Mr. Baseball* has much going for it. It has fine production values. The baseball scenes are well directed, particularly in the pitcher-and-batter duels. The film was shot on location in Japan, with huge crowds in the baseball stadium. There is some true humor in the cultural clash between Jack and Japanese society, including the Japanese slurping of food at dinner, Jack not being allowed to put a business card in his back pocket because it is like sitting on a Japanese person's identity, Jack giving out his baseball cards in response to receiving business cards from others, and the tall Jack hitting his head on a beam in his new apartment.

The movie also displays some interesting differences between Japanese and American baseball. In Japan, a baseball game can last no longer than fifteen innings; it can therefore end in a tie. It is disrespectful to take out a fielder with a slide to break up a double play. Spitting on the field is frowned upon (horror of horrors) because the field is considered sacred. A bouquet of flowers is given to a player when he walks back to the dugout after hitting a home run.

The problems with *Mr. Baseball*, however, are many. Jack's conversion from bad to good takes place suddenly, when he learns that his manager, Uchiyama, is the father of Hiroko and that Uchiyama can speak English. There is no actual motivation for Jack to change his attitude nor is there a sudden epiphany in Jack's mind about the situation. Why Jack, who is hoping to play well in Japan so that a major-league team will notice and bring him back to the States, makes no effort to improve his skills from the beginning of his trip to Japan goes unexplained.

Uchiyama finally decides to give Jack hitting advice, and Jack finally agrees to take it. However, the advice merely consists of increased calisthenics for Jack, such as running up the steps of the stadium. There is little actual hitting advice provided. Nevertheless, Jack's hitting miraculously improves, leading the team to the championship game on the last day of the season. If only it were so easy!

One would expect that once Jack moves to Japan, some of the Japanese culture and sports attitude would be inculcated in him. In fact, the exact opposite occurs. Some of American culture and sports attitude is inculcated in Uchiyama and in the team. At Jack's advice, the manager keeps pitchers in the game longer and no longer discourages the team from having fun while it plays. The fielders become more likely to take risks in the field, no longer worried about losing face. The manager argues with the home-plate umpire

Jack Elliot (Tom Selleck), batting in his last game as a New York Yankee before being sent to Japan, in *Mr. Baseball* (1992).

(including deliberately bumping him), and the team becomes involved in a brawl on the field, hardly baseball attributes that should be exported from America. Jack, on the other hand, never changes his game attitude or playing style. Thus, *Mr. Baseball* displays the worst type of ugly American attitude. Everything America does is right; everything foreigners do is wrong. That perspective may have played better in 1992. In today's world, it seems arrogant and naïve, undercutting the positives of the film.

To make matters worse, Jack comes to bat in the ninth inning of the championship game with the bases loaded, two men out, and the Dragons one run behind. Jack expects to be asked to bunt (which, even given the small-ball attitude of the Japanese, is incredible since there would be an easy force play at any base). Uchiyama tells Jack to hit away, but Jack decides to bunt anyway (which is incredible, for the reason just stated and also because he does it with two strikes). Then Jack ends up safe at first, two runners score, and the Dragons win the game!

In addition to the bunt being a ridiculous strategy, Jack actually cheats on his way to first base. Although the film is unclear at this point, Jack either pushes a fielder who has the ball and is attempting to touch first base to the ground, or he pushes the fielder who is attempting to receive a throw at first base. This is interference on Jack's part, exacerbated by the fact that he runs inside the base line on his way to first. Even without the cheating, Jack may have been safe at first, but his push of the infielder allows two runs to score on the play, not one, resulting in the Dragons winning the pennant. For the Japanese, this does not seem to be an honorable way to win the game.

The underlying premise of the film, that veteran major leaguers sometimes go to Japan to play ball near the end of their careers, is accurate. Apparently, the first athlete to do so was Don Newcombe, a pitcher who played mainly for the Dodgers. He played in Japan in 1962 after the end of his major-league career, coincidentally playing for the Chunichi Dragons, the same team for which Jack Elliot plays. Some other familiar ballplayers who played in Japan, among many other not-so-famous players, are Larry Doby, the Hall of Fame outfielder for the Cleveland Indians, Joe Pepitone, first baseman and outfielder primarily for the New York Yankees, and Cecil Fielder, a first baseman for several American League teams.

Yet, for all of the American ballplayers who have played in Japan over the past half century, none have changed the culture of the Japanese game. Thus, it strains credulity that one Jack Elliot was able to do so, making *Mr. Baseball* a very disappointing film.

American Pastime (2007)

American Pastime concerns a dark moment in American history that occurred during World War II. After the surprise attack by the Japanese on Pearl Harbor in December 1941, the United States government ordered over 100,000 people of Japanese descent who were then living on the Pacific Coast to be interned at sites far inland. Substantial numbers of the detainees were U.S. citizens. Later, in a black eye for the United States Supreme Court, the internment was upheld against a constitutional challenge in *Korematsu v. United States*, 323 U.S. 214 (1944).

One of the detention camps was the Topaz War Relocation Center in Topaz, Utah. At one time, the camp, which consisted of over eighteen acres of land just west of Delta, Utah, held more than

8,000 detainees. There they tried to reestablish normal lives, albeit inside barbwire, surrounded by several guard towers, and with their sleep interrupted at night by a moving spotlight shining through the barrack windows. The Topaz center is the primary setting for *American Pastime*.

The film's story line involves the Nomura family, comprised of two parents, Kaz and Emi, both born in Japan, and their two boys, Lyle and Lane, who were born in Los Angeles. At the beginning of the film, the family is uprooted from its typical American existence on the West Coast and forced to live at the Topaz Relocation Center. There the father tries to raise the spirits of the prisoners and bring back part of their regular lives by establishing a camp baseball team. The climax of the film is a game between the detainees and a team comprised of players from the local community of Abraham, Utah.

American Pastime obviously has a unique setting for a baseball film—a Japanese internment camp during World War II. The film is historically accurate within that setting. Baseball was played at Topaz and the other internment camps, and, of course, the Japanese had been playing baseball in Japan for many years prior to World War II, with the game introduced into Japan in the 1870s. Indeed, most of *American Pastime* is historically accurate, with its authenticity highlighted by contemporaneous footage from the era—such as the anti-Japanese banners along the Pacific Coast ("Japs Keep Out You Rats" and "Japs Keep Moving This Is A White Man's Neighborhood")—with film footage actually taken within Topaz during the war, and newsreel footage about the Japanese American battalion, the 442nd Regimental Combat Team, which fought in Europe during World War II.

While the setting and the historical context of *American Pastime* are accurate, the plot is fictional, consisting of several story arcs about the Nomura family and the camp. The primary story concerns Lyle and his relationship with Katie Burrell, the Caucasian daughter of Billy Burrell, one of the guards at the camp. Another involves the bigotry of the townspeople, particularly the local barber, Ed Tully, which manifests itself one day in the beating of Lyle on the streets of the town. A third story arc involves Lane, desperate to leave the camp, joining the 442nd combat unit, going off to war, becoming a hero but returning with a foot injury.

It would be nice to write that *American Pastime* avoids the clichés of the cinema, but it does not. The Lyle-Katie relationship is just another variation on the story of Romeo and Juliet. What a coincidence that Katie's father, Billy, is himself a baseball player, adding some extra interest to the final game. Then there is the stern Japanese father, some sibling rivalry, and the big-game finish. There is a lot that is not original in *American Pastime*.

Also, the film sometimes tries to make its points in an obvious and didactic manner. In the opening scene of the film, the Nomuras are portrayed as a typical American family, with the grilling of hot dogs, the teenage boys checking out pictures of actresses in magazines, having pictures of baseball players on the wall, and dancing to records. Of course, the quintessential American sport, baseball, is what ties the film together. Also, when Lyle and Katie fall in love, it is through the medium of jazz, another American original. The audience understands that the detainees in Topaz are actually Americans, most born and raised in the United States, with true American interests. The audience does not have to be hit over the head with the concept.

Notwithstanding those problems, *American Pastime* is a wonderful film. It covers a moment in American history with which most people are unfamiliar and which had never been addressed in the movies before, which in and of itself makes the film worthwhile. The movie is good in conveying the dreams and disappointments of the detainees, with some of the little moments made special, such as the captives patching the holes of their barracks; going to town and buying wares for the barracks to improve them; and Mr. Nomura handling a drunken episode of Lyle's at the camp, keeping the incident a family matter, not a camp issue.

The underlying theme of *American Pastime* is one of dignity. The Japanese Americans lost their dignity when they were rounded up and sent to the camps, but they try to regain it by making the physical camp into the best place they possibly can, repairing the walls, hanging curtains (and using their own cash to do so), planting, having dances, and celebrating Christmas. To show their patriotism, many of the younger males go off to war and fight in the 442nd, one of the most decorated units in all of World War II.

While the underlying theme of the movie is dignity, the underlying thread of the movie is baseball. It begins in Lyle's interest in the game before his forced removal from California; the bringing to camp of a picture of a team that Mr. Nomura's barnstorming team once played, which included Babe Ruth, Lou Gehrig, and Jimmy Foxx; the use of baseball at the camp to uplift the spirits of the detainees; a pitching/hitting challenge between Lyle and Billy that results in a cheating win by Billy; the games that Billy Burrell plays outside the camp in the hopes of being called up to the Yankees; and, of course, the big game between the detainees and the locals.

Lyle starts the game between the detainees and the locals with a brushback pitch to Tully and then strikes him out on three straight pitches. Lyle then tells Billy that he is going to throw him a pitch "straight up," which Billy hits a long way but foul. Billy then strikes out. The Abraham pitcher also starts with a brushback pitch, which puts the detainees off their hitting game for much of the rest of the contest. The game then develops into a pitcher's duel, with the only early run coming from a home run hit by the detainees' biggest player, Bambino Hirose. There are good plays in the outfield, some long foul balls, Tully acting true to form and pushing Lyle to the ground as Lyle is trying to field a dribbler off the bat, and Billy Burrell hitting a three-run homer in the top of the ninth to put the locals ahead. However, in the bottom of the ninth, with two outs, the detainees do the impossible, starting with a bunt single, a hit by pitch, a triple by Lyle, and a steal of home plate, with a controversial call that is reversed, leading to a camp victory.

While cynics may argue that the ending of the game is not believable (particularly Billy telling the home-plate umpire to reverse the call), and they would be correct, the game is enjoyable throughout, with personal stories woven into the game action, which includes some good baseball plays. The game provides a great climax for the film.

At the big game, the theme of dignity and the thread of baseball come together. Mr. Nomura, the manager, lays it out to his team before the game. He says, "But today is not just about winning. Today it's about dignity, dignity of the game and dignity that we have [tapping his heart] here." Also, Lyle is pushed in the ninth inning by the fans yelling at him, "Go for broke," the motto of the 442nd. It is a heartwarming moment when the Japanese Americans stand up and shout the saying of their combat unit at their team, encouraging the team to win.

Then there is the bet between the detainees and the Abraham team. The detainees collect over $2,500 in quarters from their fellow captives, but the Abraham players do not have that kind of money to bet on the result of the game. The locals therefore bet something different, and, on its face, the bet is nothing special—a haircut for Lane. However, when Lane returned from the war, a decorated hero with a war injury, who just wanted a haircut before he returned to camp, Tully refused to do it, saying he does not cut Jap hair. Thus, when Tully is required to cut Lane's hair after the game, it is a big moment for the detainees. Many of the detainees watch the haircut, some with their faces pressed against the glass of the establishment. It is a defining moment for the Japanese Americans. Their team won the ball game, for sure, but the captives also regained some of their dignity.

American Pastime is a little bit of history, a little bit of romance, a little bit of war, and a large amount of baseball, all within a solid drama of family life and coming-of-age story. It is a mixture that is hard to beat, making the film both enjoyable and worthwhile.

The Yankles (2009)

The Yankles fits squarely within the standard format of youth sports films made after *The Bad News Bears* (1976). In this case, the story concerns Charlie Jones, a former Major League Baseball player whose main claim to fame, or infamy, is dropping the fly ball that would have been the last out in the World Series, resulting in his team (the Spirits) losing the series. Charlie is also an alcoholic, and after that World Series defeat, his life goes downhill, with multiple DUI convictions resulting in his incarceration in prison. Charlie is paroled for good behavior, but he must complete 192 hours of community service to satisfy the conditions of his parole. Since this is a baseball film, it is obvious that the community service will be with a youth baseball team. It is also obvious that Charlie will be reluctant to become the coach of such a team, but he will eventually relent, turning a team of misfits into a group of good ballplayers, leading them into the championship game.

By 2009 most viewers would probably have been bored watching a film with the same plot as several other youth sports films of the past forty years. However, *The Yankles* is somewhat unique. The youth baseball team is not a group of Little Leaguers; it is a college team. The college team is not just any team; it is a group of students at a yeshiva, an orthodox Jewish rabbinical college made up of young men who desire to become rabbis. The students either wear hats or yarmulkes to cover their heads at all times; they have long fringes known as tzitzit appended to their clothes, which swing against their pants as they walk; and their hair is worn as peyes, i.e., closely cut except for the area near their ears, which is untouched and tumbles down the sides of their faces in very long curls.

Once *The Yankles* gets past Charlie Jones's personal problems and focuses on the yeshiva team, it becomes quite entertaining and amusing. Rabbi Meyer coaches the team by reading instructions from a book. The team originally plays in its white shirts and black pants because Mendel the tailor has not completed the uniforms. A player has to translate some of the Hebrew words that people use, such as *mazel tov* (translated as "good luck," although commonly used to mean congratulations) and *nachas* (translated as "pride," although commonly used to mean delight or satisfaction), so that Charlie can understand. Rabbi Meyer requests that Charlie, if he has to swear at the team, at least use Yiddish swear words instead of English ones. As one player rounds second base in a game, his helmet comes off. Although he could have easily made third base, the runner goes back to retrieve his helmet because he cannot leave his head uncovered. He is tagged out. However, in a game later in the season, when that same player's helmet flies off as he is rounding the bases, he pulls a yarmulke out of his pocket, puts it on his head and keeps on going.

After a time, however, the overlong *The Yankles* begins to wear on the viewer. Once the humor is gone, the plot problems of the film become apparent. Actually, it is a complete lack of any plot that does the film in. At first, the film seems to be about Charlie's difficult rehabilitation once he leaves prison, but, in fact, he completely cleans up his act almost immediately without any problems. Then the film could have been about Charlie's difficult interactions with a new culture, but Charlie easily integrates himself with the Jewish culture and its strange customs. Then the film could have been about Charlie's difficulties in teaching the yeshiva students how to play ball, but there are almost no scenes in the film about baseball practices or drills. It is unclear how the yeshiva students became such good players, with little experience on the team.

One of the side stories involves a player named Elliot who used to play minor-league professional baseball, but who gave up the game to join the yeshiva. Elliot's father, Frankie, who once played professional baseball, has never forgiven his son for that decision. Even though the Yankles are playing well, Frankie will not accept his son until, of course, the final moments of the movie when Frankie finally sees the light.

This side story could have provided some continuity and drama, except that it is so unconvincing. Many fathers may want their sons to play professionally and may be disappointed when they give up the game, but it strains credulity for Frankie to hold a lifetime grudge when Elliot had yet to make it to the majors and the odds of him doing so were so great (just as it is for most other ballplayers). It is interesting to note, however, that the premise of the side story is the opposite of the premise of the classic *The Jazz Singer* (1927) and its several remakes. In that film, a cantor at the turn of the twentieth century is upset that his son refuses to also become a cantor and sing in the synagogue, but rather desires to become a star on Broadway. That cultural issue, while old-fashioned, makes some sense in *The Jazz Singer*. In *The Yankles*, a Jewish man is upset that his son wants to become a rabbi instead of a baseball player. Either that reversal of plot makes little sense, or it shows how religious matters have changed in this country over the past century.

Having identified the film's weaknesses, it is still easy to recommend *The Yankles*. While the baseball play in the film is not that good or convincing, *The Yankles* generally avoids ridiculous plays in the field or on the base paths, avoiding several *Bad New Bears* clichés. The film does no proselytizing, as several other religious baseball films do. Of course, *The Yankles* could hardly do that since the yeshiva students are so strange in dress, manner, and outlook, even to American Jews, that it would be hard for the film to try to inculcate other Jews or non-Jews into their beliefs.

There are some good performances in the movie, particularly among the rabbis. Kenneth F. Brown plays the very overweight Rabbi Meyer, who is out of his element trying to coach a college baseball team but tries his best, never losing his enthusiasm. Jesse Bennett plays the Rebbe, the head of the school, and the wise man of the movie. People of all faiths can appreciate his calm attitude, wise ethical principals, and his use of personal stories, scriptures, and the Talmud to guide his decisions.

The Rebbe is important to the denouement of the film. The Rebbe tells Charlie Jones early on, "One's character will earn him a place in the world to come. One's ability will only earn him a paycheck. I am not interested in winning at the expense of sinning." Later, the Rebbe tells Charlie and Elliot, "My Yankles will always be seen as Jews first and a baseball team second. . . . I know that both you and the Yankles will bring us honor."

In the championship game, in the bottom of the ninth, with the winning run on third and two men out, Elliot almost hits a home run but it hooks foul at the last minute. On the next pitch, Elliot bounces a ball to the right of the first baseman, who dives for it and then throws it to the pitcher running to first. It is a foot race between Eliot and the pitcher, but the pitcher wins in a very close play. The Yankles lose.

The Yankles are disappointed at first but then break out in a Hebrew song. As the Rebbe desired, the team played with honor and never lost its Jewishness. Thus there is no reason for the team or the audience to be disappointed. Also, probably without knowing it, the Rebbe gave the same advice, based on scriptures, the Talmud, and history, that sportswriter Grantland Rice gave many years before—"For when the One Great Scorer comes, To mark against your name, He writes—not that you won or lost—But how you played the game."

The Perfect Game (2009)

Many films over many years have portrayed an underdog sports team that finally gets it together and by the end of the movie wins the championship game. This plot scenario can be seen in films such as *Angels in the Outfield* (1951) and *The Bad News Bears in Breaking Training* (1977) (baseball), *The Mighty Ducks* (1992) (hockey), and *The Big Green* (1995) (soccer). As enjoyable as many of those films may be, their inherent shortcoming is that it is often very hard to suspend disbelief when a smaller, less experienced team beats a bigger and more skilled team, particularly in a championship game.

The Perfect Game, a film based on a book of the same name by W. William Winokur published in 2008, has the same basic plot but not the same problem, because it is inspired by a true story, and in its David vs. Goliath story line, the facts in the movie are substantially accurate.

As the film begins, Cesar Faz, a locker-room attendant for the St. Louis Cardinals, quits his job and moves to Monterrey, Mexico, where he finds work in a local factory. There he meets a group of young boys who are interested in baseball. One of the boys, Angel Macias, and the local cleric, Padre Esteban, convince Faz to create and coach a Little League team for the town. Faz is a good but tough coach. He molds the boys into a solid team, good enough to compete in a Little League tournament that commences across the border in the southern United States. Surprisingly the Monterrey team, known as the Industriales, beats all of the teams it faces in the South, leading to a trip to Williamsport, Pennsylvania. There, in the championship game of the Little League World Series, Angel pitches a perfect game, resulting in Monterrey becoming the first foreign team to win the Little League World Series.

The Perfect Game is a success for several reasons. The film is substantially based on fact, adding to its intrinsic interest, as the real Monterrey Industriales of 1957 did win every game in that year's Little League tournament and did cap their achievements with a perfect game in the finals, something that has never been done before or since. If the story were complete fiction, the writer, while he may have had the youngsters from Mexico win the World Series, would never have ended the story with a perfect game. That would have been too hard to believe.

Other positives of the film include the undeniable fact that *The Perfect Game* has an inspiring story, so much so that the people the players meet along the way, from border crossing guards to waitresses, root for the team in the last game. The kids themselves are charismatic and lovable, and their enthusiasm for the game is infectious. The movie's location shooting in Monterrey, Mexico, early in the film provides the movie with some verisimilitude, as does the cast of Hispanic actors.

In addition, *The Perfect Game* works well in its smaller moments. The movie addresses racism, with the kids not permitted to use a whites-only bathroom in Texas and the kids sitting with a young black player in a restaurant because he is not allowed to eat with his white teammates. In addition to baseball, the film, at its core, is about religious faith, as the children are inspired by Father Estaban and their Catholic upbringing. Once Father Estaban must leave the team, the players refuse to play any games without a pregame prayer led by a priest. The film displays a sense of humor as, for example, Coach Faz finding many different ways for the kids to run laps, including along the ramps of a building and beside the team bus, and the new Little League jerseys that they have to wear in Williamsport being way too big on them (based on fact). There is a mild romantic element to the film as Coach Faz courts a local woman, Maria, in an inexperienced manner, twice standing her up for dinner with her family because he is involved in his baseball team.

For baseball fans, films that display a love for the game are especially appreciated. *The Perfect Game* is one of those films. The movie opens with some newsreel footage of a 1956 game between the St. Louis Cardinals and the Brooklyn Dodgers at Sportsman's Park in St. Louis, as Sal Maglie of the Dodgers pitches to Stan Musial of the Cardinals, who smashes a ball down the first baseline that is too hot to handle for Gil Hodges, the Dodgers first baseman. Mention is made of Don Larsen's perfect game in the 1956 World Series, which is a foreshadowing of the perfect game that will be pitched by Angel in Williamsport. Angel's favorite player is Sandy Koufax of the Brooklyn Dodgers, even though Koufax is a left-hander and Angel usually throws from the right side. Mention is made in the graphics at the conclusion of the film about the perfect game thrown by Sandy Koufax, eight years after the one pitched by Angel Macias. The team finds Cool Papa Bell, a former Negro League player, working as a groundskeeper at a Little League field in Louisville. He gives them tips on the pitcher's "tell," that is, unknowing movements by the pitcher that can tell the batter what pitch is coming. With Bell's help, the Industriales win another game. The youngsters want the 108th psalm read to them before games because there are 108 stitches on a baseball.

The Perfect Game received mixed reviews when it opened, and those critics who gave the film negative reviews have a point. The core story line is clichéd and obvious, as everyone knows, almost from the beginning, that Faz will eventually coach the team and do an excellent job; the players will perform very well and win the championship, despite incredible odds; Coach Faz's romance with Maria will turn out well in the end; and Angel's father, who cannot seem to get over the sudden death of Angel's brother and takes his disappointments out on Angel, will eventually come around to love and appreciate his son. For those who cannot get past film analytics and just appreciate the story for what it is, the film will not be enjoyable. For those who can get into the spirit of the film and suspend their cynicism somewhat, *The Perfect Game* is an excellent viewing experience.

One of the main difficulties with the film is that the game action is not shot very well. For most of the film, the viewer gets no sense of time or place, as the score of the game, the inning, and the ebb and flow of the game are not provided to the viewer. Sometimes the game film just seems to be an arbitrary clip or two from a game without any context. Oftentimes, when a ball is hit in the air, the camera shoots the ball from below as it travels through the air, with the viewer not knowing until the ball lands if it is a home run or an infield pop-up.

Fortunately, this shortcoming is corrected for the semifinal game and the championship game. In the sixth inning of the semifinal game, with Monterrey leading by just one run and with runners on second and third and the opponent's best hitter at the plate, Coach Faz decides not to intentionally walk the batter. Instead, he allows Enrique Suarez to pitch to the batter. Enrique gets the third out by catching a sharp liner. Similarly, in the final game, the filmmakers take the time to set up the pitcher's duel between the two teams and the grand-slam home run by Enrique in the bottom of the fifth inning (not historically accurate), with the whole inning shown, with a hit by pitch, a bunt that gets the batter on first when the throw to second is late, a runner thrown out at home plate, and an infield hit before the big blow. In the top of the sixth inning, the perfect game is on the line, with a pop-up, a tag out of a runner at first base by the trailing catcher (not very believable, as the catcher is supposed to trail in foul territory to block overthrows at first, not to tag runners out at first, but apparently a true occurrence), and a final strikeout after the first three pitches are balls (historically accurate).

In these scenes, when the baseball is put into context and each play is important, *The Perfect Game* does a much better job with telling the story of the games. It is a shame that the earlier baseball scenes were not filmed in the same manner.

The most significant flaw in the film, the one that strains credulity the most, is that the movie never explains why the Monterrey team keeps winning all of these games. If the film were to be believed, the kids had never played a real baseball game until just a few months before the tournament, never even saw a real field until they came to the United States, and did not have real bats and gloves until just a few weeks before the tournament commenced. Yet the team continued to beat more skilled and better-funded outfits with regularity. No attempt is made in the film to explain that anomaly.

In real life, the kids started playing baseball two years before their championship season in a Monterrey league that consisted of three other teams. There were more players on the team than the nine shown in the film. Even in 1957, Monterrey was a large city, not a small town with one church and dirt streets, so there was some baseball competition for the youngsters. Nevertheless, there does not seem to be any reason why a team of small ballplayers, who were outweighed by thirty-five to forty pounds by their opponents and who had never been outside their own country before, could so dominate the United States teams. In fact, the Industriales in real life won thirteen straight games in the Little League tournament in four weeks, a hard-to-explain phenomenon.

One of the highlights of the film is the archive footage of the real players from back in 1957, playing in games, riding on the streets of Williamsport, playing at the stadium in Williamsport, and then after their win, meeting the Brooklyn Dodgers and later, President Eisenhower. Even the final credits to the movie are enjoyable, as pictures of the actors are matched with vintage photos of the real players in 1957. For all of these reasons, *The Perfect Game* is highly recommended.

Sugar (2008)

Baseball has never been an international sport as soccer, basketball, and some of the Olympic sports are, but it is an important pastime in many parts of the world outside the United States, such as Japan and Korea in Asia and Canada and the Caribbean Islands in the Western Hemisphere. The Dominican Republic is one of the Caribbean countries in which baseball is particularly prominent.

The Dominican Republic is situated on the east side of the island of Hispaniola, which is about fifty miles southeast of Cuba. The Dominican Republic shares the island of Hispaniola with Haiti.

Baseball (or *béisbol*, as it is known in Spanish) was introduced into the Dominican Republic in the late 1800s by Cubans, who fled to the country during turmoil on their island. In 1951, the modern era in Dominican baseball began, with the establishment of what is now called the Dominican Baseball League. The league plays in the winter months, attracting major leaguers who desire to play winter ball along with the locals.

The first Dominican baseball player to make the majors was Osvaldo (Ozzie) Virgil Sr., who first played for the New York Giants on September 23, 1956. Virgil played third base on that day, but throughout his ten-year career in the majors with several different teams, he was a utility player, playing in both the infield and the outfield. Subsequently, there have been so many famous major leaguers of Dominican descent that all cannot be mentioned here, but they include Felipe Alou (the second Dominican to play in the major leagues and the first one to play regularly, playing outfield for the San Francisco Giants starting in 1958, eventually becoming the manager of the Montreal Expos), Juan Marichal (Hall of Fame pitcher, primarily for the San Francisco Giants, and one of the top pitchers of the 1960s), Bartolo Colón (American League Cy Young Award winner in 2005, pitching for the Angels), Sammy Sosa (controversial slugger who hit over 600 home runs in his career, the most for any foreign-born player), and Pedro Martinez (three-time Cy Young Award winner, who was inducted into the Baseball Hall of Fame in 2015). It has been estimated that over 1,500 Dominicans play professional baseball each year in both the major and minor leagues. In recent years, there are usually more players of Dominican descent in the major leagues than players from any country other than the United States.

In fact, there is so much baseball talent in the Dominican Republic that all thirty Major League Baseball clubs have established baseball academies on the island, with playing fields, dormitories, cafeterias, and training facilities. In recent years, many of the academies have become state-of-the art facilities. The major-league teams sign promising young Dominicans at an early age to the baseball academies. The lucky few are then sent to the United States to begin their slow ascent from A-ball to hopefully the major leagues, with few making the full journey.

Sugar is about one such young player, Miguel Santos, a pitcher, who goes by the nickname "Sugar." Sugar stays at an academy in the Dominican Republic run by the Kansas City Knights, a fictional team, but comes home on weekends, where he is somewhat of a hero to the locals in his impoverished community. After Sugar learns and masters a spike curve ball, the Knights bring him to the United States and assign him to the Bridgetown Swing, a Single-A affiliate of the Knights located in Iowa. There, Sugar lives with a local family, the Higgins, and tries to improve his baseball, while struggling with the difficulties of living within a new culture, with only a limited understanding of English.

Sugar sometimes seems more like a documentary than a work of fiction, as it painstakingly records the life of Sugar, beginning at the baseball academy, where, in addition to learning baseball and baseball terminology, he learns to speak important English phrases such as "What is the problem?" and "I'll do my best." The camera accompanies Sugar when he returns home to his poor neighborhood on weekends, and when he begins his professional career in Iowa, with a strong start as a pitcher, a setback when he suffers a foot injury, and then his attempt to make a comeback. When Sugar becomes disillusioned with the game, the camera follows him to New York City, where he tries to make a new start in Manhattan. *Sugar* seems so true to life that it is hard to believe it is not based on a true story.

One of the many strengths of *Sugar* is its location shooting, particularly in the Dominican Republic, which of course adds to its documentary style. The film shows the extreme poverty in the Dominican Republic, yet the luxury of the baseball academies within its midst. The scenes in Iowa, much more open and sunny than the Caribbean, provide a nice contrast to Sugar's Dominican neighborhood. Some of the baseball scenes in Iowa were shot in Davenport, Iowa, at the home field of the Quad City River Bandits. One striking aspect of the setting is the Centennial Bridge, which is located outside the first-base side of the stadium, a bridge with five steel arches that spans the Mississippi River. It is such a striking sight that the bridge is shown in the posters for the movie. The last parts of the film are shot in New York City, in Hispanic neighborhoods, bringing back images that are similar to those from the early scenes in the Dominican Republic, although in a much more urban setting. Given the circle of Sugar's life, has Sugar accomplished anything by coming to America?

Other strengths of *Sugar* are the non-professional, Dominican actors in the movie, particularly Algenis Perez Soto, who plays Sugar. Soto had a baseball background when he was chosen for the film, but as a shortstop, not a pitcher. He is still excellent in a game setting, very realistic when he is on the mound. Soto is able to convey a range of emotions, from the cocky kid at the beginning of the movie on the island, to a sullen youth when he is alone in Iowa and bewildered by the culture, to the desperate young man who is trying to carve out a life for himself in New York City.

The use of actual settings and a non-professional Dominican cast add to the documentary style of the film, with much of the dialogue in Spanish, with English subtitles employed. *Sugar* sometimes seems like a foreign-language film, not one written and directed by Americans. *Sugar* reminds the viewer of the neo-realist films of the postwar Italian cinema, such as *The Bicycle Thief* (1948) and *Umberto D.* (1952).

Even though *Sugar* is about a baseball player who is trying to make it in the professional leagues, there is surprisingly little baseball shown in *Sugar*. The viewer watches when Sugar learns how to throw a spike (or knuckle) curve on the advice of an American scout, and the viewer observes Sugar pitching in several games in Iowa, some very successful and a few not so much. However, most of the baseball-related matters in the film are on the fringes of the game, such as Sugar's reluctance to give up the ball when his manager takes him out of the game in the middle of the inning. Sugar has to learn that there is nothing demeaning when that happens, and, in fact, the first time it transpires, Sugar has pitched such a good game that the home crowd applauds him on the way to the dugout.

The theme of *Sugar* is isolation, not success in sports. Sugar is an immigrant to this country, originally on a work visa to play baseball. He has trouble understanding the language of the Iowans as well as that of his manager. Sugar tells his girlfriend back home that it is hard to be in Iowa because no one speaks Spanish. His buddy, who plays in Arizona, has a much easier time. Sugar does not know how to deal with the Higgins's granddaughter to whom he is attracted because he does not know American ways. Sugar is involved in a slight racial incident in a bar, again resulting from his lack of understanding of Midwest culture. The effervescent Sugar of the islands quickly turns into a quiet, introverted immigrant.

The entire film is about Sugar, isolating him from the rest of the characters. All of the minor side stories in the film, such as another Dominican being cut from the team, are shown only as they affect Sugar. The camera work in the film also enhances Sugar's isolation. Most of the shots in the movie focus on Sugar, usually in extreme close-ups and often with the background out of focus, isolating Sugar in the frame. When Sugar moves into a dingy hotel in New York, there is a shot of him down a long, narrow hallway as he approaches his room, a metaphor for the isolated individual Sugar has become.

The theme of isolation in *Sugar* is related to its prime subject matter, which, once again, is not baseball. The film is primarily about immigration and the life of immigrants when they come to this country. Baseball is the tool that allows Sugar and his fellow Dominicans to come to the United States, but they still have to make it in America on their own. Sugar and the many others who are unable to continue their baseball careers but want to stay in America have to find a substitute for baseball. Sugar starts his second life by working in a diner, but his true love, after baseball, is carpentry, a skill he learned from his father. As the film ends, Sugar starts to have some success as he has acquired a mentor in that industry. Perhaps matters will turn out okay for Sugar.

The most extraordinary aspect of *Sugar* is that it avoids all of the baseball movie clichés. If this were a Disney movie, Sugar, despite the long odds, would have been in the major leagues by the end of the film. *Sugar*, however, is not a Disney movie. Sugar struggles with his pitching in Iowa, even taking drugs to mask some of the pain he is suffering. He does not fall in love in Iowa or otherwise find happiness there. Sugar suddenly leaves the Swing baseball team when he realizes that he will never make it, avoiding the humiliation of being cut. New York presents its own problems for Sugar, and there he runs out of money very quickly. The film does not end with Sugar becoming a success. It simply ends with some vague possibilities of happiness in the future.

The last scene in the movie shows a semipro baseball game played by New York Hispanics on Roberto Clemente Ballfield in New York City. Each of the players introduces himself to the camera, identifying the highest minor-league team for which he played. It is a striking conclusion to the film, highlighting how many good ballplayers have come from the Dominican Republic to the States to play baseball and how few actually make it to the big time. Of course, this is also true for American-born players, but they have not left their country, their culture, and their families to try to obtain a professional baseball career. The race to succeed in the major leagues is a much more difficult odyssey for Dominicans.

In *Making Sugar: Run the Bases,* one of the special features on the 2009 DVD of *Sugar,* José Rijo, an actor and baseball consultant for the film, says that there is an old baseball saying in the Dominican Republic, that you can only leave the island in two ways—swinging the bat or throwing the ball. That concept is subtlety handled in the film. When Sugar is in a clothing store in the States, he spots a T-shirt with a label that reads, "Made in the Dominican Republic." Sugar's face freezes for a moment, as he recognizes that if he had remained in his home country, he would probably be doing menial work for low wages, just as many of his fellow countrymen were then doing. Near the end of the film, Sugar calls his mother at home from New York City and explains that even though he is out of baseball, he is still doing fine. He then asks his mother what his younger brother is doing, and the mother replies that he is starting to play baseball.

After Sugar hangs up the phone, the film remains on the mother, a rare time in the movie that a scene is shown without Sugar in it and without Sugar being the focus of the film. The mother then looks at her younger son, who is tossing a baseball in his mitt. The mother realizes that unless her young boy can succeed at baseball, he may spend the rest of his life making T-shirts in textile factories in the Dominican Republic. The mother still has hope for her young son.

Sugar is an excellent baseball movie, beautifully photographed, directed, and acted. The plot avoids the clichés of the cinema; its story line is always surprising. *Sugar* is also an important film, as it documents an aspect of the game that is virtually unknown to baseball fans in the United States.

BIBLIOGRAPHY

Alexander, Charles C. *Ty Cobb*. Dallas, TX: First Southern Methodist University Press, 1984.

Allen, Lee. *Dizzy Dean: His Story in Baseball*. New York, NY: G. P. Putnam's Sons, 1967.

Armour, Mark. "Felipe Alou." SABR Baseball Biography Project. http://sabr.org/bioproj/person/b79ab182.

Armour, Mark. "Jim Piersall." SABR Baseball Biography Project. http://sabr.org/bioproj/person/91fce86d.

Asinof, Eliot. *Eight Men Out*. New York, NY: Holt, Rinehart and Winston, 1963.

Baseball Almanac. http://www.baseball-almanac.com.

Baseball Reference. http://www.baseball-reference.com.

Bernstein, J. B., with Rebecca Paley. *Million Dollar Arm: Sometimes to Win, You Have to Change the Game*. New York, NY: Gallery Books, 2014.

Blocker, D. A. "One-Legged Stratton Proving Winner in Hill Comeback with Texas Team." *The Sporting News* (August 7, 1946): 31.

Brashler, William. *Bingo Long Traveling All-Stars and Motor Kings*. New York, NY: Harper & Row, 1973.

Brashler, William. *The Story of Negro League Baseball*. New York, NY: Ticknor & Fields, 1994.

Brown, Joe E., and Ralph Hancock. *Laughter Is a Wonderful Thing*. New York, NY: A.S. Barnes and Company, 1956.

Burns, Ken (executive producer). *Baseball*. United States: PBS DVD Gold, 2000.

Carr, Sam. "Before *A League of Their Own*." National Baseball Hall of Fame Website. http://baseballhall.org/discover/baseball-history/there-is-crying-in-baseball.

Cobb, William R. "The Georgia Peach Stumped by the Storyteller," from *The National Pastime*, SABR, 2010. http://haulsofshame.com/Final%20SABR%20Article%20-%20as%20published_6744.pdf.

Coyle, Daniel. *Hardball: A Season in the Projects*. New York, NY: Putnam, 1993.

Cramer, Richard Ben. *Joe DiMaggio: The Hero's Life*. New York, NY: Simon & Schuster, 2000.

Creamer, Robert W. *Babe: The Legend Comes to Life*. New York, NY: Simon & Schuster, 1974.

Dickson, Paul. *Bill Veeck: Baseball's Greatest Maverick*. New York, NY: Walker & Company, 2012.

Engelhardt, Brian C. *Reading's Big League Exhibition Games*. Charleston, SC: Arcadia Publishing, 2015.

Erickson, Hal. *The Baseball Filmography, 1915 to 2001*. Jefferson, NC: McFarland, 2002.

Finkel, Jan. "Juan Marichal." SABR Baseball Biography Project. http://sabr.org/bioproj/person/5196f44d.

Fitzsimmons, Cortland. *Death on the Diamond: A Baseball Mystery Story*. New York, NY: Frederick A. Stokes Co., 1934.

Friedlander, Brett. and Robert Reising. *Chasing Moonlight: The True Story of* Field of Dreams' *Doc Graham*. Winston-Salem, NC: John F. Blair Publisher, 2009.

Gehrig, Eleanor, and Joseph Durso. *My Luke and I*. New York, NY: Thomas Y. Crowell Company, 1976.

Ginsburg, Daniel. "Ty Cobb." SABR Baseball Biography Project. http://sabr.org/bioproj/person/7551754a.

Goeben, Robert von. *Ballparks*. New York, NY: MetroBooks, 2000.

Gregorich, Barbara. *Women at Play: The Story of Women in Baseball*. San Diego, CA: Harcourt Grace & Company, 1993.

Harris, Mark. *Bang the Drum Slowly*. New York, NY: Knopf, 1956.

Herzog, Whitey, and Kevin Horrigan. *White Rat: A Life in Baseball*. New York, NY: Harper & Row Publishers, 1987.

Honig, Donald R. *Baseball America: The Heroes of the Game and the Times of Their Glory*. New York, NY: Macmillan Publishing Company, 1985.

Hubler, Richard G. *Lou Gehrig: The Iron Horse of Baseball*. Boston, MA: Houghton Mifflin Company, 1941.

Johnson, Susan E. *When Women Played Hardball*. Seattle, WA: Seal Press, 1994.

Keri, Jonah, ed. *Baseball Between the Numbers*. New York, NY: Basic Books, 2006.

King, Norm. "Pedro Martinez." SABR Baseball Biography Project. http://sabr.org/bioproj/person/a9ba2c91.

Kinsella, W. P. *Shoeless Joe*. Boston, MA: Houghton Mifflin, 1982.

Lavery, Mike. "Chasing 3000." The Baseball Page. http://www.thebaseballpage.com/community/articles/chasing-3000, August 3, 2011.

Lewis, Michael. *Moneyball: The Art of Winning an Unfair Game*. New York, NY: W. W. Norton, 2003 .

Malamud, Bernard. *The Natural*. New York, NY: Harcourt Brace and Co., 1952.

Maraniss, David. *Clemente: The Passion and Grace of Baseball's Last Hero*. New York, NY: Simon & Schuster, 2006.

McCallum, John D. *Ty Cobb*. New York, NY: Praeger Publishers, 1975.

McKenna, Brian. "Charles Grant," SABR Baseball Biography Project, http://sabr.org/bioproj/person/bd564010.

Morris, Jim, and Joel Engel. *The Oldest Rookie: Big League Dreams from a Small Town Guy*. Boston, MA: Little Brown & Co., 2001.

Morrison, Jim. "The Little League World Series' Only Perfect Game." Smithsonian.com. http://www.smithsonianmag.com/history/the-little-league-world-series-only-perfect-game-12835685/, April 5, 2010.

Nowlon, Bill. "Ossie Vitt." SABR Baseball Biography Project. http://sabr.org/bioproj/person/128a662b.

O'Neill, Brian. "Brotherly film sweet, but real story sweeter." *Pittsburgh Post-Gazette*, September 5, 2010.

Piersall, Jim. *The Truth Hurts*. Chicago, IL: Contemporary Books, Inc., 1984.

Piersall, Jim, and Al Hirshberg. *Fear Strikes Out*. Boston, MA: Little, Brown and Company, 1955.

Price, Christopher. *Baseball by the Beach: A History of America's National Pastime on Cape Cod*. Yarmouth Port, MA: On Cape Publications, 1998.

Rampersad, Arnold. *Jackie Robinson: A Biography*. New York, NY: Alfred A. Knopf, 1997.

Robinson, Ray. *Iron Horse: Lou Gehrig in His Time*. New York, NY: W. W. Norton & Company, Inc., 1990.

Ruth, Babe, as told to Bob Considine. *The Babe Ruth Story*. New York, NY: E. P. Dutton & Co., Inc., 1949.

Shaughnessy, Dan. *Reversing the Curse: Inside the 2004 Boston Red Sox*. Boston, MA: Houghton Mifflin Company, 2005.

Skipper, John C. *Wicked Curve: The Life and Troubled Times of Grover Cleveland Alexander*. Jefferson, NC: McFarland and Company, Inc., 2006.

Slide, Anthony. *The Encyclopedia of Vaudeville*. Westport, CT: Greenwood Press, 1994.

Smith, Curt. *America's Dizzy Dean*. St. Louis, MO: The Bethany Press, 1978.

Smith, Curt. "Forbes Field (Pittsburgh)." SABR Baseball Biography Project. http://sabr.org/bioproj/park/forbes-field-pittsburgh.

Smith, H. Allen. *Rhubarb*. Garden City, NY: Doubleday & Co., Inc., 1946.

Smith, H. Allen, and Ira L Smith. *Three Men on Third: A Book of Baseball Anecdotes, Oddities and Curiosities*. Halcottsville, NY: Breakaway Books, 1951.

Spink, J.G.T. "Looping the Loops" *The Sporting News* (February 12, 1947): 2.

Strasberg, Andy, Bob Thompson, and Tim Wiles. *Baseball's Greatest Hit: The Story of Take Me Out to the Ball Game*. New York, NY: Hal Leonard Books, 2008.

Vaccaro, Mike. *1941: The Greatest Year in Sports*. New York, NY: Doubleday, 2007.

Winokur, W. William. *The Perfect Game*. New York, NY: Kissena Park Press, 2008.

Wulf, Steve. "December 31: Arriba Roberto." *Sports Illustrated* (December 28, 1992).

INDEX